# Franklin D. Roosevelt

# PROFILES IN POWER

*General Editor: Keith Robbins*

# Franklin D. Roosevelt

Patrick Renshaw

Harlow, England • London • New York • Boston • San Francisco • Toronto
Sydney • Tokyo • Singapore • Hong Kong • Seoul • Taipei • New Delhi
Cape Town • Madrid • Mexico City • Amsterdam • Munich • Paris • Milan

PEARSON EDUCATION LIMITED

Edinburgh Gate
Harlow CM20 2JE
Tel: +44 (0)1279 623623
Fax: +44 (0)1279 431059
Website: www.pearsoned.co.uk

**First edition published in Great Britain in 2004**

ISBN 0 582 43803 9

*British Library Cataloguing in Publication Data*
A CIP catalogue record for this book can be obtained from the British Library

*Library of Congress Cataloging in Publication Data*
A CIP catalog record for this book can be obtained from the Library of Congress

10  9  8  7  6  5  4  3  2  1

Set by 35 in 9.5/12pt Celeste
Printed in Malaysia

*The Publishers' policy is to use paper manufactured from sustainable forests.*

*To Mary, with all my love*

# CONTENTS

# Preface

❖

This book is aimed primarily at readers who know little or nothing about Franklin Delano Roosevelt, the New Deal or United States history. Many biographies of FDR exist, the best of which are listed in my short bibliography. Why write another? Roosevelt was a key political figure of the last century. He met the challenge of economic depression and world war as president of the world's most powerful democracy, but within the constraints of a federal constitution. Yet when I taught history at universities in Britain and the United States between 1968 and 1998 I found that students were more interested in tyrants like Hitler and Stalin than they were in FDR, who as president had allied the nation he led with Stalin to help defeat Hitler. On the centenary of his birth in 1982, on the fiftieth anniversary of his death in 1995, in newspaper polls to select the outstanding political figures of the twentieth century, Roosevelt received less attention than Hitler, Stalin or Churchill. Yet he ranks with them and with Atatürk, Gandhi, Lenin, Mao and Mandela on any shortlist of politicians of the century. Moreover, other books about Roosevelt are long ones, the best of them running to several volumes. My goal has been to write, in less than 100,000 words, a profile of one of the greatest men of the last century viewed from the vantage point of this century.

In his profile of Hitler in this series – sales of which underline my point about popular interest in Hitler – my friend and colleague Sir Ian Kershaw explains why he abandoned a biographical approach. Indeed, in his subsequent two-volume biography *Hitler* he further explains why historians often reject the biographical form: covering all the facts of a man's life in date order can crowd out historical analysis. I respect this view. In the following pages, however, I have deliberately adopted a biographical and chronological approach. The reason for this is twofold. Final-year students on my New Deal special subject always explained that what they needed was a brief book which would cover Roosevelt's earlier political life and relate it to the New Deal after 1932. I have now tried to meet this need.

But beyond this I believe that history can only be understood by analysis of historical problems within a chronological framework. In short, I think that most of the mistakes historians make in analysing the past stem from forgetting that events happen in strict sequence. For example, that Roosevelt looked almost certain to lose when he ran for governor of New York in 1928; that he was by no means certain to win his party's nomination for president in 1932; that, in 1940, he was genuinely in two minds about running for a third term; and that, for a few days in late October of that year, he really feared electoral defeat. I hope that this profile will introduce Roosevelt's dramatic story to a new generation of readers.

Many people helped me write this book and I gladly thank them now. A generation of New Deal special subject students at Sheffield made me clarify my ideas about Roosevelt by forcing me to explain and rethink the causes and consequences of complex events. They further refreshed me by bringing new facts and their own interpretations of events to my attention. The American Council of Learned Societies awarded me a research fellowship at the State University of New York at Binghamton in 1981–82 while writing *American Labour and Consensus Capitalism*. I benefited greatly from talking to Professor Melvyn Dubofsky and other colleagues at SUNY, while spending some weeks reading archive material in the Franklin D. Roosevelt Library at Hyde Park. Apart from this debt to the ACLS, the British Academy also provided generously more than once from their small grants fund to help finance research in the United States. Colleagues in the department of history at Sheffield University, where I had the good fortune to work from 1968 until 1998, made teaching and research a pleasure. In particular, I wish to thank Richard Carwardine, now Rhodes Professor of American History at Oxford University, for his friendship, advice and patience over the years. When I first entered his study in 1971 I remarked that his interests were nineteenth century and sacred, while mine were twentieth century and profane. It was the perfect basis for a close working relationship between two very different people. Robert Cook, of Sheffield University, acted for years as a bridge between Richard and myself because he has published on American history of both the nineteenth and twentieth centuries. He also greatly improved the first draft of Chapters 1–5 with his comments. Anthony Badger took time out from his busy schedule as Professor of American History at Cambridge University to read the final draft, which benefited from many subtle criticisms. He also kindly sent me a copy of his perceptive article 'The New Deal Without FDR', which I have eagerly plundered. Professor Owen Dudley Edwards, of Edinburgh University, read the manuscript at a late stage to good effect, as did the series editor Professor Keith Robbins, Vice-Chancellor of the University of Wales, who picked up many slips, added commas and greatly improved my discussion of foreign policy. I am very grateful to Trevor Barnes, who helped me grapple with the mysteries of IT while preparing my draft for printout, to Michael McNay, who read the proofs, and to Beryl McKie, who compiled the index. I owe a special debt to Freda Brayshaw, who read an early draft and the final draft through the eyes of the general reader, spotted my spelling mistakes and missed even less than she does when partnering me at bridge. Other Sheffield colleagues helped in many ways. Bob Moore tracked down details of the fate of the French fleet under the Vichy government. Denise Harrison and Jacky Hodgson, in the university library, were unfailingly helpful not only in locating articles, books and titles but also in solving other problems. Dorothy McCarthy was a splendid copy-editor. They all saved me from countless errors of omission and commission but bear no responsibility for any which remain.

To save space I have used notes sparingly, mostly to indicate the source of direct quotations, although a few short or very familiar quotations remain unannotated. Though my text follows English spelling, except when quoting from an American source, I use American spelling for American institutions, such as Defense or Labor departments.

Over the years, central New York has become almost a second home and many people gave me American-style hospitality. In particular I would like to name David Bennett, Ralph Ketcham and colleagues in the history department at Syracuse University's Maxwell School of Citizenship and Public Affairs, where I have taught several times, and also Nancy Calhoun, a neighbour in 1971–72 and a friend ever since. This tribute to one of New York's greatest sons expresses my gratitude to them all. What little I understand about economics I owe mostly to years of conversations with my brother Geoffrey Renshaw, of Warwick University, while my views on history and politics generally have been shaped by talks both with him and my other brother Kerry, who teaches at Bracknell and Wokingham College. I am glad to take this opportunity to call them the best of brothers. My final debt is to Mary, my wife and companion and closest friend for more than forty years. I have tried to express my love and everything else I owe her both in this book and in its dedication.

Sheffield
June 2003

# Chronology

| | |
|---|---|
| 30 January 1882 | Franklin Delano Roosevelt born |
| 1882–98 | FDR grows up at Hyde Park |
| 1892 | Father suffers a stroke |
| 1896–1900 | Attends Groton school |
| 1900–04 | Attends Harvard University |
| 14 September 1901 | President William McKinley is assassinated. FDR's cousin Teddy Roosevelt becomes president |
| 1901–09 | Theodore Roosevelt is president |
| September 1904 | Attends Columbia Law School but leaves without graduating |
| November 1904 | FDR casts his first vote for cousin Teddy |
| 17 March 1905 | Marries Eleanor Roosevelt. Fathers five children – Anna, James, Elliott, Franklin Jr and John |
| Spring 1906 | Passes Bar examination and practises law in New York City with Carter, Ledyard and Milburn |
| 1907 | Confides ambition to become president |
| 1910–13 | Revolution in Mexico spills across Texas border |
| November 1910 | Elected to New York state assembly for Columbia, Dutchess and Putnam counties, a hopeless seat won only once by Democrats since 1856 |
| January–March 1911 | Fights Tammany Hall over nomination of new US senator |
| | Meets the journalist Louis Howe and fellow assemblymen Alfred E. Smith and Robert F. Wagner |
| 25 March 1911 | Triangle shirtwaist factory fire kills 148 young women operatives |

| | |
|---|---|
| November 1912 | Wins re-election to state assembly, despite catching typhoid, thanks to Howe's clever campaigning |
| | Woodrow Wilson elected president, only the second Democrat since 1856. Appoints FDR assistant secretary to the Navy |
| 1913–20 | Assistant secretary to the Navy |
| September 1914 | Runs for US Senator from New York but is easily beaten in primary by James Gerard, who himself loses in November |
| 1914–18 | The Great War in Europe |
| 1915 | Tours Haiti after US marines quell violence |
| 7 November 1916 | Woodrow Wilson re-elected president |
| 6 April 1917 | United States declares war on Germany |
| 1917–18 | Love affair with Lucy Mercer |
| 1918 | Goes to Europe as victory in Great War nears. Eleanor learns of love affair |
| 11 November 1918 | Armistice ends Great War |
| 1918–19 | Returns to Europe for Paris peace conference |
| June 1920 | Nominated by Democrats as James Cox's running mate in presidential election |
| August 1920 | Resigns as assistant secretary to the Navy to fight campaign |
| November 1920 | Cox and FDR overwhelmed by Republican Warren Harding. Missy LeHand becomes his secretary on campaign trail |
| | Returns to practise law with Emmett and Marvin in New York City |
| 10 August 1921 | Contracts polio and never walks again |
| 1921–28 | Howe moves into FDR's home and with Eleanor works ceaselessly to keep his name in the public eye |
| 1922 | Takes job with Fidelity and Deposit in New York City at $25,000 a year |
| | President of American Construction Council |
| 1922–29 | Active in Wall Street speculation, mostly unprofitable |

| | |
|---|---|
| 1923–26 | Takes three-month cruises in Florida waters each winter with friends on the houseboat *Larooco* in search of a cure |
| February 1924 | Death of Charles F. Murphy, boss of Tammany Hall |
| June–July 1924 | Nominates 'the Happy Warrior' Al Smith as Democratic candidate for president |
| 1925 | Dissolves law partnership with Emmett Marvin and joins racier firm of Basil ('The Doc') O'Connor |
| April 1926 | Buys Warm Springs, run-down 112-acre spa estate in Georgia for $200,000, risking his entire personal fortune and some of his mother's. Identification with its curative powers is important to his political image |
| 1928 | Nominates Al Smith again for president. Smith insists FDR must run for governor of New York. Smith is crushed by Hoover but FDR wins by 25,000 votes |
| 1929–33 | Succeeds Smith as governor of New York |
| October 1929 | Wall Street crash |
| 1929–33 | Subsequent economic depression halves national income in four years, makes one-quarter of the workforce jobless and dominates politics |
| November 1930 | Re-elected governor of New York by record plurality of 750,000 votes |
| 1930–32 | Organizes campaign to win Democratic party nomination as president |
| 1931 | Adolf Berle, Raymond Moley, Rex Tugwell, Basil O'Connor and others form 'brains trust' to formulate policy. FDR also seeks financial support from Henry Morgenthau, Joseph Kennedy, Will Woodin and others |
| March–May 1932 | Enters Democratic party primaries |
| 27–30 June 1932 | Democrats nominate FDR on 4th ballot in Chicago. Promises 'New Deal' to American people |
| September–November 1932 | Campaigns against Hoover across nation |

| | |
|---|---|
| 8 November 1932 | With 57.4 per cent of the popular votes and 42 states FDR wins a great landslide victory |
| 4 March 1933 | Inaugurated 32nd president |
| March–June 1933 | First Hundred Days reforms every major economic interest. Some $3.3 billion is appropriated for public works to create jobs |
| 19 April 1933 | FDR takes United States off gold standard. Dollar devalued by about 30 per cent to help economic recovery |
| 12 May 1933 | FDR signs Agricultural Adjustment Act including Thomas amendment, which enables him to increase money supply |
| | Federal Emergency Relief Administration (FERA) under Harry Hopkins provides grants to states and cities |
| 12 June 1933 | World economic conference meets in London |
| 16 June 1933 | Glass-Steagall Banking Act sets up Federal Deposit Insurance Corporation (FDIC) to protect small bank deposits |
| 5 July 1933 | FDR collapses London world economic conference by refusing to stabilize dollar |
| October 1933 | NRA industrial codes are drawn up, amid massive publicity campaign of 'We do our part' |
| 16 November 1933 | United States extends diplomatic recognition to Soviet Union |
| 3 December 1933 | At Montevideo Latin American conference United States launches 'Good Neighbour' policy to other nations in Western hemisphere |
| 5 December 1933 | 21st Amendment to the Constitution repeals 18th Amendment so ending Prohibition of alcohol |
| 31 January 1934 | FDR fixes price of gold at $34 an ounce, where it stays until 1971 |
| 15 February 1934 | Civil Works Emergency Relief Act provides an immediate $500 million for civil works and relief programmes |
| 13 April 1934 | Johnson Debt Default Act forbids US loans to countries such as Britain and France which had reneged on Great War debts |

| | |
|---|---|
| 29 May 1934 | Congress abrogates 1901 Platt amendment which had enabled United States to intervene at will in Cuba |
| 6 June 1934 | Securities and Exchange Commission (SEC) set up under Joseph Kennedy to regulate Wall Street |
| 6 November 1934 | For the first time in living memory a president's party picks up seats in mid-term elections. Democrats have majority of 45 in the Senate and 219 in the House |
| 4 January 1935 | In his annual message to Congress FDR outlines new programme of reform, later known as 'Second New Deal' |
| 8 April 1935 | Emergency Relief Appropriation Act (ERA) authorizes expenditure of $5 billion on public works. Works Progress Administration (WPA) set up under Hopkins |
| 1 May 1935 | Resettlement Administration (RA) set up under Tugwell and auspices of ERA to extend work of FERA and resettle impoverished rural and urban families |
| 11 May 1935 | Rural Electrification Administration (REA) established to help work of TVA by financing construction of electrical plants and power lines in rural areas |
| 16 May 1935 | Senate approves National Labor Relations Act (Wagner Act) |
| 27 May 1935 | 'Black Monday': in *Schechter* case US Supreme Court by 9–0 declares NIRA unconstitutional |
| 31 May 1935 | FDR complains that Court's 'horse and buggy' definition of interstate commerce threatens New Deal |
| 19 June 1935 | FDR asks Congress to act to reverse growing concentration of economic power and promote fairer distribution of wealth |
| 5 July 1935 | Wagner Act legalizes collective bargaining and the closed shop in industry, setting up a National Labor Relations Board to enforce this. Industrial relations are transformed |

| | |
|---|---|
| 14 August 1935 | Social Security Act gives old-age pensions and federal–state unemployment insurance funded by joint employer–employee contributions |
| 23 August 1935 | Banking Act replaces Federal Reserve Board with seven-man board of governors to give central bank greater power |
| 30 August 1935 | Revenue Act raises maximum surtax to 75 per cent |
| 31 August 1935 | Neutrality Act empowers president to proclaim a state of war and ban arms sales to belligerents |
| 8 September 1935 | Senator Huey Long of Louisiana assassinated |
| 3 October 1935 | Italy invades Abyssinia (now Ethiopia). FDR imposes arms embargo but oil and coal still reach Italy |
| 16 October 1935 | American Federation of Labor (AFL) rejects proposal of mineworkers' leader John L. Lewis to organize semi-skilled and unskilled workers in single unions along industrial lines |
| 10 November 1935 | Lewis and leaders of eight other AFL unions form Congress of Industrial Organizations (CIO) to launch industrial unions |
| 6 January 1936 | In *Butler* case US Supreme Court declares Agricultural Adjustment Act unconstitutional |
| 17 January 1936 | In *Ashwander* v. *Tennessee Valley Authority* Supreme Court upholds TVA's right to dispose of surplus power |
| 26 February 1936 | In '2.26 incident' junior officers of the Japanese imperial army mutiny in favour of aggressive foreign policy |
| 29 February 1936 | Neutrality Act tightened and later extended to cover Spanish civil war |
| 7 March 1936 | Hitler reoccupies the Rhineland |
| 18 May 1936 | Supreme Court declares Guffey-Snyder Coal Act unconstitutional on grounds that coal mining is not interstate commerce |
| 1 June 1936 | In *Morehead* v. *Tipaldo* Supreme Court strikes down minimum wages for women and children by 5–4. Four months later, in *West Coast Hotel* v. *Parrish*, Court reverses |

| | |
|---|---|
| | *Tipaldo* decision and approves minimum wage law 6–3 |
| 9 June 1936 | Republican party nominates Alfred M. Landon of Kansas to run for president |
| 23 June 1936 | Democratic party renominates FDR to run for president by acclamation |
| 17 July 1936 | Spanish civil war begins |
| August–November 1936 | Landon fails to inspire while FDR mounts confident and increasingly demagogic attack on inequality, injustice and vested interests |
| 3 November 1936 | With 60.8 per cent of the popular vote and every state but Maine and Vermont FDR wins greatest victory in history |
| | Democrats have majority of 56 in the Senate and 229 in the House |
| 25 November 1936 | Having formed Rome–Berlin axis in October, Germany signs anti-Comintern pact with Japan |
| 23 December 1936 | With Buenos Aires declaration all nations in Western hemisphere agree never to intervene in each other's internal affairs |
| 29 December 1936 | United Autoworkers members begin momentous sit-down strike at Flint, Michigan to win right to organize and bargain collectively |
| 20 January 1937 | In Second Inaugural Address FDR highlights nation's central problem: 'one-third of a nation ill-housed, ill-clad, ill-nourished' |
| 3 February 1937 | FDR sends Congress secret judiciary reorganization bill to 'pack' US Supreme Court |
| | Michigan Governor Frank Murphy refuses to order national guard to evict sit-down strikers and joins FDR in pressuring GM to negotiate |
| 11 February 1937 | In Flint sit-down strike GM capitulates and agrees to recognize UAW as union |
| 2 March 1937 | Months of work by the CIO pays off when, without a strike, US Steel recognizes SWOC as union under Wagner Act and improves pay and hours |

| | |
|---|---|
| March 1937 | AFL expels 10 industrial unions, including SWOC and UAW. CIO forms rival national labour federation |
| 8 April 1937 | After two-week occupation of its plants Chrysler agrees to recognize UAW |
| 12 April 1937 | Supreme Court upholds Wagner Act 5–4 in *NLRB* v. *Jones & Laughlin* |
| 1 May 1937 | Congress passes stronger Neutrality Act forbidding FDR to sell arms to victims of aggression |
| 18 May 1937 | Justice Van Devanter announces he will retire from Supreme Court on 1 June |
| 24 May 1937 | Supreme Court upholds Social Security Act 5–4 in *Steward Machine Tool Co.* v. *Davis* |
| 30 May 1937 | Chicago police attack pickets and kill 10 strikers at Republic Steel in 'Memorial Day Massacre' |
| June 1937 | Encouraged by economic recovery since 1935 FDR cuts government spending by 25 per cent

Subsequent recession wipes out most gains made by New Deal and lasts well into 1938 |
| 3 June 1937 | FDR urges Congress to create six more public power authorities like TVA |
| 7 July 1937 | Japan launches full-scale invasion of China to conquer northern provinces |
| 12 July 1937 | FDR asks Congress to re-create the AAA through more careful, piecemeal laws to aid agriculture |
| 14 July 1937 | Democratic majority leader Joseph Robinson, struggling to get Senate to pass FDR's Supreme Court reform bill, dies suddenly of heart attack |
| 17 August 1937 | Liberal Hugo Black appointed to US Supreme Court. Liberals now have clear majority. Senator James Byrnes urges FDR to drop reform bill. 'Why run for a train after you've caught it?' |
| 26 August 1937 | FDR drops plan to enlarge Court |
| 1 September 1937 | Wagner-Steagall Housing Act gives public housing authority capital of $1 million and $500 million borrowing capacity (later raised to $1.6 billion) |

| | |
|---|---|
| 5 October 1937 | FDR's 'quarantine the aggressors' speech alerts United States to danger posed by 'bandit nations' |
| 12 October 1937 | FDR calls Congress into special session to tackle severe economic slump |
| 6 November 1937 | Italy joins Germany and Japan in anti-Comintern pact |
| 15 November 1937 | In 'fireside chat' FDR presents American people with programme to combat recession which covers farming, wages and hours, child labour and anti-trust law |
| 16 February 1938 | Congress passes second Agricultural Adjustment Act, which reorganizes farming and seeks to restore 1910–14 purchasing power to farmers |
| 12–13 March 1938 | In Anschluss Germany annexes Austria |
| 14 April 1938 | In special message to Congress FDR announces easier credit for private spending to fill the gap left by reduced public spending |
| 27 May 1938 | Conservatives in Congress push through Revenue Act, cutting corporation tax in bid to stimulate investment |
| 16 June 1938 | Joint Congressional resolution creates Temporary National Economic Committee (TNEC) to break up trusts and monopolies |
| 24 June 1938 | FDR declares intention to take part in party mid-term primaries to purge reactionary Southern Democrats |
| 25 June 1938 | Fair Labor Standards Act establishes minimum wage, maximum hours and outlaws child labour but excludes farm and domestic workers |
| 12 August 1938 | Independent Report on Economic Conditions in South highlights region's chronic problems |
| 29–30 September 1938 | Crisis over Czechoslovakia resolved at Munich when Britain and France capitulate to Hitler's demand that Germany occupy Sudetenland |
| 8 November 1938 | FDR's bid to purge party fails as Democrats lose seven seats in the Senate and 70 in the House. Dixiecrat–Republican coalition emerges in Congress to resist further reform |

| 24 December 1938 | In Lima Declaration United States and 20 other republics in Western hemisphere agree to consult when mutual security is threatened |
| --- | --- |
| 4 January 1939 | For the first time in one of his annual messages FDR steers public attention towards foreign affairs |
| 15 March 1939 | Hitler invades rest of Czechoslovakia |
| 3 April 1939 | Administrative Reorganization Act enhances efficiency and power of president. Executive order 8248 expands FDR's staff |
| 15 April 1939 | FDR sends open letter to Hitler and Mussolini asking for assurances that they do not intend to invade any other nation |
| 30 April 1939 | Hitler responds to FDR's open letter with a devastating speech combining scorn with derision |
| 10 July 1939 | Senate foreign relations committee refuses to amend 1937 Neutrality Act to allow United States to send military aid to Britain and France |
| August 1939 | TVA buys Tennessee Electric Power Co. from Commonwealth and Southern Corporation for $79 million |
| 2 August 1939 | Albert Einstein warns FDR that Germany could develop atomic bomb and urges United States to do so first. Manhattan Project is born |
| 23 August 1939 | Nazi–Soviet pact signed |
| 1 September 1939 | Germany invades Poland |
| 3 September 1939 | Britain and France declare war on Germany |
| 5 September 1939 | United States declares neutrality in European war |
| 28 September 1939 | Germany and Soviet Union partition Poland |
| 3 October 1939 | US declaration of Panama defines Western hemisphere south of Canada a 'safety zone' and reasserts Monroe Doctrine warning Europe to keep out |
| 4 November 1939 | Neutrality Act finally amended to allow FDR to send arms to Britain and France on cash-and-carry basis |
| 30 November 1939 | Soviet Union invades Finland |
| 26 January 1940 | United States allows 1911 trade treaty with Japan to lapse |

| | |
|---|---|
| 9 April–22 June 1940 | German blitzkrieg overwhelms Denmark, Norway, the Netherlands, Belgium and France |
| 18 April 1940 | FDR extends protection of Monroe Doctrine to Greenland |
| 10 May 1940 | Churchill replaces Chamberlain as British prime minister |
| 16 May 1940 | In special message to Congress FDR calls for preparedness and orders 50,000 planes a year |
| 17 May 1940 | National Committee to Defend America by Aiding the Allies formed to spread FDR's idea of United States as Arsenal of Democracy |
| 26 May–30 June 1940 | As France falls some 330,000 British and French troops are evacuated at Dunkirk without arms or equipment |
| 28 May 1940 | Council of National Defense formed under GM boss William Knudsen with labour members |
| 31 May 1940 | FDR asks Congress to raise defence spending by a billion dollars to a record $9 billion |
| 10 June 1940 | Fascist Italy invades France |
| 12 June 1940 | German army enters Paris |
| 25 June 1940 | Congress authorizes RFC to finance new defence plants |
| 28 June 1940 | Republican party convention nominates Wendell Willkie on 6th ballot |
| 15 July 1940 | Democrats nominate FDR for third term with Henry Wallace as his running-mate |
| 16 July 1940 | Fall of moderate Yonai cabinet in Japan signals policy of breaking perceived economic encirclement by military force |
| 26 July 1940 | US embargo on export of aviation fuel to Japan |
| September–November 1940 | In election campaign FDR argues that United States can best keep out of war by helping Britain win it |
| 2 September 1940 | FDR gives 50 old destroyers to Britain in return for 99-year leases on British naval bases in the Caribbean and Newfoundland |
| 16 September 1940 | As Battle of Britain rages in the skies above London Congress votes for military conscription for first time in peace |
| 22 September 1940 | Japan occupies northern Indo-China |

| | |
|---|---|
| 27 September 1940 | Axis–Japanese military pact promises support if attacked by nation not already in war |
| 30 October 1940 | In campaign speech in Boston FDR promises, 'Your boys are not going to be sent to fight in any foreign wars' |
| 5 November 1940 | With 54.3 per cent of the popular votes and 38 states FDR comfortably wins an unprecedented third term |
| 29 December 1940 | FDR announces policy of Lend-Lease. Between January and March US Congress votes Britain $7 billion worth of arms to be returned after the war |
| 6 January 1941 | FDR's annual message says war is about defence of Four Freedoms |
| January–March 1941 | Congress quadruples defence spending to $27 billion |
| 25 March 1941 | Germany extends war zone to Iceland and Denmark Strait off Greenland. FDR authorizes repair of British ships in US yards |
| 10 April 1941 | FDR extends US neutrality patrol off coast of Iceland but including Azores |
| 15 May 1941 | German submarine sinks US freighter *Robin Moor* |
| 22 June 1941 | Hitler renounces Nazi–Soviet pact and invades Soviet Union |
| 25 June 1941 | Facing March on Washington, FDR issues Order 8802 outlawing racial discrimination in defence plants |
| 7 July 1941 | United States occupies Iceland with consent of Icelandic prime minister and Winston Churchill |
| 28 July 1941 | FDR punishes Japanese occupation of southern Indo-China by seizing Japan's assets in United States and banning export of oil and all war items |
| 9 August 1941 | FDR meets Churchill on US cruiser *Augusta* off Newfoundland and signs Atlantic Charter |
| 4 September 1941 | German submarine attacks US destroyer *Greer* off Iceland |
| 2 October 1941 | US final refusal to hold peace conference with Japan to end war in China |

| | |
|---|---|
| October–November 1941 | Hundreds of American sailors die as German submarines sink US warships |
| 7 November 1941 | On anniversary of Bolshevik revolution FDR extends Lend-Lease to Soviet Union |
| | United States sends 10-point ultimatum to Japan |
| 7 December 1941 | Carrier-based Japanese planes attack US naval base at Pearl Harbor in Hawaii, sinking 5 of 7 battleships at anchor |
| 8 December 1941 | FDR asks Congress to declare war |
| | AFL and CIO agree on No-Strike pledge for duration of war |
| 11 December 1941 | Germany and Japan declare war on United States |
| 22 December 1941 | Churchill arrives in Washington |
| 1 January 1942 | United States, Britain, Soviet Union and 23 other Allies sign United Nations declaration supporting Atlantic Charter |
| 5 January 1942 | In his annual budget message FDR asks for $7 billion in new taxes to win war |
| 12 January 1942 | War Labor Board created to prevent strikes while controlling wages, inflation and the whole war economy |
| 19 February 1942 | FDR orders arrest of 118,000 Japanese-Americans living on West Coast, most of them second generation. Many spend years in concentration camps |
| 28 April 1942 | Office of Price Administration (OPA) fixes many prices and rents at March 1942 levels |
| 6 May 1942 | Japan expels US troops from Philippines General MacArthur vows, 'I shall return' |
| 7–8 May 1942 | Battle of Coral Sea checks Japanese advance in southwestern Pacific |
| 3–6 June 1942 | US naval and air forces win key Battle of Midway |
| 16 July 1942 | War Labor Board devises 'Little Steel' formula in bid to control wartime wage inflation |
| 16 August 1942 | Special committee under Bernard Baruch probes wartime rubber shortage and urges petrol rationing and speed limits |

| | |
|---|---|
| 2 October 1942 | Anti-Inflation Act empowers FDR to limit wartime pay and prices (but not profits) to levels current on 15 September |
| 3 October 1942 | Office of Economic Stabilization freezes farm prices and takes complete control of allocation of steel, aluminium and copper |
| 21 October 1942 | Revenue Act brings unprecedented range of tax increases with some 50 million Americans now paying federal income tax |
| 24 October 1942 | British 8th Army launches decisive North African counter-attack at El Alamein |
| 3 November 1942 | Republicans make big gains in mid-term elections. Thomas Dewey is elected first Republican Governor of New York since 1920 |
| 8 November 1942 | Anglo-American forces land in strength in North Africa in TORCH operation. Axis forces now face war on two fronts |
| 18 November 1942 | Military draft age lowered to 18 |
| 19 November 1942 | Soviet counter-offensive begins at Stalingrad |
| 2 December 1942 | First controlled atomic chain reaction achieved in Chicago |
| January 1943 | Dixiecrat–Republican coalition dominates new 78th Congress |
| 14 January 1943 | At Casablanca conference with Churchill, FDR agrees to defer second front in France until 1944 and invade Sicily instead. FDR insists on unconditional surrender of the Axis |
| 30 January 1943 | German 6th Army surrenders at Stalingrad with more than 330,000 killed or captured |
| 7–8 February 1943 | Japanese withdraw from Guadalcanal in Solomon Islands |
| 1 May 1943 | When coalminers strike for more pay FDR seizes mines and orders miners back to work. Unrest lasts throughout 1943 |
| | Work on Manhattan Project moved in greatest secrecy to New Mexico, supervised by J. Robert Oppenheimer |
| 11 May 1943 | Churchill arrives in Washington for TRIDENT talks to plan bombing of Germany, invasion of Italy and second front in France in 1944 |

| | |
|---|---|
| 20 June 1943 | 34 die in Detroit race riot |
| July 1943 | Counter-attacking German armies lose greatest tank battle in history at Kursk, in Ukraine |
| 10 July 1943 | Some 160,000 Allied troops land in Sicily |
| 25 July 1943 | Benito Mussolini deposed in Italy. New government sues for peace |
| 8 September 1943 | Italy surrenders |
| 14 October 1943 | Heavy losses in Schweinfurt raid force United States to suspend daylight bombing |
| 18–30 October 1943 | British, Soviet and US foreign ministers meet in Moscow to plan postwar policy |
| 22–26 November 1943 | FDR, Churchill and Chiang Kai-shek hold Cairo conference |
| 23–27 November 1943 | FDR, Churchill and Stalin hold first wartime Big Three conference in Tehran to plan strategy. Cordial spirit convinces FDR that postwar cooperation is possible |
| 4–6 December 1943 | At second Cairo conference FDR and Churchill agree that General Eisenhower should command OVERLORD invasion of France |
| 22 January 1944 | Allied landings at Anzio in Italy |
| 23 February 1944 | United States resumes daylight bombing of Germany |
| 24–25 February 1944 | Congress overrides FDR's veto of 1944 Revenue Act. War taxes greatly reduced |
| 4 June 1944 | Rome, which had been declared an Open City to avoid war damage, is liberated |
| 6 June 1944 | On D-Day US troops take heaviest casualties launching OVERLORD – Allied amphibious invasion of France. By September 2 million men and 3 million tons of supplies have been landed |
| 15 June 1944 | United States launches sustained air war on Japan |
| 23 June 1944 | Huge Soviet offensive enters Poland and Baltic states and gets within 45 miles of Berlin by end of year |
| 26 June 1944 | Republicans nominate Thomas Dewey for president |
| 1–22 July 1944 | Bretton Woods conference agrees International Monetary Fund will stabilize currencies, |

|  |  |
|---|---|
|  | pegged to US dollar, while World Bank funds reconstruction and development |
| 19 July 1944 | Democratic convention nominates FDR. Harry Truman, with CIO support, is named running mate |
| 20 July 1944 | Well-planned bid by German officers to assassinate Hitler fails. All conspirators are summarily executed |
| 25 July 1944 | Allies break out of Normandy bridgehead |
| 15 August 1944 | US 7th Army lands in Southern France catching Germans in pincer movement (ANVIL) |
| 21 August–7 October 1944 | Dumbarton Oaks conference plans for postwar United Nations (UN) to replace League of Nations but British, Soviet and US delegates cannot agree on voting |
| 25 August 1944 | Paris is liberated |
| September–November 1944 | Presidential campaign. Hampered by good war news and general concurrence with FDR's policies, Dewey benefits from his visibly declining health |
| 20–25 October 1944 | US combined forces start to recapture Philippines and destroy most of remaining Japanese fleet at Battle for Leyte Gulf |
| 23 October 1944 | United States finally recognizes Free French government of Charles de Gaulle |
| 28 October 1944 | In Economic Bill of Rights speech FDR calls for large-scale public spending to sustain prosperity after the war |
| 7 November 1944 | With 53.5 per cent of the popular vote and 37 states FDR is easily re-elected |
| 21 November 1944 | Aachen becomes first German city to fall to Allies |
| December 1944 | In *Korematsu* v. *United States* Supreme Court upholds round-up of Japanese-Americans during clear and present danger of war. Dissenting, Frank Murphy describes the decision as 'the legalization of racism' |
| 16–26 December 1944 | German counter-attack in Ardennes is halted |
| 4–11 February 1945 | Crucial Big Three conference at Yalta agrees on partition of Germany, future government of |

|                        |                                                                                                                      |
| ---------------------- | -------------------------------------------------------------------------------------------------------------------- |
|                        | Poland, structure of UN (including voting) and Soviet control of Outer Mongolia                                       |
| 6–7 March 1945         | US troops capture Cologne and Ludendorff bridge across the Rhine at Remagen                                           |
| 9 March 1945           | US airforce firebomb raid on Tokyo destroys 16 square miles and kills 185,000 civilians                               |
| 16 March 1945          | After a month's costly fighting US marines capture Iwo Jima in Philippines                                            |
| 24 March 1945          | Anglo-American armies cross Rhine in strength                                                                         |
| 1–21 April 1945        | US marines capture Okinawa, major island in chain leading to Japan itself                                             |
| 8 April 1945           | Emperor Hirohito appoints Baron Suzuki, charging him to bring war to an end                                           |
| 11 April 1945          | US troops reach river Elbe, 53 miles from Berlin                                                                      |
| 12 April 1945          | FDR dies at 4.35 p.m. of cerebral haemorrhage. His last words are, 'I have a terrific headache.' Truman sworn in as new president |
| 27 April 1945          | US and Soviet troops meet on Elbe                                                                                     |
| 28 April 1945          | Italian Communist partisans capture and shoot Mussolini                                                               |
| 30 April 1945          | Hitler shoots himself in Berlin                                                                                       |
| 2 May 1945             | Red Army takes Berlin                                                                                                 |
| 8 May 1945             | Germans surrender unconditionally                                                                                     |
| 16 July 1945           | United States successfully tests first atomic bomb                                                                    |
| 17 July–2 August 1945  | Truman attends final Big Three conference at Potsdam, with Churchill's successor Clem Attlee and Stalin to plan for postwar world |
| 6 August 1945          | United States drops first atomic bomb on Hiroshima, killing 115,000 civilians                                        |
| 8 August 1945          | Soviet Union enters war against Japan, occupying Kurile islands                                                       |
| 9 August 1945          | Second atomic bomb dropped on Nagasaki with similar loss of life                                                      |
| 10 August 1945         | Japan offers surrender                                                                                                |
| 14 August 1945         | Japan accepts Allied peace terms which keep Emperor Hirohito on throne                                                |
| 6 September 1945       | General MacArthur takes Japan's surrender on board US battleship *Missouri* in Tokyo Bay                              |

# Abbreviations and Code Names

| | |
|---|---|
| AAA | Agricultural Adjustment Act |
| | Agricultural Adjustment Administration |
| AFL | American Federation of Labor |
| ARCADIA | Washington talks after Pearl Harbor to plan war strategy |
| BOLERO | Abandoned plan to invade France in 1943 |
| CCC | Civilian Conservation Corps |
| | Commodity Credit Corporation |
| CIO | Congress of Industrial Organizations |
| CWA | Civil Works Administration |
| EPIC | 'End Poverty In California' |
| ER | Eleanor Roosevelt |
| ERA | Emergency Relief Appropriation Act |
| FDIC | Federal Deposit Insurance Corporation |
| FDR | Franklin Delano Roosevelt |
| FEPC | Fair Employment Practice Committee |
| FERA | Federal Emergency Relief Administration |
| FSA | Farm Security Administration |
| GOP | Grand Old Party (nickname of Republicans) |
| NIRA | National Industrial Recovery Act |
| NLRB | National Labor Relations Board |
| NRA | National Recovery Administration |
| OPA | Office of Price Administration |
| OVERLORD | Code name for D-Day invasion of France 1944 |
| PWA | Public Works Administration |
| RA | Resettlement Administration |
| RAINBOW | Plane for defence of Western hemisphere 1940–41 |
| RFC | Reconstruction Finance Corporation |
| SEC | Securities and Exchange Commission |
| SWOC | Steel Workers Organizing Committee |
| TERA | Temporary Emergency Relief Administration |
| TNEC | Temporary National Emergency Council |
| TORCH | Anglo-American invasion of North Africa 1942 |
| TR | Theodore ('Teddy') Roosevelt |

| | |
|---|---|
| TRIDENT | Talks in 1943 about invading France in 1944 |
| TVA | Tennessee Valley Authority |
| UAW | United Autoworkers |
| UMW | United Mineworkers |
| WPA | Works Progress Administration |

# Chapter 1

## The Paradox of Power

The railway track which bore Franklin Delano Roosevelt's funeral train from Warm Springs, Georgia, on 13 April 1945 was crowded with mourners. As the steam locomotive rolled nearly a thousand miles via Washington, DC, to burial at the Roosevelt family estate in Hyde Park, New York, people bowed in farewell at every community it passed. Anguish, desolation and grief lined their faces. The president they knew by the initials FDR, who had led them gaily and confidently through the critical period between 1933 and 1945, had been struck down. They had elected him four times through the worst economic depression and most testing foreign war in United States history. For a whole generation he was the only president they had ever known.

As news of his sudden death spread by radio, newspapers and word of mouth, Americans were deeply shocked. Farmers, sharecroppers, the organized working class, millions of the middle class, African Americans, the long-term unemployed, lone parents, widows – millions to whom he had brought hope during hard times and patriotic purpose in war – were suddenly robbed of their leader on the eve of victory. So they flocked spontaneously trackside to say goodbye. Standing with two armed soldiers at the back of the train with the coffin, his widow Eleanor was deeply moved. 'I never really understood until then how much the people loved him,' she later said.

Watching those newsreels today one senses paradox not evident in 1945. But then FDR's whole career had been paradoxical. First, the man who used political power to such effect and with such zest had himself lacked physical power after polio appeared to have cut short his public life when he was 39 in 1921. With both legs paralysed FDR spent the rest of his days in a wheelchair, or in painful leg braces, dependent on the physical support of family and friends, or on clumsy crutches. In those days the handicapped, especially polio victims, bore a sense of shame and enjoyed far fewer aids than is true today. Polio was widely believed to be an illness people brought on themselves and was often associated with dirt and poverty. Simply returning to something like a normal domestic life, which Roosevelt did, would have been hard enough. Returning in triumph to public life, which not one person in millions would have done, revealed rare qualities, among them relentless will, ambition and resource. He was greatly helped by the willing complicity of the media which ensured that, despite the fact that Roosevelt was the most photographed and filmed American of his time, neither photograph nor film was ever published to reveal the true extent of his disability. Having slowly and painfully learned to deal with it, and been elected governor of New York twice between 1928 and 1932, he took office as president in March 1933 with the American economy in ruins.

Income had been halved in four years, one in four was jobless, agriculture had been laid waste, banking and finance were at the point of collapse, America's self-confidence – in many ways its key asset – was running out fast. Though similar conditions existed throughout the Western capitalist world, America had been hardest hit. To many American democracy seemed doomed. Communism and fascism looked like the wave of the future. Communists and fascists, both in the United States and elsewhere, certainly saw it that way. Yet, though constrained by democracy, Roosevelt's leadership between 1933 and 1945 showed that tyrants like Hitler and Stalin did not have all the answers. Free government could find efficient and compassionate solutions to the deepest problems of the age. When FDR became president unemployment was 25 per cent; when he died it was less than two. America, an ailing giant in 1933, was now the arsenal of democracy, improbably allied with Stalin to defeat Hitler in the most terrible war in history, a war which determined the direction world history took for the rest of the century. When he died Roosevelt had become the greatest president of the twentieth century, a leader who inspired democratic nations to defend freedom against the tyranny of fascism.

His closest companions sought in vain to explain how an amiable cripple had achieved this. Few of those who watched his political career before he became president in 1933 believed he would become the great president history recalls. Moreover, the man loved by millions was himself unable to open his heart to others. Neither his remarkable wife Eleanor, until Hillary Clinton in the 1990s the only first lady in American history to have a significant political life of her own, nor his five children, nor his mistress Lucy Mercer, once Eleanor's secretary, who was in Warm Springs when he died, nor his closest confidantes like Louis Howe and Harry Hopkins ever penetrated 'his heavily forested interior', as

FDR's speechwriter Robert Sherwood vividly called it. 'I could never really understand what was going on in there,' Sherwood added. On the surface FDR was to all appearances open, genial, fun-loving, easy-going, a charming man. But beneath the surface different forces were at work which no one, least of all FDR himself, has ever been able to fathom. 'The most complicated man I ever knew,' wrote Frances Perkins, who knew him for years. He appeared easy-going. Yet his core was diamond hard. 'It's the hard surface that takes the high polish,' his long-time cabinet colleague Harold Ickes explained.

Roosevelt's relationship with the American electorate was equally puzzling. He was not simply supported but idolized by millions of Americans from every social class, especially the poorest. 'He was the only president who understood that my boss is a son-of-a-bitch,' said one workman. Millions of others thought the same. Yet this champion of the poor, the greatest vote-winner in US history, had been raised in lonely splendour, the only child of one of the nation's oldest, proudest and richest families. Though loved more than any American president of the twentieth century, he was hated too. 'Kill FDR' was often scrawled on walls during his 12-year term. Nor was he just hated by those who scrawl slogans. Many of America's richest and most powerful people loathed 'That man in the White House' and his New Deal reforms. They feared FDR because they believed that by spending to end unemployment, launching federal provision of social security, backing welfare reform and labour unions and attacking monopoly he had sent America down the slippery slope to socialism. His attempt to reform the Supreme Court in 1937, and so make it more pliant to his New Deal, was seen by many as proof that Roosevelt was a twentieth-century Caesar. That he then broke the two-term convention to become the first president to be re-elected for a third term in 1940 merely confirmed their suspicions. FDR had become what the Founding Fathers had most feared: an elected king.

Other critics attacked his foreign policy with equal gusto. They charged him with having dragged America into war with Japan and Germany despite repeated promises that he would not do so. Worse, he had then betrayed democracy by giving Stalin control of central and eastern Europe at the 1945 Yalta conference. In short, his critics, many from the same patrician background as Roosevelt himself, despised him as a traitor to his class and nation. This was further irony. No one did more than FDR to save democratic capitalism. In the deepening world crisis of the 1930s the United States had been firmly isolationist, preoccupied with domestic problems. Yet Roosevelt had seen the danger. If the efforts of Germany and Japan to redraw the world map by force led to world war then the

United States would inevitably be involved. He tried to alert America to the danger posed by fascism and militarism but with small success.

His Four Freedoms – freedom of speech and religion, freedom from want and fear – defined what the war was about. In the end the nation was driven to fight in December 1941 only when Japan attacked Pearl Harbor. Roosevelt, proving himself as effective in war as in peace, used 1942 to bring America's full industrial and military might to bear. In the next three years, while the Red Army tore the heart out of the German invader, the United States aided both Britain and the Soviet Union, fought in North Africa, the Pacific and later Europe and developed the atomic bomb which ended the war with Japan in August 1945. Not only had Germany and Japan been crushed. America had become the world's economic, financial, military and political powerhouse. War in the 1940s in fact completed the process FDR had begun in the 1930s with his New Deal. He had saved American capitalism. Yet these hectic events did not change American institutions nor redistribute wealth and power in the nation. Indeed, he used political power precisely to prevent that happening. In fact, during the New Deal and the war, agriculture, banking, business, finance and industry were restored to health. Reforms which helped the working class and the poor were real and effective. But they were designed not so much to stimulate significant change as avert it. So the United States emerged from depression and war with its economic, political and social systems essentially unscathed, with personal wealth distributed in roughly the same proportions and, more important, with a share of world power unparalleled in modern history. Liberals and conservatives alike could applaud that. As the historian A.J.P. Taylor says of the war years, 'Of the three great men at the top, Roosevelt was the only one who knew what he was doing: he made the United States the greatest power in the world at virtually no cost.'

From the vantage point of this century, however, we can see that Roosevelt's leadership left a legacy which, during the Cold War between 1945 and 1990, enabled world capitalism, led by the United States, to resist and finally vanquish the challenge of world Communism. Moreover, however much historians may differ about Roosevelt and his use of power, some fundamental points are plain. Between 1933 and 1945 his administration saved the American system of democratic capitalism and made the United States accept the full responsibilities of world power. Abroad between 1941 and 1945 he helped liberate 'captive nations' in Asia and Europe from alien military dictatorship. At home he helped both capital and labour, landlord and tenant, creditor and debtor, rich and poor. The grieving crowds lining the railtrack in April 1945 came from every social class, which was convincing and moving testimony both to his stature as political leader and to his use of political power. Yet many Americans knew that, though he had helped all his fellow citizens, he had not helped everyone equally. Hence it was in the way people perceived their dead president that the greatest irony of all about Franklin Roosevelt was revealed. The real work he did for the poor, for organized labour and the birth of the American welfare state must be set against even more solid help for banking, big business and finance. In that sense there was always some truth in the left-wing jibe that he was loved by those for whom he had done least and hated by those for whom he had done most.

## Chapter 2

※

# The Power of Patrician Upbringing, 1882–1911

I

Franklin Delano Roosevelt was a key figure in the critical years of the twentieth century who acted on the world stage with Hitler, Stalin and Churchill. In what was popularly called the American century or the century of the common man FDR became champion of the common people not just of America but the world. Yet not the least of the many paradoxes about his life was that, from the very start, aristocratic birth set him apart from the American people he came to lead. The political power he won and used with such zest and effect must be first examined within this context.

Roosevelt is a Dutch name. The first Europeans to settle in New York were fur traders from Holland. In 1624 they established a small community on Manhattan Island which, until 1664, remained a Dutch colony. With little or no backing from Holland, the small province of New Netherlands grew slowly, failing to establish the effective self-government that other colonies, planted by English settlers, were able to evolve. But it did leave a permanent mark in the patroon system of plantations which grew along the Hudson river, and in the 'Knickerbocker' families who were to play an important role in the history of New York and the United States.

Roosevelt was born into such a family of landed aristocrats on 30 January 1882. His father James was not simply a millionaire. His was one of the proudest and oldest names in the land. More important, he represented 'old money'. His mother Sara Delano came from another old-established family. The Roosevelts had made their fortune from land and trading in the eighteenth century and increased their wealth during the nineteenth. James owned copper lands, iron and coal mines, acreage on New York harbour and a fleet of clipper ships, but managers ran his businesses for him so he could enjoy his country estates and, like his father, dabble in Democratic party politics.

Franklin Roosevelt grew up keenly aware of the tradition which he had inherited. In a student history thesis on 'The Roosevelts in New Amsterdam' he explained, 'Some of the famous Dutch families in New York today have nothing left but their name – they are few in numbers, they lack progressivism and a true democratic spirit. One reason – perhaps the chief – of the virility of the Roosevelts is their very democratic spirit . . . They have felt . . . that . . . there was no excuse for them if they did not do their duty by the community . . .'.[1]

As a political friend told him when he ran for national office in 1920, 'We want gentlemen to represent us. Frankness, and largeness and simplicity, and a fine fervour for the right, are virtues that some must preserve, and where can one look for them if not from the Roosevelts and the Delanos?'[2] This sense of *noblesse oblige* was one reason Roosevelt entered politics. He believed it the duty of progressive reformers to seek power and tame corporate interests which, as he grew up in the 1880s and 1890s, were challenging established landed families like the Roosevelts.

## II

But for the moment such power struggles left no apparent trace on Frank's charmed world. When he was born, his father James was 53, his first wife having died in 1876. James then married Sara Delano in 1880 when she was 26, the same age as James's son by his first marriage. So while Frank's father treated him like a grandson, Sara lavished quite remarkable, yet possessive, love on her only child. He was brought up on the beautiful Hyde Park estate with indulgence unusual even for his social class. He had governesses and tutors; he owned a pony and a 21-foot sailboat; he toured Europe eight times before adolescence.

His childhood was idyllic but lonely. He did not go to school until he was 16, when he became a boarder at Groton, where the headmaster Endicott Peabody mixed the lessons of Greek democracy with Christian ethics. Further, between the age of 10 and 18 Frank's conduct was constrained by the fact that his father became an invalid after a stroke. Throughout the crucial years of adolescence, rebellion against parents, a key part of normal teenage development, was not part of his. This desire to please, especially to please his loving mother, and not to be seen doing anything which might upset people, became an important part of Roosevelt's personality in adolescence and adult life. Moreover, it is not without significance that, throughout his life, a common description of Roosevelt's eager, happy demeanour was that it was 'boyish'.

All this seems to have played a part in making him lonely and unhappy at Groton. His peers devalued a fellow pupil so determined to please his elders. Moreover, the long years he had spent alone growing up at Hyde Park had not prepared him for the rough and tumble of school, the playing fields and dormitory. He was not used to being ragged, made fun of, challenged to fight like most schoolboys. Worse, he had started at Groton two years after the rest of his class, when everyone else had made their friends. At this stage of his life he was an outsider and he made no close contacts at Groton. Moreover, sport played an important part in the life of the school, and young Roosevelt was not good at games.

He grew into a big, strong, handsome man who enjoyed the physical side of life and was a good yachtsman, swimmer and outdoor person, but he never made a mark at team games. 'I never could understand all this fuss about Frank,' Groton's captain of baseball Geoffrey Potter wrote when his former schoolmate became president in March 1933. 'He never amounted to anything much at school.'³ One biographer, Arthur Schlesinger, argues that too much can be made of his failure at Groton. It contrasts with so much success everywhere else in his life. But as his wife Eleanor wrote fifty years later, 'He felt left out. It gave him sympathy for people who are left out.'⁴ Whatever the truth of the matter, he himself knew at the time that something had gone wrong, and vowed it would not happen again when he went on to Harvard in 1900.

Nor did it. His four years at one of America's most illustrious universities were far happier. Though by no means a high flyer, he impressed his tutors and finished a four-year course in three, spending his final year editing the student newspaper *Crimson*, an experience which gave him lifelong rapport with journalists and his first taste of adult politics. In short, at Harvard Roosevelt started to find himself as a person and became a self-confident young man who was taken seriously by serious people.

III

Other more significant events were shaping the adult world of work and politics into which Frank was moving. The Democratic party, to which Hyde Park Roosevelts like his father had belonged, could trace its origins back to Andrew Jackson in the 1830s, or even Thomas Jefferson in the 1790s. But the modern two-party system had been created by the conflict over slavery which began in the 1840s and destroyed the earlier system.

The old Whig party of Henry Clay and Daniel Webster broke into pro- and anti-slavery factions and disappeared in the early 1850s. The Democrats, increasingly divided into Northern and Southern factions, struggled unsuccessfully to preserve unity of party and nation. The Republican party, which emerged in the 1850s from this break-up and realignment, was a coalition determined to resist slave expansion into territories west of the Mississippi. When the Democrats finally split in 1860, the Republican Abraham Lincoln was elected president with less than 40 per cent of the poll and without a single popular vote in ten Southern slave states. When these states seceded, Lincoln fought the Civil War to save the Union and, in defeating the South, helped destroy slavery.

Reconstruction after the war, between 1865 and 1877, set a pattern for American politics which lasted until the 1890s and in many ways until the 1930s. The Republicans – the Grand Old Party (GOP), the party of abolition, civil war and military occupation after defeat – did not exist in the South. By giving millions of freed African-American slaves the vote, Republicans had hoped to win black support in a new, democratized South. But local white resistance proved invincible. By contrast, the GOP won support elsewhere. They passed the 1862 Homestead Act, which gave settlers in new states in the West free land, hoping grateful settlers would vote Republican. By 1870 it was no longer the purely Northern sectional party which had elected Lincoln and won the war.

Nevertheless, now that former Confederate states had been restored to the Union, the Democrats were once again a truly national party, with support in every region. The disputed presidential election of 1876 showed what this meant. The result was too close to call, and fraud by both sides further put the result in dispute. So Congress brokered the Compromise of March 1877. Both sides agreed that the Republican, Rutherford Hayes, with only 48 per cent of the popular vote, had defeated the Democratic New Yorker Samuel Tilden, with 51 per cent, in the electoral college 185–184. This dubious victory settled the political balance of power for a generation. The Republicans won control of national politics; Democrats were given control of the South where they established white supremacy. This proved a lasting settlement. Nationwide, Republicans won every presidential election between 1860 and 1912, apart from Grover Cleveland's two narrow victories in 1884 and 1892.

Elections were still closely contested, while partisan rivalry in politics remained intense. The GOP had become not just the party of Union victory, but of industrial and Western expansion, high tariffs and post-war prosperity. They were backed not only by big business, banking and finance, but also by the middle class, skilled workers and farmers in most places outside the old South. Such support in the more populous states of the North and West meant Republicans usually controlled the White House, Congress and nominations to the US Supreme Court. Democrats, by contrast, not only monopolized Southern politics but also had political presence in every state of the Union. This meant that, while enjoying the benefits of a one-party system at home, Southern Democrats, re-elected to Congress without real opposition, could win seniority and influence on key committees, such as Rules, Appropriations and Judiciary, when they occasionally won a national majority there.

Since Republicans usually won support from rich, mercantile landed families like the Roosevelts it is not immediately clear why Frank's father James should have been a Democrat. The Oyster Bay branch of the family, into which Frank's cousin Theodore Roosevelt was born in 1858, was after all Republican. Yet American politics were not primarily ideological. Both parties were broad coalitions designed to make the widest possible appeal across social class and sectional interests. Party preference often became a matter of personal taste. James was growing up when the Democrat Andrew Jackson dominated the scene and matured when his style dominated politics. He had remained a Union Democrat during the Civil War. Moreover, since many of James's interests were in New York City, which was ruled by Democrats through its formidable political machine Tammany Hall, it made sense for Hyde Park Roosevelts to be Democrats too.


IV


Party politics did not fully reflect more important forces which were changing the nature of power between 1877 and 1900 when Roosevelt was growing into manhood. Industrialization, immigration, Western expansion and white racism were transforming America. Old postwar political slogans lost their force, although in race relations Southern whites extended segregation and second-class citizenship for African Americans across the nation as a whole. Blacks in the South were denied the vote or access to law, forced to sharecrop with white landowners, confined to the least secure, lowest paid jobs and liable to lynching at any time.

The 14th Amendment to the Constitution was passed during Reconstruction to define and protect citizenship for freed slaves. Yet in a series of legal decisions, culminating in the landmark 1896 case *Plessy* v. *Ferguson*, the Supreme Court ruled Southern segregation constitutional and imposed it on the whole nation. The fate of the 14th Amendment revealed the real balance of power in America as Roosevelt grew to manhood. For the courts which struck down the rights of black Americans with such gusto eagerly used the same amendment to uphold the property rights and political power of corporate interests. Roosevelt became a progressive, Northern reformer but did so in a party where Southern white supremacists were the solid core.

Roosevelt was uninterested in seeking a cure for poisoned race relations. The reforms he came to embrace were designed to tame the growing power of corporate America. This new corporate power sprang from industrialization, which was further transforming the nation. Between 1870 and 1900 the United States grew from fourth to first place among the industrial nations of the world. Exploiting her abundant natural resources, a new class of capitalist entrepreneurs made America not just a rival nation to Britain, France and Germany, but a rival continent to all Europe. By 1900 free competition was creating consolidation. With the weakest economic enterprises driven to the wall, mergers led to a system of cartels, monopolies and syndicates known as trusts. Largely formed in the late 1890s and early 1900s, trusts were the symbol of corporate power. The first 'billion dollar trust' was United States Steel, formed in 1901. Trusts not only revolutionized industrial production, transport and communications but also increasingly controlled America's services and public utilities, her financial and economic life. The old middle class – doctors, lawyers, preachers – had been swept aside. The new captains of industry – Andrew Carnegie, John D. Rockefeller and the financier J.P. Morgan – dwarfed even old families like the Roosevelts.

Moreover, the Roosevelts and other established landowners felt threatened not only from above but from below. Industrialization was in part the creation of a vast new working class. Unrestricted immigration from Europe provided an endless supply of labour, ethnically diverse and often unused to life in a modern, urban industrial democracy. Some struggled to form trade unions to protect their wages, hours and conditions, but with little success. The interests of skilled workers were opposed to those of unskilled. Competing amongst themselves, the working class were exploited not only by employers but also by those who ran the politics of America's teeming cities. The first great wave of immigrants had been Irish fleeing famine in the 1840s. Political forces created by anti-Catholicism, xenophobia and party break-up over slavery and secession combined to make Irish-Americans vote overwhelmingly Democrat, the first ethnic group to give such solid support to one party.

Other immigrants, such as Germans, who eventually outnumbered all others, voted Democrat or Republican according to time, place and circumstance. But whichever party they joined, the main point was that within a generation such ethnic groups were tending to run the politics of big cities. Bosses organized political machines to control municipal democracy. Tammany Hall, which ruled New York City in Roosevelt's own state, was the oldest and most notorious political machine in America; but similar machines flourished in other cities such as Boston, Chicago, Philadelphia and St Louis. Machine politics grew when services and favours were traded for votes, with bosses supplying somewhat ramshackle welfare and institutional structure to burgeoning municipal government.

So, as the twentieth century opened, those who had traditionally provided political leadership, like the Roosevelts, believed American democracy was now under increasing attack. In the South, largely untouched by industrialization and immigration, white supremacists ran politics and race relations. In the national economy the new captains of industry stifled free enterprise and bought influence wholesale. In the cities, which were growing at such phenomenal pace, corrupt political bosses ruled. In industry, labour unions clamoured for more and led strikes. Faced with all this, campaigns for reform, often led by the American middle class, began to emerge. Such reform was essentially conservative, designed to enhance middle-class control of the American system of democracy and free enterprise, thus restoring a largely imaginary past when these virtues were believed to have flourished.

Yet reform began in rural America. In 1890 Congress had passed the Sherman Anti-Trust Act to attack monopoly. Since Reconstruction currency reform had long been popular with Western farmers, anxious to relieve their crushing burden of debt. What a farmer could have repaid with 1,000 bushels of wheat in 1865 now cost 3,000 bushels. In the 1890s chronically indebted farmers launched the new Populist political party in Western grain and silver states, and in parts of the South, which urged farmers to demand that the dollar be backed by silver as well as gold. Free silver, by increasing money supply, would ease the pain of chronic debt. At first it proved so irresistible that Democrats merged with Populists to back the great evangelical orator W.J. Bryan in the 1896 presidential election. But the Populist demand for free silver terrified bankers and the urban middle or skilled working classes, who were frightened into voting for Bryan's opponent William McKinley, giving the GOP the biggest share of the popular vote won by any party since 1872. Populism rapidly declined and free silver became a heresy, like free love.

But other reformers took up the rest of the Populist programme of reform. Calling themselves progressives, these reformers entered the twentieth century demanding more effective anti-trust measures, primary elections to defeat political bosses, women's suffrage, direct election of senators, federal income tax, a federal reserve bank, railway regulation, greater popular control of the political economy. Populists had been agrarian and sectional, confined to the Dakotas, Nebraska, Kansas and parts of the South, only briefly influencing the Democrats. The new progressives were predominantly urban, small businessmen, professional middle class and skilled working class who successfully penetrated both parties nationwide. They concentrated on two goals: breaking the monopoly power of the trusts; and ending the political corruption of the bosses and their machines. The theme of progressivism was regulation and control of the economy and the political process in the public interest. As Roosevelt came of age and went up to Harvard, progressive ideas were shaping his approach to political power.

V

Then something unexpected happened which dramatized the importance of political power both to the Roosevelt family and the nation. His cousin Theodore ('Teddy') Roosevelt suddenly became president of the United States when McKinley was assassinated on 14 September 1901. Teddy Roosevelt, or TR as he was known, came from the Oyster Bay Republican branch of the family. He had been elected governor of New York in 1898 and then McKinley's vice-president in 1900. His accidental transition to the White House personified the arrival of progressivism centre stage. For although at 42 the youngest president in history, TR was clearly already a great man, combining first-class brains with tireless energy, ambition, vision and a policy which he later orchestrated into the New Nationalism. 'Bristling with buck teeth and jingoism', Teddy Roosevelt also had remarkable physical presence and a genius for self-dramatization. Such was his fame as a hunter that the 'teddy bear' was named after him.

Seizing leadership of the progressive reform movement as president after 1901, TR embarked on a series of high-profile anti-trust suits, like the Northern Securities case, ostensibly to break up monopoly capitalism. Billion-dollar trusts were being formed by corporate takeovers and mergers despite the Sherman Anti-Trust Act. Progressives believed that these monopolies, such as Standard Oil and American Tobacco, threatened free enterprise, free institutions and the whole American concept of the public good. So in the first decade of the new century progressives in both parties were struggling to establish popular political control over corporate capitalism. Using the White House, in his own words, as 'a bully pulpit', Teddy Roosevelt was not just the first progressive president, but first of the modern presidents, expanding the power and influence of both presidency and federal government. He also combined demands for social reform at home with jingoism abroad. Having famously led his 'Rough Riders' in the 1898 Spanish–American war, as president he forced Colombia to cede territory on which America built the Panama Canal to expand her naval and imperial ambitions.

An overbearing but essentially kindly man, he found time too to show an affectionate interest in young cousin Frank's life, writing letters and meeting him. There is no doubt either that Frank was strongly influenced by the older Roosevelt's example. Though he belonged to the opposing political party Frank, in common with many college men of his generation, saw himself as a progressive. He supported Teddy's attack on monopoly, labour unrest and political corruption. He voted for him in 1904 (his first vote for a president) not from family affection but 'because I thought he was a better Democrat than the Democratic candidate', the conservative nonentity Alton Parker.[5] Since Teddy Roosevelt was president until 1909, during which time he dominated political debate, Frank's agenda as he began his own quest for power was partly set by TR. He supported the president's florid attacks on 'malefactors of great wealth' who monopolized American capitalism and thus denied democratic opportunity.

As president, Teddy Roosevelt's attacks on the trusts were largely moral and ceremonial in character, designed to relieve middle-class anxiety about monopoly and scare capitalists into accepting self-regulation for fear of being forced to accept something worse. Frank learned a lot about the importance of appearance in American politics from this and later became a master at applying that lesson himself. Both Roosevelts also believed that conservation of America's natural resources against the predatory instincts of those who sought to exploit them for gain was the key political issue of the day. Indeed, throughout his life conservation was the issue closest to Frank's heart. He liked to copy his cousin in other ways too, while evolving his own political beliefs, style and voice. He took to wearing Teddy's type of eye-glasses, used the term 'bully' to express approval and pronounced himself 'dee-lighted!' when something pleased him. Many American men of the progressive period did the same. Franklin Roosevelt alone could already nurture serious ambitions that one day he might follow in his cousin's footsteps. When as a small boy his father had introduced him to Grover Cleveland, the president had dolefully hoped Frank would never grow up to become president himself. Years later, when asked how he enjoyed the job, cousin Teddy had flashed his teeth at his young cousin and replied, 'Ripping, simply ripping!' Gleefully recalling this contrast, FDR left no doubt which view he took of being president.[6]

## VI

Though his cousin's dazzling example in those years helped focus Frank's aim on winning political power, something of more short-term significance was happening in his private life. While studying at Harvard, he had met and fallen in love with Teddy Roosevelt's niece Eleanor, his own fifth cousin two years his junior. Unlike Frank's idyllic childhood, Eleanor's had been miserably unhappy. Her beautiful mother Anna brought little Nel up to believe she was ugly. Her father Elliott, Uncle Teddy's brother, whom she adored, was a drunk. When she was eight her mother died so Nel was sent to live with the grandmother. Two years later her father also died. Now an orphan, Eleanor's salvation came when at 15 she was sent to Allenswood, a British girls' boarding school. Her gifted French headteacher, Marie Souvestre, saw her talents, helped her find them and encouraged her to use them in adult life. But when she met Frank this socially prominent debutante was not interested in politics. She was seeking the happiness and security she had lacked as a child. As their courtship progressed she believed that, beneath his easy-going, fun-loving exterior, Frank could give her what she craved. All his life, in his own or in America's greatest crises, FDR always loved a good time. Eleanor soon discerned that, beneath this surface hedonism, the playboy Harvard graduate, dilettante and editor of *Crimson*, was a serious and dependable young man.

His mother Sara, however, knew nothing about Eleanor until they announced their engagement. Possessive love made her oppose the idea; but though she tried to break it up she was finally reconciled. They were married on 17 March 1905: St Patrick's Day, such an important political holiday in New York City that the sound of the Tammany parade nearly drowned the responses. Yet they had picked that date so that Eleanor's uncle Teddy could attend to give away the bride in a ceremony conducted by Frank's former headmaster, Endicott Peabody. For the fashionable guests it was the wedding of the year. No one could then see, except by clairvoyance, that it was the start of the most important American political marriage of the twentieth century.

Eleanor eventually bore her husband a daughter named Anna and five sons (one of whom died in infancy) to add lustre to the Roosevelt name. Meanwhile Frank was taking the first steps in his political career. After

Harvard, he went to Columbia Law School, but with no great enthusiasm. When he got married it did not seem necessary to complete the university law course. So in 1906 he passed the New York state bar exam but did not graduate from Columbia. Much later, joshed by university president Nicholas Murray Butler that, 'You will never be able to call yourself an intellectual until you come back to Columbia and pass your law exams', FDR laughingly retorted, 'That just shows how unimportant the law really is.' The idea that he was remotely interested in becoming an intellectual shows how little Butler understood him. Yet later FDR explained, 'You know you don't learn law at our law schools. You learn how to think.'[7] Unlike cousin Teddy, voracious reader and writer of substantial historical works, he was not interested in books, though he later came to value the company of those who were. Meanwhile, having passed the state bar exam he played at rather than practised law in New York City. With his great fortune and family name he might have done what young men from the leisure class commonly did by joining the idle rich and dabbling in politics as his father had done. But that was not FDR's way. True, he joined Carter, Ledyard and Milburn at 54 Wall Street, a bluechip firm whose best clients, big corporations like Standard Oil of Ohio and American Tobacco, were the very people who were vigorously fighting Theodore Roosevelt's anti-trust suits in federal court.

That his law firm should be in the vanguard of resistance to the central thrust of progressive reform was yet another FDR irony. But the young lawyer was too junior to take part in these legal battles against trust busting. Instead, he became interested in municipal court work, where cases involving poorer clients, rather than those who could afford to pay fat fees, went to trial. Municipal court involved the daily life of New York City; and this meant daily involvement with city politics, run most years by the Democrats through Tammany Hall, the oldest political machine in America. Tammany's boss, Charles F. Murphy, became an example of the new kind of more responsible urban politician emerging during the progressive period in contrast to crooks like his predecessor Richard Croker, who usually ran affairs in urban America. Municipal court helped Roosevelt understand the way American politics worked in the real world, as opposed to Harvard textbooks.

During this period he expressed for the first time political ambitions. A fellow law clerk remembered him saying at work one day in 1907 'with engaging frankness' that he planned to run for public office soon and that he wanted to be president. Cousin Teddy supplied the model: first the state assembly, then assistant secretary of the Navy, then governor of New York. 'Anyone who is governor of New York', he concluded, 'has a good chance to be president with any luck.'[8] The last part was certainly true. In nine of sixteen campaigns between the Civil War and 1932, one of the two leading candidates was either a governor or former governor of New York: Seymour, Tilden, Cleveland (three elections), Theodore Roosevelt (twice), Hughes and Smith. Of this group five were Democrats.

So there it was. At the age of 25 Roosevelt was seriously seeking political power. As a New Yorker he knew that this meant he must learn to work with men like Murphy. But at the same time he aspired to walk in the footsteps of cousin Teddy who, in 1907, dominated the American political scene. In so far as he had a political agenda at this stage of his life, he aimed at tackling both bosses who ran machine politics and plutocrats who ran the trusts, forcing both to accept new responsibilities. However, conservation of America's environment and its resources was the issue closest to his heart and as he matured he orchestrated a policy of management of American resources for the public good. Yet it is important to grasp that at this stage FDR was already bored with the life of a lawyer and wanted the fun and excitement politics would bring.

Nevertheless, his chance to campaign for political power came sooner than he had expected. When Teddy Roosevelt left the White House in 1909, the progressive movement in New York and across the nation was on the crest of a wave. An irresistible demand for reform was building up and, in 1910, local New York Democratic party managers asked FDR to run for election to the state senate for rural Columbia, Dutchess and Putnam counties.[9]

This was not surprising. Rich men, especially rich men with famous names, were often asked to run for hopelessly unwinnable seats like this, not least because they could pay for their own campaign. But this year was different. Not only did progressivism give Roosevelt the chance to campaign for the kind of clean government which would appeal to the conservative farmers of upstate New York, but also across the whole nation it was a Democratic year, the first for nearly two decades. The Republicans, their national power intact since 1892, were now badly split over reform, the tariff, conservation and much else. A little-known 54-year-old university professor, president of Princeton, named Woodrow Wilson, who was running as progressive Democratic candidate for governor in the adjoining state of New Jersey, was expected to win.

Since the founding of the Republican party in the 1850s only one Democrat had won the district Frank was now contesting. At this stage Roosevelt was a bad public speaker, his grating, upper-class English-sounding accent often punctuated by long pauses. But he always loved campaigning, and did so now with great gusto, touring the district in an open red motor car. This, plus the fact that some farmers may have thought a Roosevelt must be a Republican, plus heavy rain on polling day, which kept some die-hard opponents at home, plus the rising tide of political reform, all helped him run well ahead of the Democratic ticket and beat his Republican opponent by more than a thousand votes.[10]

In some respects, FDR's first political victory was the result of luck – the Roosevelt luck which followed him most of his life. The important point, however, was that FDR always anticipated his luck with careful groundwork, and capitalized on it afterwards. To see the truth of this, one need only compare him with Theodore Roosevelt Jr, Teddy's son. An amiable young man, bearer of the same famous name, he had ambition, brains, charm and every opportunity to become his father's successor. After a spell as assistant secretary of the Navy he ran in 1924 for governor of New York when Republicans were riding high. But he was defeated and never heard of again.[11] In this light, FDR's success depended on something more than mere chance. Whatever it was, the 1910 election meant that at the age of only 28 the world of political power was already at his feet.

## Chapter 3

# Power in Albany and Washington, 1911–21

I

When Roosevelt went to Albany as a freshman state senator in January 1911, state politics counted for much more than they do today. This was particularly true in New York, the most populous and prosperous state in the Union. Its economy combined strong agricultural, manufacturing and mercantile interests. New York City was the largest in America. It was also one of the world's most profitable manufacturing centres, a city of garment, printing and many other small firms producing specialized goods. Manhattan alone was the site of over half a million manufacturing jobs, while the sprawling districts of Brooklyn, the Bronx and Queens were home to a largely Irish, Italian and Jewish working class. As America's busiest port, New York handled one-third of US international trade and was also centre of the nation's financial life and its cultural capital. America's dominant trusts in railways and utilities and most effective political machine, Tammany Hall, operated there. But though New York City tended to dwarf the state, there were other important urban centres, such as Buffalo, Rochester and Syracuse. Yet, with more farms than Kansas, agricultural interests dominated upstate New York. As noted above, six major party candidates for president since the Civil War had been a governor, or former governor, of New York. No state exercised more influence on national politics.

This was Roosevelt's first taste of political power, and his use of it was revealing. His approach was bold, high-spirited, dramatic but essentially conservative. On arrival in Albany he spurned his father's old friends, Cleveland Democrats from the 1890s. The new Democratic governor, John A. Dix, was a dull and unimaginative manufacturer. Nor did FDR seek to make friends with Robert Wagner, who at 33 was Tammany's choice as the new senate leader, or Alfred E. Smith, at 37 a seasoned veteran of seven terms, chosen by Tammany as new majority leader in the assembly.[1] Both Smith and Wagner were to play crucial roles in American politics and in Roosevelt's own career. Eventually he outshone them. But at this stage he was still finding his way.

Yet his victory in 1910 had already revealed the central fact of FDR's political career: he was a great vote-winner. The big corporations – Standard Oil, pulp and water power producers, the railways, the insurance institutions, the gas companies and the New York traction interests – among them had control of the state's services and regulatory bodies. They were powerful opponents of reform. Moreover, the Republican political machine, run by Thomas C. Platt, usually kept control of New York. Tammany could not win control of the whole state, as it had just done, without the support of reform Democrats from upstate like FDR. So he immediately embarked upon the kind of turbulent, high-profile political battle his cousin Theodore Roosevelt loved.

## II

There were sound reasons for doing this. FDR was only the second Democrat elected from his district since 1854. His victory alerted Louis Howe, soon to become his closest friend, but for the moment simply an objective journalist. 'A perfectly hopeless fight,' Howe said in wonder, 'yet Roosevelt won it.' Still he could not immediately expect to make a mark. Winning a freak victory is one thing. Gaining re-election would be much more unusual. As Howe explained, 'A new senator in Albany is of an importance somewhere between a janitor and a committee clerk.'[2] So if FDR wished to go any further in politics he would have to make a bigger reputation in two years than the average state senator achieved in two decades. If he kept his head down, hanging on for re-election, he would probably lose. So he decided to take on Tammany and try to make his name that way. It showed that Roosevelt was already a shrewd political operator. The publicity would only add to the power of his famous name and he loved a good political scrap.

The issue on which he fought simply fell into his lap. New York lagged behind more progressive states in not yet having direct election of US senators. So the most important task facing the new Democratic majority was electing a successor to the retiring Republican Chauncey M. Depew. Tammany's boss Murphy wanted William Sheehan. Young Roosevelt chose to see the selection of 'Blue-eyed Billy' Sheehan as a betrayal of his party's commitment to progressive government. Not only was Sheehan a wealthy businessman and law partner to Alton Parker, the conservative

Democrat Roosevelt had refused to vote for in 1904, but he was also sponsored both by Tammany and by railway and utilities interests. 'The Democratic party is on trial,' Roosevelt announced on New Year's Day 1911, 'and having been given control of government chiefly through upState vote, cannot afford to surrender its control to the organization in New York City.'[3]

The new legislature would appoint the new senator. Of 200 legislators, 114 were Democrats so 101 would elect. Thus Murphy only needed to manipulate 50 to 60 votes in the Democratic caucus to elect a US senator. This was so outrageously undemocratic that FDR could have campaigned on that and made popular, direct election of senators the issue. Instead, he hoped that fighting Tammany's choice of senator would remind New York voters of the fact. Other Democrats had similar doubts and though FDR at first did not want to break openly with the party, the anti-Sheehan faction, which coalesced when the party caucus met, made him their chairman. Ten weeks of bitter struggle began.[4]

Leadership had little to do with the force of Roosevelt's personality. His wealth meant that, unlike the other state legislators, he could afford to rent a large house in Albany for his family which served as headquarters for the insurgents. The tall, slim, intense young man with his good suits, high collars and gold-framed pince-nez spectacles emerged as their spokesman. He had a habit of throwing his head up when talking. Later, as president during the New Deal, this became a gesture of courage and self-confidence. But in the early days of his career it made him seem to be looking down his nose. 'Awful arrogant fellow, that Roosevelt,' commented Tammany's affable Timothy ('Big Tim') Sullivan.[5]

Despite this, the fight against Tammany brought him publicity. His name and easy accessibility were a gift to the newspapers, and for the first time his reputation began to spread beyond New York. 'There is nothing I love so much as a good fight,' he told the *New York Times*. 'I have never had so much fun in my life as I am having right now.' The issue, he told the *Times* was 'bossism'. As he explained to the Toledo, Ohio, *News-Bee*, 'Business must get out of politics. The people must make a stand against it. The Murphys, who represent business, must be cleaned out.'[6]

There was not much chance of this. Murphy was far too powerful. Though the insurgents might stop him from doing something he wanted, they could not force him to do something he did not want. Moreover, Roosevelt had no man he wished to become senator and no compunction about consorting with Wall Street lawyers himself in the fight against Sheehan. His first law firm had defended some of America's biggest corporations in anti-trust suits, while he had just become partner in another such firm, Emmett and Marvin. 'All Wall Street is not bad,' he explained privately, 'as a residence here of four years has shown me.'[7] This was a forecast of his future ambivalence towards financial power. Even more important, he already understood the importance of symbols in politics. His words and actions now in the fight against Sheehan helped create a powerful symbol: the battle against bossism and the trusts.

As this rancorous political row continued into February and March, boss Murphy began to look for a compromise, at which Roosevelt was already an expert. Murphy's support for Sheehan had always been half-hearted and in the crunch was slipping. Most of the insurgents were equally eager for a way out. As legislators, they were used to coming to Albany only for Monday evening sessions and perhaps a day or so more. Lacking Roosevelt's money, they relied entirely on a small salary and were soon suffering serious financial loss. Other candidates were suggested by both sides and then discarded until on 29 March fire struck the Capitol building, forcing legislators to meet in cramped quarters in city hall and so seek a quick solution. Eventually, as their unity crumbled away, the insurgents reluctantly accepted, as a substitute for Sheehan, Justice James O'Gorman, a former Grand Sachem of Tammany, more closely identified with Murphy than Sheehan had been.

The press almost unanimously judged this an ignominious defeat for Roosevelt and the insurgents.[8] But Al Smith and Robert Wagner promised the rebels there would be no reprisals and restored Roosevelt to the party. Characteristically, throughout the rest of his career he always presented this defeat as a triumph. It was characteristic too that people believed him. In his first year in politics FDR had already revealed some of his most important attributes: that he was a great vote-winner; that he loved political conflict; that he also enjoyed compromise; and that he was a master at using surface appearance to mask underlying reality. Yet the real significance of the Sheehan episode was that it had shown the essentially cosmetic nature of most progressive reforms. Up to about 1911–12, progressivism was still primarily concerned with political change aimed at ending political corruption. Soon conflict about working conditions and welfare would seize the reform agenda and transform the nature of political power in the progressive period.[9]

III

This transition from cosmetic to social reform marked a decisive shift in early twentieth-century reform politics. One of its catalysts was the

Triangle shirtwaist factory fire in New York City which occurred on 25 March 1911 while the insurgent movement against Sheehan was reaching its climax. Most of the 148 who died were young women and some 150 more were injured.[10] Hundreds of other factories and buildings, in New York and across the nation, were similarly at risk. Public outcry forced the legislature to set up a state factory investigating commission, on which such senior politicians as Smith and Wagner played leading roles. The subsequent series of safety laws proved landmarks not only in factory legislation but also in transforming the nature of social reform.

Yet Roosevelt took no part in the commission, while his copious correspondence for 1911 makes no mention of the Triangle fire.[11] Given his background this is not really surprising. Not simply his aristocratic upbringing, but his Hudson river district meant that he concentrated on rural Republican rather than urban Democratic issues. Progressivism in both New York and the nation was still primarily the programme of middle-class farmers, or business and professional men. They supported clean government, conservation and aid to the farmer. Farmers were concerned about the price the canneries paid them for their produce, not the wages canneries paid their employees nor the hours and conditions of their work. Laws limiting hours, or regulating health and safety in factories, were still likely to be seen as unwarranted government interference with free competition.

Frances Perkins, the fire commission's most resourceful investigator, was Roosevelt's secretary of labour between 1933 and 1945. But in 1911–12 she complained of FDR's lack of interest in fighting for better conditions for working women. Not that he did not vote the right way, but that his main attention was elsewhere. Hard-bitten Tammany men like Tim Sullivan, or legislators like Smith and Wagner, on the other hand, showed growing support for social reform. Both Smith and Wagner were of recent immigrant origin but neither had fully realized, before the Triangle fire commission, the aching hours of labour in dark lofts, the filth and stink of washrooms and toilets, the callous exploitation of child labour. Perkins, investigating for the commission, took Smith to see thousands of women, pale and exhausted, coming off 10-hour night shifts. In another factory she made Wagner crawl through a tiny hole in the wall, marked 'Fire Escape', to the steep ladder covered in ice which ended 12 feet above the ground. She got both politicians up at dawn to watch six- and seven-year-old children snipping beans and shelling peas at a cannery.

Neither Smith nor Wagner ever forgot that lesson.[12] Their alliance in the New York assembly was critically important to progressive reform. Wagner was a German immigrant from a Manhattan neighbourhood similar to Smith's who had managed to put himself through law school at night. They roomed together and taught each other. Smith, who had grown up in the Fulton fish market, self-made and self-taught, became unmatched master of the details of law making and New York's outstanding reform governor. No other New York politician came near him in his command. Yet Wagner became the most effective US senator of his generation, author of the landmark 1935 Wagner Labour Relations Act, social security and much other reform legislation.

By 1912 Perkins herself knew that even boss Murphy supported factory reform when he saw how many votes Tammany gained from a law limiting women to 54 hours' work a week.[13] The important point for Murphy was that these votes were likely to last for life. A decisive political realignment was taking place, of which Roosevelt himself was at first completely unaware. He was still the kind of progressive his voters wanted him to be. But he came to realize that his Tammany colleagues were not everything progressive propaganda painted them as being. They were not simply a corrupt group, cynically using politics for graft and plunder. Partisan politics were important; favours and services were still traded for votes. But younger Tammany men had given voters a surprise by backing social reforms which cut into the pockets of employers – factory laws, workmen's compensation, the protection of women and children in industry. As a Republican told Roosevelt, 'Smith and the others represent a new spirit in Tammany Hall, are organization followers, of course, but they seem to have discovered that there is something more important than ward picnics and balls.'[14]

A basic shift was taking place in the direction of American politics. Reformers were becoming more realistic, political bosses more responsible. A symbiotic relationship was developing between them. In consequence, American reform politics were transformed. Working men and women began to support welfare legislation through labour unions and urban political machines. A new voting configuration was emerging about 1911–12 which was to sweep Perkins, Smith, Wagner and Roosevelt himself into a reform coalition which culminated a generation later in the New Deal. Machine politicians backed social reform because it won votes. Yet as government took on more of the welfare functions which political machines had hitherto supplied, in however rough-and-ready a way, the power of machines began to wane.[15] The working-class vote, however, became a burgeoning reality which transformed the machines, urban liberalism, government welfare provision, indeed the whole of American politics. Roosevelt was the greatest beneficiary of this change, but only came to appreciate what had happened much later.

For the moment, as a freshman senator in 1911, his beliefs, dress, policies and whole demeanour were, in the words of Billy Sheehan, 'The silly conceits of a political prig'.[16] To politicians like Tim Sullivan, Roosevelt was a baffling figure. In June 1911, for example, an item of $381, to repair a bridge in FDR's district, appeared in an appropriation bill. He asked to have it thrown out, as he knew no need for such a sum. 'Frank, you ought to have your head examined,' Sullivan exclaimed.[17] At this stage, Tammany and Roosevelt did not speak the same language. Perkins has left an indelible impression of him standing back at the brass rail arguing with two or three Democrats, his small mouth pursed up, his nostrils distended, his head in the air, his cool, distant voice saying disdainfully, 'No, no, I won't hear of it!'[18] Looking back, Roosevelt told her, 'You know, I was an awfully mean cuss when I first went into politics.'[19]

But in time Roosevelt came to learn from Tammany politicians. He patterned his own conduct after their good fellowship and naturalness. His famous charm, with which, much later, he even tried to woo Joseph Stalin at Yalta in 1945, also came from watching Tammany men. He grew to understand city Democrats and even learn from them. In 1937, when as president he was discussing an immigration problem with Frances Perkins, he suddenly said, 'Tim Sullivan used to say that the America of the future would be made up of people who had come over in steerage and who knew in their own hearts and lives the difference between being despised and being accepted and liked.' Then he added, 'Poor old Tim Sullivan never understood about modern politics, but he was right about the human heart.'[20]

## IV

If Roosevelt was not as responsive to social reform as city politicians like Smith or Wagner, the wonder was that this upstate aristocrat from a rural district should have bothered himself with such questions at all. At this stage his attitude towards organized labour was essentially paternalistic. While deploring exploitation, he disapproved even more strongly of giving unions weapons with which workers might win concessions for themselves, and he especially disliked strikes. In time, his tepid interest in labour questions grew warmer so that he sponsored labour legislation and by 1916 played a more active part in helping the urban workers. No one knew better than FDR that they could vote too and vote in large numbers. But his progressive beliefs meant he aimed at the elimination of the sources of industrial conflict through arbitration and so forth rather than enhancing the power of labour unions through collective bargaining. Even during the New Deal, which saw a step change in union power, he never showed that instinctive rapport with labour leaders (and still less with the workers they led) that he always had with farmers.

The urban working class was far down FDR's list of priorities as a political issue compared with his lifelong belief in conservation. From his earliest days, growing up on the estate at Hyde Park, until the catastrophe of the Dust Bowl in the 1930s, FDR saw landscape and the environment as something which had to be protected against private greed. So about 1912 he started planting thousands of trees at Hyde Park. Then, as chairman of the state forest, fish and game committee, he crusaded for conservation in New York. When he invited Gifford Pinchot, cousin Teddy's intimate friend and chief forester of the United States, to lecture the state assembly, Pinchot projected two slides. One was an old Chinese painting of a green valley in the year 1500. In the corner a small logging chute could be dimly discerned. The second slide showed the same valley four centuries later, parched and deserted, bare rocks glaring in the sun. Greed for profit through logging was achieving the same result in America. The task was to manage and control forests in the public interest: in that sense it summarized progressivism as a political force. Roosevelt never forgot Pinchot's lesson and hoped to imprint it on the people of New York and the nation.[21]

Other issues he tackled with varying degrees of success. The campaign for the direct primary, like that for direct election of US senators, was successful. Women's suffrage, however, though a central progressive policy, proved thornier. Roosevelt strongly favoured votes for women. The celebrated women's college Vassar in his district was a bastion of support. But the majority of male farmers were equally strongly opposed. Facing this Roosevelt did what his whole career showed he was incomparably good at: he fudged. The expedient of advocating local option gave him the chance. He treated divorce reform similarly and hedged with such success over Prohibition of alcohol that the story persisted right down to 1932 that at heart he was a Dry when in fact he was not. Similarly, where Tammany worked to end Prohibition and legalize horse racing, Sunday baseball and prize fighting, Roosevelt opposed all three reforms. Personally, he liked drinking, horses and racing; but publicly he never drank and deplored sport which was dependent on gambling. There were votes in being strait-laced. Though alien to his nature and upbringing, it paid to be puritan in Albany.[22] As a state senator Roosevelt was revealing the abiding qualities in his approach to politics. He was patrician, energetic, opportunist, pragmatic and willing to compromise. When it came to resisting Tammany on major issues, however, his record looked less good. Over three questions – reorganization of the state highway commission, drafting a new city charter for New York and electoral reapportionment – he fought and lost. Tammany tried the usual kind of political persuasion: they would favour him over reapportionment if he would give way over the charter. In the end he lost on both counts: his district was later redrawn and went Republican again, while the new charter weakened the civil service and strengthened Tammany's ability to plunder the public purse. As his biographer Frank Freidel puts it, 'No matter how skilful, clever and popular Roosevelt had been, he was Canute before the Tammany tide.'[23]

The legislature had increased the New York City payroll by $350,000, apparently proving the old Republican election cry that when Democrats won the state the city ran it and upstate taxpayers paid for it. Not surprisingly, the upstate political pendulum began to swing back in its normal Republican direction with only four of the 23 insurgent assemblymen who had backed FDR against Sheehan being re-elected. Yet as the presidential election of 1912 approached, Roosevelt's chances of re-election to the state senate looked good. Conservation (FDR's strongest suit) was now a major national issue. The Ballinger–Pinchot scandal had revealed corrupt sale of public lands in Alaska and split the Republican party. Theodore Roosevelt led an insurgent 'Bull Moose' Progressive party against President William Taft as a third-party candidate, so splitting the Republican vote and enabling the Democrats to win the White House for only the third time since the Civil War. Such was the ardour of TR's crusade for president and the New Nationalism in 1912 that political realism was forgotten. 'Roosevelt bit me,' one of his Republican supporters explained, 'and I went mad.'[24]

Franklin Roosevelt had remained a loyal Democrat, but one who believed Tammany was corruptly conservative. What the Democrats needed, he thought, as the party convention approached, was the kind of liberal progressive leadership Woodrow Wilson promised. Boss Murphy, backing Champ Clark of Missouri as the party's candidate for president, was opposed to Wilson. So Roosevelt took Tammany on once again, leading an insurgent movement to nominate Wilson. Again the insurgent power was strictly limited. While they could keep Tammany from winning, they could not win themselves. Clark won a majority of delegates but not the two-thirds needed.

After Wilson was nominated on the 46th ballot at Baltimore in 1912, he ran as centre candidate for president between Taft on the right and TR on the left to win the White House. Yet FDR's re-election to the New

York senate in 1912 was by no means assured by Wilson's victory and in many ways his campaign was closer to cousin Teddy than to Wilson. Wilson's New Freedom aimed at dissolving the trusts and restoring competition between many firms. Teddy Roosevelt's New Nationalism, by contrast, implied this was impossible. Even if government could restore the old competitive model of American capitalism, TR argued, it would inevitably end by re-establishing monopoly, since in a perfect competition there is only one winner. TR believed that there were good trusts and bad. The task of government was to encourage the good and discourage the bad. FDR agreed, calling it 'The struggle for the liberty of the community rather then the liberty of the individual' and urging government intervention. 'If we call this method regulation,' he explained, 'people hold up their hands in horror and say "Unamerican" or "dangerous." But if we call the same identical process co-operation the same old fogies will cry "well done." '[25]

It did the trick in Dutchess county in 1912. The 'old fogies' who voted for him in 1910 put him in again. Despite reapportionment and the fact that he caught typhoid and spent most of his campaign flat on his back in bed, FDR won re-election, thanks largely to the efforts of his new campaign manager Louis Howe, who bombarded voters with 'personal' letters, thus anticipating FDR's later election style. He had shown once again that he was a winner. Woodrow Wilson had read about Roosevelt's exploits in New York since 1910 and was sufficiently impressed by the young politician to offer him a job as assistant to the secretary of the Navy, Josephus Daniels. 'How would you like', he asked, 'to come with me as assistant secretary of the Navy?' 'How would I like it?' Roosevelt beamed with pleasure. 'How would I like it? I'd rather have that place than any other.'[26] He had a job at the heart of the federal government. It was another step on his road to power.

V

As a junior member of Wilson's government, Roosevelt was to become part of the most successful reform administration since the Civil War. Constitutional amendments for direct election of US senators and federal income tax, passed during Taft's regime, were not ratified until 1913, while creation of a central bank, the federal reserve board, along with federal income tax, vastly enhanced the power of the US government to tax and spend. Farmers got government credits through the Federal Farm Loan Act, while the Warehousing Act gave them several provisions of the old Populist demand for an independent treasury. The middle class got the federal trade commission, designed to end 'illicit competition', and the Clayton Act, which beefed up the Sherman Anti-Trust Act and also exempted unions from harassment by anti-trust suits. The La Follette Seaman's Act, and the eight-hour day for railwaymen in the Adamson Act, were further working-class gains. Lastly Wilson's administration saw the first tariff reduction since the 1850s.

Roosevelt was pleased to be part of this culmination of progressive reform. But Wilson's early domestic victories contrasted with bitter defeats later in foreign affairs. Once the Great War broke out in August 1914, Wilson's pro-British neutrality failed and America joined Britain and France in April 1917. But though Germany finally sought an Armistice on the basis of Wilson's Fourteen Points in November 1918, he was bamboozled by Clemenceau and Lloyd George at the Paris peace conference. The subsequent Versailles treaty was rejected by the US Senate so that America could not join Wilson's League of Nations. Roosevelt thus saw at first hand the fickle and tragic nature of political power.

Though no one could foresee this outcome in March 1913 it was plain that Roosevelt loved his new job. Cousin Teddy once held it, so Frank was following the route to the White House he had planned as a law clerk. Moreover, Roosevelt really loved the sea. Much of the family fortune came from mercantile interests; his American ancestors had been sailors; Dutch maritime traditions seemed to have entered his blood. He had even thought briefly as a teenager of running away to the US naval academy at Annapolis instead of going to Harvard. The crack yachtsman with his encyclopaedic knowledge of maps and charts was in his element.

More significant, he had real grasp of the strategic importance of the Navy. Brought up on A.T. Mahan's seminal study, *The Influence of Sea Power upon History 1660–1783*, he knew that command of the world's oceans was key to world power, as Britain showed. With world war approaching, the international naval race heightened tension. The Panama Canal, built largely on cousin Teddy's initiative, was about to open, enabling the US Navy to shift more swiftly from Atlantic to Pacific and making American control of the whole Caribbean and Latin-American region paramount. Roosevelt was an ardent proponent of a Big Navy and in 1913–15 in his new job he was now dealing not just with national but with international politics.

To help him, he inherited a loyal and competent permanent secretary, Charles H. McCarthy, who had served under several of Roosevelt's predecessors. But he brought with him from Albany the man who, as his campaign manager, had won him re-election in 1912, Louis McHenry Howe. Apart from Eleanor, Louis Howe became the crucial influence on Roosevelt's career. About ten years older than Roosevelt, Howe was his complete opposite. A veteran newspaper reporter, he grew up in New York's race-track country at Saratoga Springs, its plush hotels crowded with sportsmen, gamblers and politicians. To the end of his life, with his high, stiff collars and watchful eyes, Howe conveyed this racy atmosphere of the era before the Great War. Personal familiarity with the seamier side of life, which Frank's own patrician background precluded, was the quality Roosevelt most valued in him. Short, thin and untidily dressed in suits which appeared second- or third-hand, Howe looked like a medieval gargoyle with a twentieth-century cigarette dangling perpetually from his small mouth. He himself said he was 'one of the four ugliest men . . . in the State of New York . . . Children take one look at me on the street and run.' Eleanor Roosevelt at first disliked this 'dirty little man', but came to see he was invaluable to her husband and eventually to herself.

His sharp wit, cynicism, love of intrigue, strange oaths (such as 'Mein Gawd') and creased face hid a sensitive spirit. Expressive brown eyes, together with love of art and theatre, hinted at this. More important, Howe lived for politics and had excellent political judgement. His favourite historian was Carlyle, and like him he believed in the hero in history. As he watched Roosevelt lead the fight against Sheehan in 1911 scepticism had turned to admiration and then ardour.[27] Howe had found his hero. The young, tall, vigorous politician pacing the floor while he outlined his tactics in defeating Sheehan so impressed Howe that he came to a remarkable conclusion: 'nothing but an accident could keep him from becoming president'.[28] Making sure he did so became the purpose of Howe's life. As his secretary explained, 'Louis was small, ugly and insignificant looking. Roosevelt was big, handsome and dramatic. Louis Howe closed one eye and saw the two divergent personalities merge into a political entity and the picture fascinated him.'[29] By June 1912 he began a letter to FDR with an only half-sardonic 'Beloved and Reverend Future President' (it reminded Roosevelt they had a date to go swimming).[30] By autumn, campaigning for re-election when flat on his back with typhoid, FDR had hired Howe full-time to run his campaign. Victory in November 1912 sealed the closest kind of political friendship which lasted until Howe died in 1936. When polio struck Roosevelt in 1921, Howe helped nurse him through pain and paralysis to a triumphant return to public life as governor of New York in 1928. Four years later both men played for the highest stakes and won.

VI

For the moment, in 1913 Howe and McCarthy made an excellent, though not always harmonious, team. 'Howe goes to Newfoundland tomorrow,' Roosevelt confided to his wife, 'and I shall try to clean up his back work for him! He is so wonderful on the big things that he has let the routine slide. I need a thoroughgoing hack without brilliancy like the faithful McCarthy to keep things going.'[31] Later Roosevelt often worked with similar duos, one who gave careful attention to detail, the other relying on intuition and flair: Ickes and Hopkins, in the early New Deal, Morgenthau and Currie later, or Hull and Welles at the state department. The years 1913–15, when FDR was supervising the business affairs of the Navy, made him familiar with the realities of power in the progressive period. He dealt with the trusts which built the ships, supplied them with coal, food and generators for electric power, or brought tobacco and spirits to the sailors. He tried to stop collusive contracts and give the taxpayer value for money. Soon the team of Roosevelt and Howe were fast winning a reputation for speeding up procurement and construction. Customarily, FDR was in charge of personnel, including thousands of civilian jobs in the navy yards where new warships were built.

Here, more than anywhere else, Howe led the way by explaining the political importance of good relations with organized labour. He insisted FDR attend hearings on labour problems in person rather than delegate labour relations to someone else. He spent hours that he might have spent playing golf with his social-register friends learning instead the union viewpoint. 'The friends Franklin made among labour people during his Navy days', Howe explained, 'stayed with him for the rest of his life.' Eleanor believed Howe's greatest service was impressing on her husband the significance of labour and in getting him to include labour leaders in his circle – and there were more labour voters than officers. Young FDR was not snobbish or undemocratic. But it would simply not have occurred to him before 1914 that an ambitious young politician should spend less time in elite social circles. Now he kept his door open for labour leaders, understanding their problems, winning their friendship and evolving enlightened labour policy in the navy yards.[32]

In consequence, no major strike occurred there while Roosevelt held office. Good labour relations in the yards meant better working conditions, and vice versa. It also meant, as Howe had foreseen, that he was building political support there. With Brooklyn navy yard in New York, he could send contracts there, keeping Tammany happy, and clear contracts in other yards with Democratic congressmen. Moreover, while labour leaders and naval officers were often at opposite poles, FDR, through Howe, managed to maintain cordial relations with both. This was another characteristic of his use of power. Naval officers took out their resentment against the department's pro-labour policies on Howe, while union leaders gave full credit for favours to Roosevelt.[33] By 1915 FDR was handling all contracts which did not involve policy and sharing preparation of annual estimates for the budget. He had more power than most assistant secretaries. 'I get my fingers into everything,' he explained, 'and there's no law against it.'[34]

In summary, transition from New York to Washington, from legislative to executive power, had increased Roosevelt's experience of dealing with big business, organized labour and political machines which, apart from farming, were the three central areas of politics in the progressive period. He had developed another trait in his subsequent use of power. He took credit when he succeeded in securing what petitioners wanted, but shifted blame when he failed, with Howe gladly acting as scapegoat. Moreover, while in Washington he still kept in contact with events in New York.

Politics in New York were becoming more hectic than ever. First, in November 1913 Tammany suffered one of its cyclical defeats when an insurgent Democrat, J.P. Mitchell, was elected mayor of New York City with the largest vote in history. Recovering from this reverse, Tammany managed to get Democratic Governor William Sulzer impeached for using campaign funds to speculate on the stock market and then became suspicious of FDR's attempts to build an organization in the state. Tammany suspicion deepened when he seemed to be seeking the Democratic nomination for either governor or US senator in 1914. William McAdoo, Wilson's secretary of the treasury and son-in-law, gave FDR the quite wrong impression that Wilson wanted him to enter the Senate race, so he entered. But McAdoo had his own quarrel with Tammany; Daniels opposed Roosevelt running; and FDR did not consult Howe or major party leaders. When Tammany boss Murphy asked Wilson's ambassador to Germany, James W. Gerard, to enter the primary he beat Roosevelt by more than 2 to 1 without even leaving Berlin, only to be badly beaten himself at the general election in November.[35]

Everyone learned from this. Roosevelt respected the power of Murphy's machine in primaries. But Gerard's defeat showed Murphy the appeal an 'independent' candidate could exercise at general elections. Howe urged FDR that now was 'The right time for you to show you don't hate all

Tammany'[36] while Wilson was also keen to improve his relations with Tammany. So in 1915 FDR abandoned his bid to build an upstate anti-Tammany machine, made friends with Smith, helped Wagner get a federal postmastership in New York City and by 1917 was being photographed with Murphy at Tammany's annual Fourth of July celebration. As a practical politician Roosevelt was learning a lot – about patronage, about party organization, about working with congressmen, about power.

American diplomacy contributed to his expanding political education. Chronic disorder in the Caribbean had long worried the Navy and in 1915 an outbreak of violence in Haiti was quelled by American marines, who took control of the Haitian government. Such imperial power was quite compatible with progressivism; indeed, it was central to cousin Teddy's combination of imperialism with social reform. FDR made an appropriately proconsular tour of the island, noted with satisfaction the benefits American occupation had brought and returned with a sense of personal proprietorship. This all fed his well-established habit of embellishing the truth. Five years later he felt able to claim, quite falsely, 'You know I had something to do with the running of a couple of little republics. The fact is that I wrote Haiti's Constitution myself, and, if I do say it, I think it is a pretty good Constitution.'[37]

What such events showed was that foreign affairs was becoming increasingly decisive, and that FDR understood international power politics. Mexico was in the throes of revolution, which was spilling over the Texas border. Tensions with Mexico and Japan made FDR renew his backing for a Big Navy and urge intervention in Mexico. Cousin Teddy warned him, 'I do not anticipate trouble with Japan, but it may come,' adding prophetically, 'and if it does it will come suddenly.'[38] Once world war began in August 1914 FDR urged preparedness, which President Wilson accepted in 1915 after German submarines sank the British liner *Lusitania* with the loss of 126 American lives. But he increasingly despaired of Wilson's neutrality. Despite the resignation of his near-pacifist secretary of state, W.J. Bryan, Wilson could not face the possibility of Allied, especially British, defeat; and Frank believed America would eventually have to fight alongside Britain and France. Running against the powerful progressive Republican Charles Evans Hughes, Wilson won re-election in 1916, one of the closest contests in history, on the slogan 'He kept us out of war.' But in April 1917 unrestricted German U-boat sinkings and British publication of the Zimmermann telegram, in which Berlin tried to bribe Mexico into invading the United States, forced Wilson to declare war. America had entered the world stage.

## VII

The crisis of war in 1917–18 coincided with a crisis in Roosevelt's private life. In 1914 Eleanor had employed as social secretary her friend Lucy Mercer, a young Virginia girl of impeccable background. She was sweet, womanly, slightly old-fashioned but spirited and outgoing in a style Frank admired. Eleanor usually took herself and the children away from the insufferable summer heat of Washington to their holiday home on Campobello island between Maine and New Brunswick. Roosevelt had to stay at war work, but remained free in the evenings to cruise on the Potomac with his fun-loving friends, including Lucy. They fell in love. When Eleanor found their letters in 1918 she was deeply hurt. Lucy was not just her secretary but her friend. Moreover, Eleanor felt she had been betrayed once as a child by those she loved. She wanted a divorce. But as this would have been death to Roosevelt's political career he refused to consider it. So she agreed to stay married, on strict condition that he never see Lucy again, while Eleanor would be free to live her own life. The impact which the Lucy Mercer affair had on the quadrilateral tension which linked FDR, his wife, his mother and Louis Howe will be examined more fully in the final chapter. But it was a defining episode, most clearly to Eleanor and Frank. They remained on terms of affection and deep mutual respect, but the love they had shared was gone for ever. Theirs was to remain one of the most remarkable marriages in American political history, but after the Lucy Mercer affair it was profoundly changed.

Chastened by this emotional crisis, Roosevelt found escape in war administration which extended his experience and personal powers. Regulation and control which progressives like FDR had long urged became acceptable during wartime. As they would in 1933, the depth of the economic depression, people flocked to Washington in 1917 to help tackle the emergency. Federal agencies like the war industries board, headed by his old friend Bernard Baruch, or modern managers like John J. Raskob at Du Ponts and General Motors, were transforming the economy on progressive lines. Roosevelt himself was a Washington celebrity. His boss Josephus Daniels, a senior Democrat, helped him make vital contacts with the party's Southern wing. Moreover, his vital intellectual relationship with Felix Frankfurter, of Harvard Law School, dates from these wartime years. Daniels remembered him as 'Young and debonair, striding and strong', while Bainbridge Colby thought him 'The handsomest and most attractive man in Washington'. Questions remained about his depth. Justice Oliver Wendell Holmes recalled 'A good fellow with rather a soft edge' and Roosevelt's friend William Phillips said he was 'Likeable and attractive but not a heavyweight, brilliant but not particularly steady in his views. He could charm anybody but lacked greatness.' Or, as the mother of his banker friend James Warburg put it, 'He's a really beautiful looking man, but he's so dumb.'[39]

Such was the judgement of most political observers before 1932. Roosevelt thought of running for governor of New York in 1918, but was happy to let Al Smith take it – the start of Smith's matchless record as reform governor and of his creative rivalry with Roosevelt. But domestic politics seemed minor when Roosevelt was sent in 1918 to Europe to inspect American naval operations. He met Clemenceau, Churchill, Lloyd George, General Joffre, King George V and Lady Astor. Still only 35, Roosevelt wanted more than anything to resign and enlist, but Daniels and Wilson insisted he was too important to the war effort and flatly refused. So when Germany sought peace on the basis of Wilson's Fourteen Points in November 1918 he returned to Europe for the peace talks. FDR's insignificance here contrasted sharply with Herbert Hoover's power as chief US administrator, feeding starving millions in Germany and the whole of postwar Europe. Despite this, the peace talks proved a disaster for Wilson, who in 1919 was outmanoeuvred by Clemenceau and Lloyd George. As 1920 approached it was plain that the mood of America had changed, that Wilson's political power at home had crumbled, that the Senate would not ratify the treaty nor let the United States join the League of Nations. The idealism which had marked Wilson's domestic reforms and driven him to fight a war 'To make the world safe for democracy' had been replaced by isolationism and the primacy of big business.

The year 1920 began badly for Roosevelt. He had his tonsils out, his children fell sick with the influenza pandemic then sweeping the world, he was in political trouble with Daniels and Wilson, while in February he read that Lucy Mercer had married Winthrop Rutherfurd, a much older widower. Most important, the Republicans were plainly going to win the approaching 1920 presidential contest. They had done well in the midterm elections in November 1918 and had majorities of 237 to 190 in the House and 49 to 47 in the Senate. Although gravely ill, Wilson had entertained the foolish idea that his party would choose him to run for a third term. When they refused, Wilson hoped the campaign would be a 'solemn referendum' on the League issue, but these hopes were ruined. Since Theodore Roosevelt had died in 1919, Republican party managers had at last regained complete control of their party and, determined to keep it, in June 1920 nominated the unknown mediocrity Warren Harding to run for president.

Franklin Roosevelt and other Democratic liberals tried to persuade Hoover, who had supported TR's Bull Moose campaign in 1912, to run as a Democrat in the primaries in 1920.[40] Like Bernard Baruch and John J. Raskob, Hoover personified the new managerial elite which had come to the fore in the progressive era and was now running American capitalism. In 1920, as the man who had organized economic relief for postwar Europe, Hoover had a matchless reputation and could have had the nomination of either party. Had he won as a Republican in 1920, it is intriguing to think counterfactually for a moment. Presumably he would have presided over the prosperous 1920s and left office in March 1929 one of the most admired and successful presidents in history. Even more intriguing, in view of what was to happen in 1932, FDR's old Harvard friend Louis Wehle briefly tried to promote a Hoover–Roosevelt ticket for the Democrats.[41] Yet for the men who really ran the party the question was: should the Democrats nominate a reactionary, a party hack or W.J. Bryan?

When the convention met in what in 1920 was the remote city of San Francisco, it took 44 ballots to nominate a hack, James M. Cox, whose choice Wilson had said would be 'a joke'.[42] By picking Roosevelt as his running mate Cox surprised not only the party, but Roosevelt himself. True, cousin Teddy had run with McKinley in 1900. But that year Republicans had been confident of victory. More important, the whole point of nominating TR then was the desire of party managers to shunt a dangerous insurgent into the obscure siding of the vice-presidency. The accident of McKinley's murder in 1901 had ruined their plans and made TR president. But in 1920 the Democrats were going to be badly beaten. What could Franklin Roosevelt hope to gain by going down in a big defeat? In fact, he had thought about other offices – either New York governor or senator. He would have been a credible candidate for either, with a good record in wartime Washington. But New York already had a Democratic governor, and a good one, in Al Smith, while the senator up for re-election, James Wadsworth, was unbeatable in a Republican year which in the event proved to be so solid that even Smith lost.

Yet the most recent example for FDR was Hiram Johnson, TR's running mate in 1912, who was a strong Republican contender in 1920. Finally, Cox wanted Roosevelt, but his manager, Edmund H. Moore, had to consult Tammany's boss. 'Young Roosevelt is no good,' Charles Murphy said. But the rest of his reply, which decided the issue, sheds light on the nature of power and deference in the Democratic party. 'I don't like him,' Murphy told Moore. 'He is not well known in the country, but, Ed, this is the first time a Democratic nominee for the presidency has shown me courtesy. That's why I would vote for the devil himself if Cox wanted me to. Tell him we will nominate Roosevelt on the first ballot as soon as we assemble.'[43]

Running with Cox in a losing year, the best FDR could expect was to enhance his name and hope to cash in at a later election. So he campaigned vigorously all over the nation, making more than a thousand speeches and far more good political contacts, while the contest degenerated into a dull and hopeless farce. Warren Harding, handsome, genial, ignorant and weak, did not campaign yet won 61 per cent of the popular vote, the greatest share in history. The era of progressive reform was over; one of speculative capitalism was about to begin. In the decade of economic boom which followed, the Republicans, closely identified with big business, monopolized power. As Roosevelt returned to private life for the first time in a decade, his political career seemed at an end.

True his campaign had given him national stature and he had admirers across America. Tammany's failure to get Smith elected might make Roosevelt the Democratic candidate for governor in 1922. The fact was that no defeated vice-presidential candidate in history had ever returned to make a name for himself in national politics. He started to make fun of himself, heading his letters, 'Franklin D. Roosevelt, Ex V.P., Canned. (Erroneously reported dead).'[44] This joke stopped being funny for FDR on 10 August 1921, on holiday at his beloved Campobello. Dog-tired after helping fight a forest fire and then swimming in the ice-cold Bay of Fundy, he went up early to bed and woke the next morning unable to move his legs. Though correct diagnosis was delayed, he had contracted infantile paralysis, or polio.[45] That handsome, energetic figure, 'striding and strong', who had won Howe's heart and paced about Albany and Washington to such effect, never walked again. The man who had enjoyed political power for ten years was now physically powerless. Somehow he was able to struggle back from the abyss. But for the moment this was the darkest night of his soul. His ordeal had begun.

※

## Chapter 4

# The Fight to Regain Power, 1921–29

I

Roosevelt's struggle against infantile paralysis was the central episode in his life. He had been struck down very late. Correct diagnosis had been delayed partly because doctors did not think a man of nearly 40 could contract it. At first, he was in such distress that the mere pressure of bedsheets was unbearable. In addition, the original medical treatment, which included deep massage, was not only excruciatingly painful but also the exact opposite of what was needed. At this stage too he was partly paralysed from the chest down, while his thumb muscles were so weak he was unable to write. Fortunately, this passed. He was soon able to sit up and write, while eventually years of exercise gave him a very powerful torso. The greatly increasing strength of his back, shoulders and arms, which transformed his appearance from slender to stocky, was critically important later in helping him disguise the reality of his paralysis.

After early months of pain and strain this reality became starkly clear. In January 1922, the muscles behind his knees began to tighten and pull his legs up under him. His doctor had to put both legs in plaster and then, during two weeks of agony, drive wedges in a bit deeper each day to stretch the tendons back.[1] In February FDR put on steel braces, weighing seven pounds each and stretching from hips to shoes. Thus he slowly learned to stand up and walk with crutches. Yet he was not really walking at all but manoeuvring himself with his hips. Even so it took Frank years of exercise and practice to learn. A few tantalizing seconds of moving film exist which show him doing this, helped by a strong male companion and a walking stick. He had no balance or power in his legs and was never able to walk, or even stand, again without support. Even when he did he was in constant danger of falling.[2]

Roosevelt's wealth gave him every state-of-the-art piece of equipment and aid available, such as private railway carriages, lifts, wheelchairs, ramps and handrails. Later he had a special car built with hand controls so he could drive. Speaking at a podium he was fine: braces and the lectern itself gave him support. He could even gesture carefully with hands or arms. But getting to the platform was a problem. He usually arrived very early and, even so, could not stand for the national anthem, which caused criticism he was unable to answer without admitting he was a cripple.[3] Moreover, moving from one secure position to another was always difficult. Eyewitnesses, like his friend and cabinet colleague Harold Ickes, have described the shock they felt when he had to be carried from his car like a sack of potatoes. In short, after August 1921 Roosevelt spent the rest of his life in a wheelchair, on crutches or in painful leg braces.

Most men would have given up. His mother Sara wanted that. As far as she was concerned his political career was over. He must accept reality, as his father had done after his stroke, and settle for a quiet life as squire of Hyde Park, with his hobbies, stamps, wildlife collections, maps and manuscripts. Business and public life were out of the question. Frank would be under his mother's domination, which was what his mother wanted. That he refused to do this is central to understanding Roosevelt's attitude to power. Simply returning to normal private life would have been difficult enough. Returning in triumph to public life and becoming a key figure in twentieth-century world politics, which not one man in millions would have done, shows relentless fortitude and ambition. Yet why he strove so hard to return to public life, and what he aimed at achieving with political power, remains a mystery. If he ever spoke about this to Eleanor or Louis Howe, the two people closest to him, they left no record. The solution must be sought in those seven crucial years between the onset of polio in August 1921 and his election as governor of New York in November 1928. Close examination of events in those years is the key which unlocks the door to Roosevelt's subsequent career.

II

He knew despair at times in the early years of his illness. Though not a pious Episcopalian Christian, he did believe and felt at first that God had deserted him. Yet he also knew he had been lucky: polio often killed or struck its victims harder than it had struck him. If God had spared him it must have been for a purpose. The private nature of FDR's religious beliefs, in sharp contrast to their often unconvincing public expression by every president since Jimmy Carter in the 1970s, does not mean they were less significant – indeed the reverse would be nearer the truth. Nevertheless, there is an enigma at the heart of his political career: the personality of Roosevelt. Though still light-hearted ('boyish' remained the most common description of him even as president), Roosevelt became more serious and determined to live out his destiny. First, he refused to accept his paralysis himself. He never believed he was crippled for life and always thought a cure possible. To the end of his days he felt that exercising his leg muscles would restore them to full strength. Second, in his long struggle with his mother, Frank had powerful allies. His wife Eleanor, his closest friend Louis Howe and his Groton classmate Dr George Draper, who took over his treatment, all believed it would be 'a terrible waste' for Roosevelt to retire.[4] Finally, he entered into an open conspiracy with press and film journalists not to publish pictures which revealed how disabled he was – which was of critical importance in spreading the idea that he had recovered and was lame, not crippled.

Only two days after polio struck, he authorized the president of Vassar College to place his name on an endowment committee, while a month later he accepted membership of the Democratic party state executive.[5] So literally at no time was he out of public life. He even maintained his golf club membership for some years.[6] Eleanor and Howe were absolutely tireless in keeping Roosevelt in touch with political events and his name in the public eye. With her five children away at boarding school and the freedom that settlement of the Lucy Mercer affair had given, Eleanor had embarked on her own career as teacher and writer. Yet she still devoted much thought and time to her husband's fight. It was a way of paying him back, in good coin, for the Lucy Mercer betrayal. Meantime Howe, who when FDR became ill had been winding up Navy department affairs and considering lucrative business offers, moved into the Roosevelt home. Though he had a wife and children, he only saw them at weekends. For the rest of his life he lived with him, not simply chief-of-staff but to all intents and purposes one of the family.

Resuming the role he had played when Roosevelt had been in government, Howe became press agent, political guide and administrative assistant, spending the next ten years helping to make him president. One of the ways he kept his crippled boss's spirits up was by his flair for amateur theatricals, which combined perfectly with Frank's own love of spoofs and parties. Another key member of the little team working to bring him back to power was Marguerite ('Missy') LeHand. FDR had met Missy, a young, strikingly beautiful Southern Catholic, working in New York headquarters during the 1920 election. She loved him and became his devoted personal secretary. His feelings for her are harder to determine, though she remained by his side as his secretary until she died, only months before he did, in 1944. For their part Eleanor and Louis Howe acted as FDR's eyes and ears round New York and the nation, keeping the Roosevelt name in the forefront. Until polio struck FDR Eleanor had had little interest in public life. His 1920 campaign for vice-president had been her first exposure to politics. But in the 1920s her political career advanced spectacularly. Her causes – working conditions, the exploitation of women and child labour, racial discrimination – were those Frances Perkins had tried to educate Frank into supporting.

Full female suffrage had been granted in 1920, and a woman of Eleanor's ability soon held key positions in women's divisions of the Democratic party which influenced half the electorate. As early as 1922, FDR saw what this meant. Thousands of upstate districts were dominated by Republicans. 'Get the right kind of women in the various rural counties,' he told Eleanor's friend Caroline O'Day, 'to restore the prestige of the [Democratic] party.'[7] Eleanor was in general politically far to the left of her husband. But on national Prohibition, which began in 1920, given that alcohol had destroyed her father, she was firmly Dry. So a trend developed which Roosevelt exploited with great skill in pursuit of power. He could take credit with African Americans, feminists, Drys and the left for his wife's opinions, while persuading Wets or opponents of civil and women's rights that, although her views were not his, he could not repudiate her in public. Many conservatives thus came to believe that Roosevelt was essentially one of them, which in a sense he was.

Howe's influence on Eleanor's political career was at first as important as it was on FDR's. He advised her on campaigns, committees and meetings. His political judgement was excellent, but his unimpressive demeanour made it imperative he be kept from public view. Like her husband, Eleanor was not a natural speaker, but Howe sat at the back, making notes, and turned her into one. 'He used to make fun of me,' she explained, 'and then tell me where I had gone wrong and what I should do to put it right.'[8] Amongst other things he helped suppress her nervous girlish giggle. Moreover, Howe steered her towards other women who were to become her political partners and closest companions – to Marion Dickerman, an instructor at the Todhunter School in New York, Mrs James Laidlaw, of the Women's Trade Union League, and Nancy Cook, who was on the Democratic State Committee.

With politically experienced, independent women like these, who often lived alone or together, Eleanor blossomed in the 1920s to become political activist, teacher, journalist and businesswoman at the furniture factory she founded at Val-Kill, close to Hyde Park. She flew with the pioneer aviator Amelia Earhart and went on to become an outstanding political woman of her generation, seen by opponents as a crank, but an influential crank. The vital and unique political partnership between her and Frank was being forged. She became her crippled husband's eyes and ears. Yet she also became a formidable figure in her own right on the liberal wing of the Democrats in New York and nationally. The centre of a dynamic group of women reformers who were college-educated, who had worked helping the urban poor in settlement houses and were social feminists, she gave this network a dynamic role model. But she gave much more. Effective advocates of social reform in the 1920s, these women in the 1930s enjoyed access to the White House through Eleanor and thus could influence policy during an unprecedented economic crisis.

The distance between Eleanor and FDR in their private lives while all this was going on makes this political partnership all the more remarkable. In fact, since the Lucy Mercer affair and then polio she was living a separate life, not just with a separate bedroom but a home of her own at Val-Kill. Yet the principal purpose of all her activity remained helping FDR. Between them, Howe and Eleanor had succeeded by 1928 in keeping Roosevelt in touch with public affairs, keeping his name alive and persuading politicians and voters alike that he had recovered, partially or in full, from polio when in fact he had not. Characteristic of Roosevelt, inasmuch as appearance masked reality, this achievement was the crux of his whole career. Without it he could not have returned to political power.

III

At first, in 1921 and 1922, thanks to Howe and Eleanor, Roosevelt could lend his name to political enterprises without leaving home or office. For several years, while he built up strength and mobility, it was impossible for him to appear in person at dinners, rallies and meetings which are the stock-in-trade of politicians. But while his wife attended these and did the public speaking, FDR and Howe were formulating the issues which would bring voters back again to the Democratic party and eventually to him. This was not easy. The party was deeply and seriously divided throughout the 1920s. Prohibition, immigration restriction, farm support, the Ku Klux Klan, anti-Catholicism and other issues had Democrats at each other's throats.[9] At times it seemed as if Southern bigots were fighting Northern crooks for control of a party whose national support in presidential elections was vanishing. In such a situation, Roosevelt's place on the sidelines was an advantage. It saved him from having to take sides, from being identified too closely with any faction. Indeed, as we shall see, he carefully cultivated contacts with all sources of power within the Democratic party.

To start with, he addressed himself to small-business, middle-class Americans who had formed the backbone of the progressive movement since 1900 and were the most important group of active voters. Though no longer so keenly interested in progressive reform, partly because the movement had achieved what many progressives wanted by the 1920s, these voters still harboured prejudice against the money power. This fear was part of Roosevelt's political vocabulary and he regularly expressed it, despite his own close associations with Wall Street. So in a letter read at a Jackson Day dinner in Portland, Oregon, at the end of 1921, he declared that the significance of Jackson for the 1920s was his 'Earnest determination to keep control of our government out of the hands of professional moneymakers and keep it in the hands of the people themselves'.

Given, as soon emerged, that members of President Harding's cabinet were selling Navy oil leases in what became known as the Teapot Dome scandal, such warnings proved politically timely between 1922 and 1924. Roosevelt backed Al Smith's successful campaign for governor in 1922, while his own return to public life closely followed Smith's career and, quite literally, the steps he took on Smith's behalf at the Democratic presidential conventions of 1924 and 1928. Yet for most of 1922–23 Roosevelt had to work on his legs at Hyde Park, combining strenuous exercises to build shoulders and arms with sunbathing and much swimming in warm water. Vincent Astor gave him use of his nearby pool and Roosevelt was certain this would do the trick. 'The water put me where I am and the water has to bring me back,' he explained.[10]

For the time being the quest for political power was no longer central to Roosevelt's life. His prime objective before 1928 was somehow to regain power over his own body: to learn to walk again or, failing that, to persuade people to believe that he could walk. Every day, helped by family and friends, chatting and joking, he struggled on crutches from the house down the drive aiming to reach the gates of Hyde Park some 200 yards away. He never did. Out of office he also needed a salary again; and by the end of September 1922 he was spending two or three days a week at the New York City office of Fidelity and Deposit, the third largest surety bonding company in the country, where his name greatly increased business and justified his handsome salary of $25,000 a year. Steep steps at his law partnership with Emmett and Marvin, which he had joined after his election to the New York senate in 1910, were too much for him and he could not bear the thought of being carried up in public. Moreover, the work he did there was mostly on wills and inheritance which bored him. So in 1924 he dissolved his partnership and joined Basil D. O'Connor. 'The Doc', as he was known, did a racier and more lucrative line of work in corporate, municipal and political law – much more congenial to FDR's character and useful to his career. O'Connor became a close friend, valued adviser and prominent financial backer.

Spending time in New York City was politically important for Roosevelt. During the progressive period between 1900 and 1920 the political centre of gravity had shifted to Washington. In the booming 1920s it shifted back to Wall Street. Many former progressives were dazzled and disillusioned by this change, but not FDR. Though he could not manage the steps at his law firm, he was more at home in the financial world than most progressive reformers, and in a career sense he went to Wall Street in the 1920s. Roosevelt's business ventures during that decade have attracted little comment from historians. Yet throughout the 1920s FDR was feeling the financial pinch. When a politician like Al Smith won elective office his salary was far less than he could have earned as a private citizen. Later, as we shall see, Smith paid a high political price for this fact. Of course, Smith had no money of his own while FDR had a private income and large family fortune. Their cases, it might appear, could not have been more contrasting.

Yet in the 1920s the Roosevelts were finding it hard to live as they wished. Eight years entertaining in Washington between 1913 and 1921 on an assistant secretary's salary had eaten into his income so much that he had to turn to his mother Sara to recoup lost capital. Though this topic will be explored more fully in the final chapter, the point to grasp here is that polio added to these money problems. Despite his means, FDR felt the financial pain of all his cures and treatment, especially as he had five children to bring up in upper-class style. He worried about this and had a reputation within the family for parsimony. He felt so financially embarrassed in January 1925, for example, that he auctioned some of his prized maritime prints, though they raised less than a thousand dollars, and he always economized by wearing clothes bought several years before. In 1928 his son James made a point by throwing away one of FDR's suits which his father James had worn, while Eleanor's letters to him throughout the 1920s are full of talk about unpaid bills and allowances to their children.

But though penny-pinching in private, he was quite the opposite in business, where he plunged into speculative markets typical of the 1920s. Buying and selling securities was a delightful game which he played on a sizeable scale. Like poker and politics, business was a form of adventure for FDR. Speculators found it so easy to make money in the 1920s that one of the biggest – Joseph Kennedy – commented, 'We'd better get on with it before they pass a law to stop it.' This was ironic. As president in the 1930s FDR did indeed set up the Securities and Exchange Commission to regulate Wall Street and made Kennedy its head. But in the 1920s things were different. Kennedy made a huge fortune investing. By contrast, the ventures with which FDR was associated – chiefly for the promotional value his name brought – were highly speculative. With one exception – dealings in the spectacular collapse and recovery of the German mark in the mid-1920s – they all failed. The fate of all these speculative business ventures reveals he had no special insight into the approaching economic depression.

For example, FDR lost $26,000 – more than a year's salary – trying to corner the lobster market. Yet another venture was even more revealing. With his rich neighbour Henry Morgenthau, whose son later became his treasury secretary in 1934–45, he was founder and director of Consolidated Automatic Merchandising Corporation. Camco was a holding company which promoted the typically American idea of a chain of clerkless stores selling standard goods by means of automatic vending machines. A large store operated by such machines opened in New York City in 1928 but, although it promised fabulous returns to its investors, it lost more than two million dollars in three years and went bankrupt. Since Roosevelt promptly resigned his interest when he became governor of New York in January 1929 his personal connection with Camco was brief. Later he claimed, with accuracy but without conviction, that it was unimportant; that Camco was only one of several such ventures, taken over by a stamp machine company where he had an interest, of which he knew nothing. The important point was that in the booming 1920s the idea of the automated store, freeing store clerks from drudgery, had seemed liberating. In the 1930s, with 15 million jobless, it looked quite different. FDR's later denials served only to highlight the serious social implications of the clerkless store and jobless clerk, while the casually speculative way it had been launched was typical of FDR.[11] Economic depression in the 1930s threw harsh light on such activities. As Roosevelt said when his secretary of the treasury Will Woodin was in 1934 accused of insider trading in the 1920s, 'Many people did things before 1929 that they would not think of doing now.'[12]

More significant than his connection with Camco, as part of his business activities Roosevelt became president in 1922 of the American Construction Council. This was a building industry trade organization, conceived under Republican secretary of commerce Herbert Hoover's philosophy of self-regulation by business. Though a typically progressive idea, it was ironic, in light of future events, that Hoover actually chose FDR for that post. Yet in 1922 the political ideas of Hoover and Roosevelt were in general harmony. As late as 1929 Roosevelt, like his cousin Teddy before him, was still warning of the dangers inherent in 'Great combinations of capital', but explaining, like a New Nationalist progressive, that 'industrial combination is not wrong in itself'. The danger was in taking government into partnership. 'I want to preach a new doctrine,' Roosevelt concluded, 'complete separation of business and government.'[13] Far from being new, this message was as old as the Republic itself. More important, it did not indicate that within a few years FDR would become architect of the National Recovery Administration which aimed at planning all US industry during the New Deal.

## IV

Unlike his business adventures in the 1920s, the effect of Roosevelt's polio on his character and values has received much comment. Speculation has centred on the extent to which suffering changed him. Frances Perkins, who knew him before his illness, thought like many people that he was a pleasant but somewhat supercilious young man. Later she worked for him as governor and in his presidential cabinet. She got to know him well; and she believed his illness accomplished spiritual transformation. He was purged of 'The slightly arrogant attitude' he had shown before and became 'completely warm-hearted'. Most important, Perkins concluded, 'He understood the problems of people in trouble.'[14] Eleanor agreed, and in a sense it was true, that after polio he could identify with powerless people in a way he had not been able to do before.

Yet it is easy to make too much of this. People who are powerless in an economic, political or social sense generally attract less sympathy than those who lack power because of physical illness. The two cases have little in common. Anyway Roosevelt had always been a man of warm human sympathies, with a genuine liking for all sorts of people, who loved to exercise his charm on them. Personal charm is always an advantage to a politician and by the 1920s Roosevelt had it in abundance. Partly for this reason Louis Howe genuinely believed that had 'the boss' not been crippled he would have spread himself too thin on too many activities – political, social, sporting, his many hobbies – and so wasted himself. He would certainly have had to take sides in the bitter political conflicts which rent the Democratic party in the 1920s instead of enjoying the independence, immunity from criticism and glamour which polio brought.

Moreover, before paralysis struck, he had already learned the knack, thanks to Howe's prompting, of understanding people with whom he had no natural sympathy, such as machine politicians or labour leaders. As we have already seen, work at the Navy department had sharpened his political skill. Yet his writings and speeches in the 1920s reveal no dramatic transformation or identification with those excluded from the promise of American life. They reveal a mind general and sensible, but superficial and complacent. Once again, in FDR's struggle for political power, appearance masked reality. By placing emphasis on the way suffering had made him appear more compassionate, it is important to grasp that Frances Perkins, Eleanor Roosevelt and others were helping to fabricate a powerful political myth, realized on stage and screen in Dore Schary's *Sunrise at Campobello.*

One striking but little-noticed aspect of his handicap was his complete lack of self-pity. Roosevelt's personal triumph over polio was real and remarkable. Politically, however, his struggle gained even more importance. For when the economy smashed to smithereens in the 1930s his ordeal seemed to harmonize with desperate times, in stark contrast to Hoover's impressive personal success. Yet even here the extent of his handicap was in reality carefully concealed. People were persuaded to believe that he had largely recovered. While he walked on a cane, with leg braces and a strong man's arm, no photograph or moving film was published of him in a wheelchair or being carried to show how badly he was still crippled. That age was less voyeuristic than our own. But the message which came across was clear: the nation might recover from economic depression much as he had recovered from polio. For the crucial point about Roosevelt's thinking was that, throughout his life, all his ideas and policies were designed to help a capitalist economy which, as Frances Perkins put it, he took as much for granted as he did his own family.

V

Nevertheless, from 1923 until 1928 his real attention centred on the practical problem of his own physical recovery. Exercise had to be combined with rest. For this purpose Fidelity and Deposit, in addition to paying him $25,000 a year, gave him generous vacations. After he contracted polio there in August 1921 Roosevelt did not visit Campobello again for seven years. Instead, he took long winter cruises through Florida waters in search of a cure. For this purpose in 1923 he rented a houseboat. The experiment proved so successful that the next year, with his friend John S. Lawrence, he bought a houseboat and renamed it the *Larooco*, a contraction of Lawrence, Roosevelt and Company.[15] Between 1924 and 1928 he spent at least three months each year soaking up warm winter sunshine, cruising the Florida Keys, swimming, sunbathing, working and loafing with congenial friends. Shipboard life suited him. He learnt new ways of moving on deck, or in and out of boats or sea, which greatly improved his mobility.

He liked being skipper: his vice-president in the 1930s, John Garner, always called him 'Cap'n'. His companions in this voyage to seek recovery were revealing too. Though this topic will be discussed more fully in the final chapter, neither Eleanor nor Howe liked the sea. Moreover both were too busy, Howe in advancing FDR's political career, Eleanor advancing both his and her own independent life, to spend much time on board. Between 1925 and 1928 FDR spent 116 of 228 weeks away from home. Eleanor was with him four of those weeks, his mother Sara for just two, while his beautiful and adoring secretary Missy LeHand was with him for 110 weeks, living in his house and on the houseboat. Yet all was not plain sailing. Missy said that there were days on the *Larooco* when it was noon before FDR could pull himself out of depression and greet his guests with his usual lighthearted façade.[16]

As we have seen, the cost of all this was a strain even on a man of Roosevelt's means. Simply leasing the first houseboat in 1923 had cost $1,500; he was bearing most of the *Larooco*'s expenses; and he had five children to raise and educate. Yet in this situation, despite strong opposition from Eleanor, FDR took for the only time in his life a serious risk with money. As noted, his mother Sara had inherited the bulk of her fortune from her father. Her husband James had left $300,000 equally to her, her stepson and FDR. He now persuaded Sara to help him buy a rundown 112-acre spa estate in Georgia called Warm Springs for $200,000 – his entire personal fortune and Sara's matrimonial legacy. Development and running costs, at this stage unknown, would by any estimate be a further chronic burden. If anything went wrong Eleanor feared that, at the very least, they would not be able to put their sons through college.[17]

Buying Warm Springs was not just a big financial step; it was significant in other ways. Though FDR had held public office he had never actually run anything before. At the age of 45 he finally got the chance.

Moreover, its location meant he could forge crucially important political contacts in the South, without which no Democrat could succeed in national politics. Finally, the Warm Springs baths brought hope of recovery not just for him but for thousands of other victims of paralysis, many of them poor children. So, while in the long run Warm Springs was a financial investment which at least broke even, its real importance was revealed in other ways. It soon became central to the Roosevelt myth. It was his second home; it helped others who had been stricken; it played a vital role in the drama of his career. Crucially it enabled FDR himself to regain control of both his private and public life.

## VI

For recovery from polio was only a means to an end: Roosevelt's pursuit of political power was relentless. The first test of recovery came in 1924, presidential election year. When President Harding died suddenly in August 1923, Calvin Coolidge succeeded him and was duly nominated by the Republicans for president on 10–12 June the following year. Though Coolidge worshipped business and so fitted the dominant mood of the 1920s he was really one of the most limited men ever to become president. Yet this devout conservative was undoubtedly popular. Facing a popular conservative it would have made sense for Democrats to nominate a progressive liberal. The party did not see this. Indeed, the Democratic convention, which opened in New York City on 24 June, was a disaster. The Democrats, like the nation, had been split since Prohibition of alcohol in 1920 into Wet and Dry factions. Now for three weeks, in searing summer heat, the galleries packed with a Tammany claque, rural South fought urban North not just over Prohibition, the Klan, ethnicity and religion but for the soul of the party.

A motion to condemn the Ku Klux Klan by name failed by 543 votes to 542. W.J. Bryan, hero of rural Populists in the 1890s but now hero of the Klan, was mercilessly jeered by city delegates. Deadlock set in between the South's candidate, William McAdoo, and Al Smith, champion of New York and urban America. White, Anglo-Saxon, Protestant, rural, small-town America was in mortal combat with an ethnically diverse, metropolitan and cosmopolitan culture. As a Catholic, a Wet and scion of Tammany, Smith with his brown derby hat and rasping Eastside accent personified the city and so was completely unacceptable to the South.

By contrast McAdoo, born in Georgia, then from New York and now California, Wilson's son-in-law, mildly progressive, a Dry and an experienced politician, looked favourite to win the necessary two-thirds majority.[18] But then it emerged that Edward Doheny, who paid the Teapot Dome bribes, had hired McAdoo as his lawyer in the continuing legal proceedings. President Harding's death had helped Republicans escape further blame for Teapot Dome. Now it was the turn of McAdoo and the Democrats to be punished. Despite the clear need to name a liberal progressive to challenge Coolidge, on the 103rd ballot exhausted delegates finally picked John W. Davis, a conservative lawyer whose clients included the archetypal big business financier J.P. Morgan. As a Midwesterner told FDR, the only choice the convention offered was 'between Doheny's attorney and Morgan's attorney'.[19]

For the party nothing good came out of this experience. For Roosevelt, however, the convention was a personal triumph. When Tammany boss Charles Murphy died in February 1924, FDR assumed active leadership of Smith's campaign. Delegates cheered for three minutes as he swung on crutches to the speakers' lectern – his first important public appearance since contracting polio – to nominate Smith as 'The Happy Warrior of the political battlefield'.[20] Roosevelt made other significant interventions during the three-week calamity, while Smith's failure to win the nomination was clearly not FDR's fault. Nor was Davis's overwhelming defeat in the presidential election. When Robert La Follette ran in November as candidate for a new insurgent Progressive party, Roosevelt feared he might do well enough to deny anyone a majority in the electoral college and throw the decision into the House of Representatives for the first time in a century. In fact, La Follette pinched progressive votes from Davis and frightened moderates who might have voted Democrat into voting Republican. The nation at large wished to 'Keep cool with Coolidge', who won easily. Davis, who won only 28 per cent of the popular vote, did worse than any Democrat since the Civil War.

The Democrats were in deep trouble. Nominating a conservative like Davis they failed to win conservative support but lost progressive support instead. Yet they were afraid that if they ran a liberal Catholic like Smith they would do even worse. No one could blame Roosevelt for this though. As far as his personal career was concerned, the 1924 convention revealed that he was back on the front rank of politics. In a sense, his aim when the party convention ended in July was simple: next time he must walk to the podium without crutches. So his priority remained improving his mobility, which he did with regular cruises on the *Larooco* and later immersion in the bubbling waters at Warm Springs. Though wonderful for his spirits it did not enable him to walk again. Talk of throwing away his crutches in two years remained a will-o'-the-wisp – always ahead, tantalizingly out of reach.

Likewise, his political ambitions always seemed to be two years away. Yet here he was much more successful in achieving them. Having failed to win his party's nomination for president in 1924, Smith ran again as governor of New York, easily defeating Theodore Roosevelt Jr. First elected in 1918, another disastrous year for Democrats, Smith had become an outstanding governor, championing civil rights and progressive reforms such as an eight-hour day for women workers, state ownership of hydro-electric power and health care for the rural poor, all carried over the unbending opposition of a conservative legislature dominated by Teddy Roosevelt's old nemesis, Republican boss Bill Barnes. Despite Smith's success though, it was apparent that both Roosevelt and the Democrats were suffering from serious disability. So throughout the Coolidge admin-istration, FDR continued to develop his broad strategy of moderate pro-gressivism and a mildly Wilsonian foreign policy, seeking to advance his own and the party's fortunes.[21]

Bitterness over Prohibition and the Catholic issue was just part of the party's overall political problem. Between 1924 and 1928 Democrats did not even have a national headquarters. Yet there were reasons why Demo-crats might hope to win a future presidential election. Progressivism went into eclipse after Wilson's re-election partly because it had achieved so much. America in the 1920s had in many ways fulfilled the progress-ive dream. Yet Western Democrats and many Southerners too, like FDR's old boss Josephus Daniels, were still appealing to those middle-class, small businessmen, the professions and farmers who had found pro-gressive ideas attractive before the war. In addition, the limited welfare legislation the party favoured attracted Catholic (or Jewish) immigrant working-class voters who formed the backbone of city Democratic party organizations. All these voters who leaned towards the Democratic party had one thing in common in the 1920s: they were failing to share in the Harding–Coolidge prosperity. Yet by 1926, while they might be a major-ity in the party, they remained a minority in the country.

However, when 1920s prosperity collapsed after 1929 they spearheaded a new majority in the nation which would sweep Roosevelt to power. Few saw that at the time. Even Howe saw 1936 as the earliest year in which his idol FDR might fulfil his destiny. In fact, he would not win the presidency until the economy collapsed, which even fewer people pre-dicted. For the moment, in the 1920s FDR's sincere loyalty to Smith, and his inability to use his legs, helped disguise the central fact that, however long it might take, he was working steadily towards the time when he would become Democratic candidate for the White House. All major political figures – Baruch, Hoover, Raskob and Smith himself – seriously underestimated FDR. For what Howe alone knew was that in one vital respect Roosevelt resembled Lincoln. His ambition was a little engine that knew no rest.

At this stage, moreover, FDR's refusal to seek nomination was key to his outwardly cordial relations with Smith. The latter, who (as noted) was building an unparalleled record as reform governor of New York, was re-elected in 1926 by an even greater margin than in 1924. Despite Smith's obvious shortcomings as a national leader, FDR respected him and took him very seriously. Such feelings were not reciprocated. To Smith, who never read a book, Roosevelt's sweeping political discourses and glittering generalizations were the sign of a hopelessly impractical intellectual. In fact, Roosevelt did not read much either, but loved to pick the brains of those who did and was fascinated by ideas well beyond Smith's horizon.

Money meant power to Smith and already by 1927 he clearly preferred the company of rich people. He had gone into politics to join them. Roosevelt, of course, took wealth for granted and knew that little separated the rich from the rest of humanity but their money. Smith did not think like that. He was starting to idolize the rich, though he was never comfortable at Hyde Park. He believed Sara patronized him and knew Eleanor kept him short of alcohol. In summary, he was mildly contemptuous of FDR the country squire with his airy plans and many hobbies. For Smith, FDR was a crippled millionaire playboy, permanently out of politics, a genial and rather useful patron of the party, but not someone to be taken seriously.

Roosevelt for his part genuinely hoped to help Smith by trying to persuade him to make more speaking tours outside New York and, on the few occasions when he did, spend less time talking about New York's problems. He also sent him plenty of data trying to make good his deficiencies on domestic issues, such as farm relief, and his even greater ones on foreign affairs. In addition, Roosevelt tried to make Smith grasp the critical importance of improving party funding. He wanted to stimulate small financial contributions from millions of Democratic voters so that the party became less dependent on a few rich backers like Baruch and Raskob. But Smith paid little attention to such attempts at party reform. He was quite happy to be dependent on rich backers like Raskob, the type of anti-Prohibition, anti-statist political sponsor he admired so uncritically and who came to influence him so greatly during the 1930s. Busy being governor, Smith paid little or no attention to what Roosevelt was saying or doing. Ultimately, this was Smith's most serious political mistake.[22] Had he foreseen that in time Roosevelt would usurp him he could have made things much harder for him than they already were.

## VII

Against this background the Democrats approached the presidential election of 1928. At the end of 1927 it appeared to most observers that the likeliest outcome would be similar to 1924: another deadlock between Smith and McAdoo, with the convention eventually nominating an available man as compromise candidate. Expecting this, Howe had for years been pushing Roosevelt's claims to be the man who could bridge the gap between the party's two factions. But as Howe saw things, Roosevelt's candidacy must not under any circumstances develop until Smith had been eliminated. This would probably not be clear until 1936, when Smith had been defeated twice for president. So 1936 remained the date Howe aimed at having FDR run. Meantime, as things turned out, in 1928 Smith was unbeatable as party nominee. The Democrats had no comparable vote-winner, nor anyone who could remotely equal Smith's executive experience or record as a reformer. True, when FDR's old Harvard classmate Louis Wehle, who had mooted a Hoover–Roosevelt Democratic ticket in 1920, mentioned Roosevelt to Southern conservatives like Carter Glass they seemed enthusiastic. What Wehle failed to see was that, unlike Howe, these Southern Democrats wanted to use Roosevelt to stop Smith's nomination in 1928 so that Roosevelt could run and lose.[23] Apart from all considerations about FDR's health, however, neither Howe nor Roosevelt wanted to fight and lose in 1928, because losing would end his career.

Moreover, when delegates arrived at the convention in Houston, Texas, at the end of June, it was plain that Smith and his New York organization had locked up the nomination. Though they were playing this time in the South, Tammany would sweep the board with no repeat of the 1924 stalemate. For the first time since 1916 the Democrats nominated their candidate on the first ballot. By then the Republicans had already nominated Herbert Hoover, who personified the permanent triumph of American capitalism which most Americans confidently believed had occurred in the 1920s. Smith knew Hoover would be impossible to beat; the best he could hope for was to run a campaign so strong that grateful Democrats would run Smith again in 1932. Howe, on the other hand, expected Hoover to beat whoever he ran against in 1932, finishing Smith's career and leaving FDR to fight a weaker opponent in 1936. What neither Smith nor Howe could see in 1928 was that by 1929 Roosevelt would be much better placed for 1932 than Smith and that by 1930 he would be better placed for it than Hoover.

This unexpected outcome began in June 1928 at the Democratic convention in Houston, with FDR no longer Smith's pre-convention manager, nor even at first his floor manager. It was typical of Smith's shortcomings as a national leader that Frank Hague, brutal boss of Jersey City, was his choice for that post, for there could have been no one worse from the standpoint of winning Smith rural support in either party or nation. Knowing this, other senior Democrats stopped Hague. When Roosevelt was named instead, Howe exclaimed, 'Thank God.' What delegates learned too was that FDR had at last become a good public speaker. More important, as he walked from floor to platform to place Smith's name in nomination again, he appeared to have regained the use of his legs. The crutches were gone; in their place he walked in braces, using a stick and leaning on the arm of his strong son Elliott. To thousands of watching delegates he seemed not crippled but lame.[24] It was a popular perception which helped him through the rest of his political career.

Roosevelt's 1928 convention speech was the culmination of all his work since polio had struck in 1921. Howe made sure it got maximum publicity, sending advance copies to all the newspapers. The speech was also broadcast live and aimed, in Roosevelt's words, at 'The 15,000,000 radio listeners rather than at the 15,000 in the convention hall'.[25] In this he was successful, anticipating his later 'fireside chats' broadcast over the radio when he became president in the 1930s. Millions more read it in their morning newspaper. Once nominated Smith chose Senator Joseph Robinson of Arkansas, later Senate majority leader from 1933 until 1937, as his running mate. Roosevelt was not even considered: no national ticket can consist of two residents of the same state.

Nevertheless, FDR's role turned out to be crucial. Smith had to win his own state of New York. He believed he could only do that if Roosevelt agreed to run for governor and help Smith take the vital upstate Republican districts. In a sense, he would run on FDR's coat tails. Roosevelt's position was quite different. Howe was certain he must not run for governor. He needed another four years to improve his strength and mobility. Worse, on the same ticket as Smith he would probably lose. Defeat would finish him. For his part FDR still considered Hoover a personal friend and had been careful not to criticize him in public. This was ironic. When the two men contested the presidency in 1932, FDR was forced to attack Hoover, who in turn made it clear in private that he despised Roosevelt. Yet though in 1928 Roosevelt regarded Hoover as a great man, he thought Smith a greater one. Tired after the Houston convention, Roosevelt went as usual to Warm Springs expecting to be asked to work on Smith's national campaign. Instead, Smith made it plain that all he wanted was FDR to run for governor.

This was a real problem. If he agreed he would face a double bind. Going down in defeat with Smith would be disastrous. But even if he won the governorship in 1928 the Democrats might pick him to run against Hoover, who would be unbeatable in 1932 if Republican prosperity continued. Indeed, Howe's real problem in making FDR president was that any Republican looked unbeatable while the good times rolled. Roosevelt was not one of the few who saw the prosperity of the 1920s ending. Like most Americans he believed it to be permanent. Howe, as we have seen, wanted to wait until Smith had been beaten. Then FDR could run for governor in 1932 and president in 1936. At least he would not then have to run against Hoover, a far stronger candidate than Harding or Coolidge had been.

But Smith's easy nomination in 1928 had put him in a strong position. Rich party backers like Raskob emphasized the vital importance of FDR helping Smith carry New York. So suddenly everything depended on him. This was the kind of situation he loved. He had apparently agreed with Howe and Eleanor that he would refuse, making his health the non-negotiable reason. But significantly, as pressure from Smith and Raskob mounted, Eleanor and Howe were in New York and Roosevelt was in Warm Springs. Howe wanted Roosevelt simply to say no. He must wait patiently until 1932 when he could throw his crutches away for good and run for governor. But at the most critical point in his career, he discarded Howe's counsel. When Smith offered him the nomination over the telephone several times Roosevelt hedged. On one occasion Missy LeHand, who was standing beside him, told him sternly, 'Don't you dare.' Then his daughter Anna wired, GO AHEAD AND TAKE IT. Roosevelt replied, YOU OUGHT TO BE SPANKED. MUCH LOVE. PA.[26]

What he failed to do, though, was make the definite, final and irrevocable refusal Howe had urged to run for governor in any circumstance. When he said his health was a problem, Smith said the lieutenant-governor would take over while FDR spent three months each year at Warm Springs. When he pleaded that his main worry was the $200,000 he had invested in Warm Springs, Raskob, chairman of the Democratic national committee (whose appointment FDR had opposed in July), immediately underwrote the debt with a personal cheque for $350,000. (Roosevelt returned the cheque, but by 1932 Raskob had contributed some $200,000 to Warm Springs.) When Smith asked FDR what he would do if nominated by acclamation he replied weakly that he did not know and, when the convention immediately did this, he agreed to run. 'Mess is no name for it' a disgusted Howe telegraphed. 'I suppose you could demand time to reconsider . . . For once I have no advice to give.'[27] Against all advice FDR had got what he really wanted. At last he was back in the game he loved best. Yet it was a big risk. Had he lost in 1928 his career would have ended. He would not have become president in 1932.

In fact events could not have worked out better. The 1928 presidential election became a by-word for religious bigotry, racism and prejudice of all kinds. The opposition Smith had attracted from Southern Democrats at the 1924 convention was now magnified on a national scale. While campaigning in the South, Smith was burned in effigy and Klan crosses blazed while Catholics were vilified for letting blacks worship in the same churches as whites.[28] But the underlying forces at work were more complex than ignorant religious and racial prejudice. Religious prejudice was allied to fears that the Pope would exercise influence on a Catholic president and undermine that separation of Church and State on which the American republic had been founded. As the influential progressive journalist Walter Lippmann wrote, 'Quite apart from the severe opposition of the Prohibitionists, the objection to Tammany, the sectional objections to New York, there is an opposition to Smith which is as authentic and, it seems to me, as poignant as his support. It is inspired by the feeling that the clamorous life of the city should not be acknowledged as the American ideal.'[29] Lippmann was right: what the election showed was that the clamorous life of the city was becoming the dominant theme in American politics. Since the 1920 census had shown that, for the first time, a majority of Americans lived in urban places, the campaign against the city was all the more strident because it was like the last round in a lost fight.

What everyone noticed about Hoover's huge victory over Smith was that for the first time since the Civil War the solid South split: Texas, Florida, Tennessee, Kentucky, Virginia and West Virginia voted Republican. Few noticed that Smith's total of 15 million votes, which surpassed that for any other Democrat in history, was more than Coolidge had polled in 1924, or that his 40.8 per cent share of the popular vote compared favourably with Cox's 34.1 per cent in 1920 or Davis's derisory 28.8 per cent in 1924. Moreover, Smith got little credit for his surprisingly strong showing in some farm states, like those in the Midwestern grain belt, where anti-Catholicism was less virulent. Even fewer noticed the crucial point about the 1928 election. For the first time, the total Democratic vote in America's 12 largest cities exceeded the Republican total there. That small majority of 210,000 was the tip of an iceberg which sank the Republican party without trace during the 1930s. The same cities gave the Democrats majorities of 1.7 million in 1932 and 3.4 million in 1936.[30] Moreover, not only had America's 12 largest cities gone Democratic; women in those cities, who went to the polls in numbers for the first time in 1928, also voted heavily Democratic. The sons and daughters of the last great wave of immigrants to arrive before unrestricted entry ended after 1914, who lived in those cities, were already voting for Democrats.

What destroyed Smith in rural America – his religion and recent ethnic origin – was his making in urban America. When economic catastrophe struck after 1929, these new Americans were seeking their first job and casting their first vote as Republican prosperity crashed in ruins. That they should vote disproportionately for Democrats was not surprising. Roosevelt and the New Deal were the beneficiaries of this demographic change. But it remained true, as political analyst Samuel Lubell points out, that 'Before the Roosevelt Revolution there was an Al Smith Revolution'.[31] Smith failed to benefit from this fact. For just as the fiasco of the 1924 convention had eliminated McAdoo, leader of the Dry, rural anti-Catholic wing of the party, so Hoover's victory in 1928 buried the Wet, urban Catholic leader Smith.

What Democrats learned between 1928 and 1930, however, was that in the right circumstances, and with the right leader, they could become the party of this new majority. In the search to find that leader, the 1928 election was also significant. For while Smith failed by more than 100,000 votes to carry his own state, Roosevelt was elected governor. Energetically chasing votes and rounding up ballot boxes after the polls closed, FDR won by just 25,000 votes in four and a quarter million cast, defeating Albert Ottinger. As Republican attorney general, Ottinger had built up a formidable record for busting criminal rackets to become the first Jew to run for New York governor.[32] As Howe immediately saw, Ottinger's narrow defeat meant that the relative political positions of Smith and Roosevelt had been transposed. In the right circumstances, Roosevelt rather than Smith would be the leader to put the Democrats back in power in Washington.

## Chapter 5

※

# Power as Governor, 1929–33

I

Franklin Roosevelt returned to elective office as governor of New York on 1 January 1929 after eight years in the political wilderness. It was a major turning point. Defeat would have meant oblivion, but victory meant – we can now see – that he was on his way to the White House. Yet just as he had been overshadowed at his own wedding by the presence of Theodore Roosevelt, so now he was overshadowed at his inauguration by the presence of Al Smith. Smith, elected four times since 1918, was the most effective Democratic reform governor in America. But he had been permanently scarred by the religious bigotry which overwhelmed him in 1928. Disinclined to relinquish office, he was unable to reconcile himself to FDR's victory and lacked respect for his successor's strength, whether intellectual, moral or physical. Moreover, he had taken Roosevelt's infirmity so seriously that a friend told the new governor that Smith had said of him, 'He won't live for a year.'[1]

In these circumstances, Smith started out as if FDR was merely his proxy. He had his own special adviser Belle Moskovitz start work on FDR's inaugural address, pressing her reappointment as governor's secretary and that of Robert Moses as secretary of state. Smith even reserved a hotel suite in Albany to help with the big decisions. FDR saw things very differently. As governor, another item in the timetable he had outlined as a law clerk 21 years before had been achieved. Once again he sat in Theodore Roosevelt's chair. Like his cousin before him he knew that he had to run his own administration and like him he was confident he could do it.

Belle Moskovitz was one of the most remarkable women of her generation. Her value to Smith in making policy is hard to exaggerate while, as a woman in politics, she at this stage outranked Frances Perkins and Eleanor Roosevelt with wider experience than either. Her paternalistic progressive politics meant she could have worked with Roosevelt. But the new governor understood that he could not employ her as his secretary and still run his own administration.

Instead, he appointed Guernsey Cross, whose only qualification was that he was the kind of physically strong man who could help him walk at public appearances. To add to Moskovitz's discomfort, FDR did not read the draft inaugural she sent him, nor consult her about anything. Indeed, though, initially at least, Roosevelt largely continued Smith's policies and kept on most departmental heads, Smith felt he had been deliberately ignored. 'Do you know, by God,' he said angrily some two years later, rising and stamping his foot, 'he has never consulted me about a damn thing since he became governor.'[2] As Roosevelt explained to Frances Perkins, 'I've got to be governor of the State of New York and I've got to be it myself.'[3] So having dropped Moskovitz and Smith he replaced Robert Moses, the most gifted town planner of his generation, as secretary of state with Edward J. Flynn, Democratic boss of the Bronx, who became a key aide, while appointing Perkins industrial commissioner.

Yet his programme essentially continued Smith's remarkable record as governor since 1918. To surpass him would have been difficult. Against the prevailing conservative tide of the 1920s Smith had sustained progressive government in New York, made it more efficient, and forced through a reluctant Republican legislature measures limiting rents and encouraging construction of low-rent housing in crowded cities. Smith had obtained bond issues to eliminate dangerous railway grade-crossings, improve state hospitals and build state parks and parkways. State appropriations for teachers' salaries increased tenfold and he won equal pay for women teachers, plus a law which limited all women's work to 48 hours a week. All this was a remarkable demonstration of the efficacy of what might be called materialist progressive politics, the more so as rapidly rising prosperity in the 1920s enabled him to cut direct taxes substantially and, above all, achieve the complete reorganization of state government. The hodgepodge he had inherited of 187 agencies, many of them virtually independent, became 18 administrative departments, for the most part responsible directly to the governor. This reorganization, which had been in place for only two years, gave Roosevelt the perfect opportunity to run New York as he wished and run it more efficiently.

II

Yet Smith had left much unfinished business. The legislature, as always, had a Republican majority. This remained true even at the high-tide of

Roosevelt and the New Deal in 1936. Roosevelt had to force his programme through a hostile legislature and then campaign on it for re-election in 1930. First among these issues was one destined to loom large in Roosevelt's subsequent political career – the public development of hydroelectric power. But there were many others. Smith had denounced the outgoing legislature as the most fruitless in 25 years. Aside from grade-crossing legislation, it had ignored every one of his specific proposals, which included further aid to women and children, especially the physically handicapped, improvement of education, protection of labour. It had also resisted efficient reorganization of town, country and state government.[4]

Superficially, then, FDR's programme as governor was at first Smith's with the emphasis shifted somewhat from urban to rural matters. To New York's Democratic leaders, all this seemed sound. He was not abandoning policies which would appeal to city voters, but simply putting more stress on those which might make upstate Republicans vote Democrat. Smith, for his part, had apparently given up public life. As late as 1931 he repeatedly said that nothing would induce him to enter the political arena again. Flynn vividly described Smith spreading a sheaf of papers on his desk and saying, 'Ed, these are all debts that I must clear up. Financially, I am in an extremely bad position.'[5] He told others the same. Yet though FDR had now replaced Smith as leader of progressive Democrats in New York, nationally he had yet to win the goodwill, if not active support, of bitterly antagonistic pro-Smith and anti-Smith factions still struggling to control the party. He was well placed to do this. No politician of Roosevelt's generation had a better sense of the realities of political power. The long struggle to re-establish himself after polio struck was transforming the political playboy into a tough, calculating operator.

For example, FDR loved being introduced at meetings as a farmer. Though a great landowner he was really a big city lawyer. The New Deal forced painful solutions to America's farm problem but he gave no hint of such radicalism, or indeed of any New Deal thinking, in the 1920s. His real strength then was to act in both state and national politics as mediator. In a decade where surface appearance often masked underlying reality, FDR, so adept at doing this himself, was in his element. He held the balance between city and country, progressive and conservative, Catholic and Protestant, Wet and Dry wings of the Democratic party. His vast and systematic correspondence with politicians throughout America was carefully designed to do this. Now, within weeks of becoming governor he was putting together the equipment he needed to conquer the highest political peak.

That he did this without anyone except Howe fully seeing what he was up to shows matchless skill in pursuit of power. Even Howe, who could see that 1932 might be the year, feared the danger of a premature dash for the summit. Only when economic depression began to bite so fiercely in the early 1930s did this danger subside. Even then FDR was not seen as a strong contender. He was still underestimated: pleasant, superficial and, in Bernard Baruch's phrase, 'wishy-washy'. Even Sam Rosenman, formerly an ardent Smith supporter, who in 1928 played a crucial part in FDR's election as governor, had no idea at this stage of the new governor's aim. This is all the more surprising, since Rosenman's early doubts about Roosevelt's patrician manner had soon been stilled. He was not the lightweight Smith described so pungently. 'The broad jaw and upthrust chin, the piercing, flashing eyes, the firm hands,' Rosenman wrote, '– they did not fit the description.'[6]

## III

As he planned this stealthy bid for power Roosevelt made some policies clearly his own. Public power was the first such initiative. He had originally become concerned about the importance of cheap electric power at Albany in 1911 and his interest steadily increased. In 1921 he had begun talking about using tidal power in Passamaquoddy Bay, near his holiday home at Campobello, to generate hydroelectricity. When the lower Mississippi valley was hit by yet another serious flood in 1927, he outlined to Smith a solution which anticipated what he eventually did as president during the New Deal with the Tennessee Valley Authority. Control of flood waters would 'develop hydroelectric power for the benefit of the people of the United States'.[7]

Aside from the importance of building dams for flood control, the political side of his fight for cheaper electricity had two distinct parts: the promotion of public power; and the effective regulation of private utility monopoly. Here, he took advice from Gifford Pinchot, the progressive Republican who had taught him the vital importance of conservation in 1912. Pinchot was now governor of neighbouring Pennsylvania and FDR brought Morris Llewellyn Cooke, another Pennsylvanian and a power expert, to New York to give advice. He also appointed the economist Leland Olds to the New York state power authority to advise on rate reduction. He proposed public power development on the St Lawrence river, an idea he had inherited from Smith, but he went further than Smith had done by insisting that the state build its own transmission lines if utilities buying state power would not cut rates. He also imposed more rigorous methods of evaluating utility company stocks, investments and costs.

Conservation was much the same story. This was the political issue closest to Roosevelt's heart and, over the years, it had come to mean more than simply planning for land and resource use. 'Broadly speaking,' he explained, 'its implications of saving and protecting what we own that is of genuine worth, whether of wealth, of health or of happiness, is inclusive enough to take in all the functions of government.'[8] Even before the ravages of depression and the Dust Bowl of the 1930s, Roosevelt looked to regional planning to improve the farm situation. This meant withdrawing submarginal land, reforestation and related land use as well as simple conservation measures.

His constitutional amendment authorizing the state to buy up abandoned farms for reforestation, later sustained by the people in a referendum, was denounced by Smith in a way which hurt him personally. 'What a queer thing that was for Smith to fight so bitterly,' he commented, remembering that when Smith had been governor he had kept quiet about measures with which he had disagreed.[9]

FDR was angry and depressed about his disagreement with Smith, which was a significant parting of the ways. By distancing himself from his predecessor FDR was already throwing down the gauntlet to possible future opponents for president, like Smith. More important, after the Wall Street crash in October 1929, when President Hoover sought to restore business confidence in November by assuring everyone that the depression was over, Roosevelt began to square up to his biggest opponent. He asked Frances Perkins to produce figures which revealed that unemployment was actually rising, not falling as Hoover tried to pretend. He also considered radical plans to help rescue its jobless victims, in contrast to Hoover's passive reliance on market forces to give hope to the desperate and feed the hungry.

## IV

Roosevelt had been governor for less than a year when the Wall Street crash was followed by the worst economic collapse in US history. The great depression, together with the Second World War, shaped the rest of his life as it did the lives of millions of his fellow Americans. Roosevelt's importance stems solely from the fact that throughout the critical period of the twentieth century – from 1929 until 1945 – he was governor of

America's most populous state and then president of the world's greatest power. In common with most of those millions, Roosevelt had not seen depression coming. Moreover, he was slow to grasp that this was more than the usual temporary downturn in the trade cycle. Yet the next four years provided painful education. Events revealed that surface prosperity in the 1920s, with the spread of consumer goods like motor cars and household appliances, had disguised serious weaknesses in the American economy.

For a start, the Great War had transformed America's position in the world. Britain and France had paid for victory by running up huge debts in the United States. From being the world's largest debtor nation in 1914, the United States was now its greatest creditor. But this fundamental transformation had not been accompanied by any change in thinking or in trading policy. America had always believed in high tariffs to protect domestic manufactures from foreign competition, using the revenue to pay for internal improvements. The only way European nations could repay war debt was by selling goods in the American domestic market. Yet far from reducing tariffs, Congress raised them to unprecedented heights in the 1920s. This was bound to disrupt world trading and financial arrangements and eventually inflict grave damage on the United States too.

Weak banking and poor corporate structure made this more likely. There was no effective national banking system. State banks were often under-capitalized and badly managed. The central problem, however, was reliance on market forces and lack of effective regulation. From the 1830s until the progressive period there had been no central bank to take care of credit nationally or act as lender of last resort. The federal reserve board, set up in 1913 to do this, was untested in a serious crisis. Even in the 1920s boom bank failures averaged more than 600 a year, which meant that over a dozen banks failed every year in every state. Corporate structure, though it looked impressive, was in reality just as ramshackle. Much of it had been put together without thought, often to throw federal trust-busting agencies off the scent. Corporate structure was like a huge inverted pyramid: comparatively small amounts of cash underpinned huge amounts of paper wealth. In good times this was not a problem; but if failure occurred in parts of the system it would short-circuit through the rest bringing the whole unstable edifice down.

More serious, the rising prosperity of the 1920s was not well distributed. Farming had failed to share it. The chronic problem of falling agricultural prices was being masked by the McNary-Haugen Act, which forced the federal government to pay agreed prices for farm surpluses at home before using subsidies to dump them abroad. Though FDR accepted McNary-Haugenism in the 1920s he completely dismantled it during the New Deal. Meantime, in industry another chronic problem lurked: while real wages of industrial workers rose by about 10 per cent in the 1920s, productivity rose by more than 40 per cent. Semi-skilled and unskilled workers in mass production, who were not unionized, lagged far behind skilled craftsmen. The real problem was that in both agricultural and industrial sectors of the economy America's capacity to produce was tending to outstrip its capacity to consume. This gap had been partly bridged by private debt, easy credit and hire purchase. But this would collapse if anything went wrong in another part of the system.

Finally, the stock market insanity which characterized the years between 1927 and 1929 might have been designed to make this a certainty. Investors no longer bought shares in companies for the dividends they might bring but for their paper value. Indeed, the shares which rose most rapidly in value in the 1920s were often those, like radio, which did not declare dividends. Something similar happened during the dot.com madness of the 1990s. Paper values could be used to borrow more money, to buy more shares on margin by placing only 10 per cent of their cost with the broker. Such shares in turn would then be used to borrow more money to buy more shares and so on. With more buyers than sellers, prices rose inexorably. But if anything went wrong – if people started to sell in large numbers rather than to buy – stock market prices would collapse. Brokers would put pressure on clients, banks on both and a vicious downward spiral would follow. This is exactly what happened after October 1929, the most serious financial crash in American history.

Yet this financial crisis did not necessarily have to trigger economic collapse. The Panic of 1907 had not caused an economic downturn; the depression of 1920–21 did not damage the stock market. But, as we have seen, there were many weaknesses in the economy in the 1920s which rendered it liable to serious downturn, while the stock market vortex was so severe it sucked significant spending power out of the economy. The combined effects were devastating. By mid-November 1929 stocks listed on the New York exchange had fallen more than 40 per cent in value, a loss on paper of 26 million dollars. Bad as this was, the serious damage occurred later in the real economy. In the next four years manufacturing output halved, farm prices fell by 40 per cent from the low base of 1928, exports declined by a third in value. National income had fallen from 83 billion dollars in 1929 to just over 40 billion dollars in 1931. By conservative estimates, unemployment in 1933 stood at 13 million. This meant that about one-quarter of the workforce, and nearly 40 per cent of wage and salary earners, were jobless. With no federal social security, and state systems, local welfare, savings and charity long since exhausted, purchasing power was at an all-time low. Capacity to consume was gone and millions of Americans were on the brink of starvation.[10]

## V

The worst economic disaster in American history was also a crisis of American individualism. Yet Roosevelt had foreseen none of it. It was typical of his luck that economic depression should so greatly improve his personal political prospects. Depression and what to do about it dominated events until at least 1940. Moreover, no blame could be attached by voters to Roosevelt and the Democrats for the catastrophe. Voters punished the Republicans, who had monopolized federal power during the 1920s, and President Hoover. Moreover, as usual FDR used the opportunity the depression provided in his tireless pursuit of political power. No governor in the nation – apart from Huey Long in Louisiana – was more responsive to the challenge of the depression. On welfare issues, his programme was initially an extension of earlier beliefs; but in modifying these he found ready advice from old New York colleagues like Frances Perkins and new ones like Harry Hopkins, a lively social worker and expert on unemployment relief who, after Howe's death in 1936, ultimately became FDR's closest adviser.

Even before the depression Roosevelt, Perkins and Hopkins had begun to advocate state old-age pensions in New York. When unemployment began to rise steeply in January 1930 Perkins and Hopkins supplied FDR with figures which revealed the magnitude of the crisis both in New York and the nation, exposing as false Hoover's optimistic reports. By March 1930 Roosevelt had appointed a commission on the stabilization of employment in New York and later, at a governors' conference in Salt Lake City, he finally endorsed the principle of unemployment insurance.[11]

But federal unemployment insurance was a long-term goal not achieved in the nation until 1935 under the New Deal. As local relief broke down in New York and the whole United States, the immediate need was to fight hunger and cold as the first depression winter deepened. So in New York FDR set up the temporary emergency relief administration (TERA). He became the first governor in the United States to establish state aid for unemployment relief and TERA was the first state relief agency to go into action. Despite limitations, it gave aid to jobless citizens 'not as a matter of charity but as a matter of social duty'.[12] With TERA Roosevelt and Hopkins gave America a significant lead. It anticipated Hopkins's later role running federal emergency relief administration (FERA), one of FDR's first New Deal measures to help America's jobless.

In tackling the gravest economic crisis in New York history FDR faced a Republican legislature hostile to all his pet projects – public power, work creation, conservation and social reform. The governor further antagonized Republicans in April 1930 by vetoing three segregated lumpsum items in the executive budget. Opponents argued that this was unconstitutional, a view which the courts later upheld, but which the US Supreme Court reversed on appeal, handing FDR a big political victory. Through all these political conflicts he made deft use of radio, anticipating his tactics later as president, to rouse voters to force the legislature to accept his measures. This was an important shift in the nature of political propaganda in the twentieth century, which Roosevelt shrewdly observed and exploited. 'It seems to me,' he noted, 'that radio is gradually bringing to the ears of our people matters of interest concerning their country which they refused to consider in the daily press with their eyes.'[13]

Meantime, efforts to live on good terms with his old enemies at Tammany Hall were sabotaged by bitter divisions within Tammany and by the scandalous behaviour of New York's mayor Jimmy Walker. When it became clear that playboy Walker could not wisecrack away the corruption which flourished so luxuriantly in his administration, FDR was forced to set up an inquiry under Judge Samuel Seabury. The Seabury inquiry and the Walker affair were to embarrass Roosevelt until his campaign for president began in earnest in 1932, when Walker resigned. For 18 months, Governor Roosevelt could not escape the problem, made worse by the fact that he personally liked Walker, who had placed his name in nomination for governor at the 1928 Democratic convention. FDR liked a good time so Walker probably appealed to the playboy in his own character. Yet he quickly saw that this was not just another Tammany scandal: Walker had become a symbol of the evils of machine politics. 'How would it be,' FDR mused as late as summer 1932, 'if I let the little mayor off with a hell of a reprimand?' Suddenly, as if answering himself, he said sharply, 'No. That would be weak.'[14]

Before Walker's resignation Republicans fired their big guns to try to make a political breakthrough. But when Hoover sent his secretary of state, Henry L. Stimson, secretary of war, Patrick J. Hurley, and undersecretary of the treasury, Ogden Mills, to New York, FDR counter-attacked with sharp, satirical speeches which roused Democrats.[15] In November 1930, New York voters had given their verdict on Roosevelt as governor. They returned him for a second term with a plurality of 750,000 votes, by far the largest in history, surpassing even the victories of Al Smith. James A. Farley, the Democratic state chairman, soon to become FDR's presidential campaign manager, issued a public statement drafted with Howe. 'I do not see', it declared, 'how Mr Roosevelt can escape becoming the next presidential nominee of the party, even if no one should raise a finger to bring it about.'[16] But more than fingers were going to be raised. A few days later Roosevelt invited the professional politician he trusted most, his secretary of state Edward Flynn, to meet him and Howe at the governor's mansion in Albany. 'Eddie,' FDR explained, 'my reason for asking you to stay overnight is that I believe I can be nominated for the presidency in 1932.'[17]

## VI

If the Jimmy Walker scandal overshadowed FDR's reform programme and general performance as governor in his second term, his developing presidential candidacy overshadowed it even more. Not least of the many things Roosevelt had going for him as he reached for the presidency was – somewhat surprisingly – his health. Though, as he had anticipated, the governorship had hit his search for a cure – the three months a year he had spent at Warm Springs was now cut to six weeks – his health was excellent. Running for re-election he took out life insurance worth a million dollars. Insurance company doctors told the press that his condition aged 48 was that of a man of 30. When a doctor said his chest expansion was better than that of Jack Dempsey, a recent heavyweight boxing champion of the world, FDR added, 'Dempsey is an "ex"; I'm not.'[18] Such public relations hid the fact that Roosevelt still could not use his legs and, barring a miracle, never would. It helped spread the idea many people had taken from the 1928 Democratic presidential convention in Houston: that FDR had recovered from polio and was not crippled but lame.

Politically speaking Roosevelt was in rude health. First, the deepening depression made it every month more likely that a Democrat would be elected president in 1932. Despite headlines about the Walker scandal or ending Prohibition, it was collapsing farm prices and bonds and above all unemployment which dominated the political agenda. As a white, Anglo-Saxon, aristocratic landowner with impeccable upstate New York credentials, Roosevelt's appeal to farmers and conservatives generally was strong. He was a progressive with Wall Street connections and (rare even today and more so then) unusual knowledge of foreign affairs. He had effective, informal political relations with Tammany Hall, while not being closely associated with Tammany in the public mind. He had a name known all over America. Moreover, long stays in Warm Springs in search of a cure had cemented Southern political friendships crucial for a progressive Democrat. Living in the South helped him understand its problems as few New Yorkers did. As we have seen, polio had also kept him from taking sides in the rancorous conflicts which had rent the Democrats in the 1920s over Prohibition, immigration, Catholicism and the Klan. He was the available bridge between city and country. Finally, he had just shown he was the greatest vote-winner in New York political history.

His political experience – state senator, federal government, New York governor – was unmatched by any other presidential candidate in history since Teddy Roosevelt succeeded McKinley in 1901. Yet as an experienced office holder and political operator, Roosevelt knew in 1930 that he must assemble a team to win in 1932. His wealth would buy him expert consultants. Howe, who had lived for Roosevelt since 1912, and Eleanor, who had lived with him even longer, were at the heart of the team. His wife was now effectively living a separate life; but she had become a political operator in her own right with strong links with the political left. Newer members of the team were Edward Flynn, Sam Rosenman, Basil O'Connor and James Farley.

Flynn, Roosevelt's secretary of state, came, as was common among New York Democrats, from an Irish family; less commonly, the family was rich and so socially at ease with FDR. After law school and a spell in the New York assembly, Tammany boss Murphy had made him Democratic leader in the Bronx. As immaculate in dress as Howe was scruffy, Flynn was a courteous but tough politician. To Flynn corruption was worse than immoral: it was stupid. 'Bosses are inevitable under our system of government,' he liked to say, 'bad bosses are not.'[19] His money and flourishing law practice gave him independence and power. He was FDR's only reliable ally in New York City. Sam Rosenman was also a New York lawyer who had become indispensable when Roosevelt ran for governor in 1928. His careful files on every political issue, which characterized his whole approach to politics and life, helped win that wafer-thin victory and so impressed the new governor that Rosenman became his counsel in Albany and eventually archivist of the Roosevelt papers. Roosevelt admired Rosenman's orderly mind, fluent writing and sound political judgement. Rosenman was fascinated by Frank's flair and ability to bring dull prose to life in personal speech.

Flynn and Rosenman were essentially political friends. Basil O'Connor by contrast was, as we have seen, a business friend and FDR's law partner who became vital to his attempt to reconstruct himself. FDR found much legal work boring.[20] But his new practice with 'Doc' O'Connor was much more to his taste. O'Connor operated boldly in the corporate and political field where he was speculating with such gusto in the 1920s. FDR loved politics, business and the law for much the same reason: each combined pursuit of power with intoxicating sense of risk. Minimizing that risk in politics was the speciality of James Farley. Engaging and friendly, Farley had worked his way up in the New York Democratic organization from town chairmanship at Stony Point through the county chairmanship to state assembly and state chairmanship. Even less familiar than Howe or Flynn with the national picture, Farley's orderly mind, integrity, memory, modest and decent life – he was a devoted family man who neither smoked nor drank and faithfully attended Sunday mass – had made their mark.

In the great American hinterland, Roosevelt felt, Farley's personal qualities would disarm people who might otherwise mistrust a big, bald, glad-handing Irish-Catholic politician from New York. 'You have done a wonderful piece of work,' FDR told him after the 1930 re-election campaign. 'I have an idea that you and I can make a combination which has not existed since Cleveland and Lamont.'[21] No need to add that Lamont had helped put Cleveland, an earlier New York governor, into the White House. At this stage, though, Roosevelt could only guess that he and Farley were to become one of the most successful campaign combinations in history.

## VII

Next came money. As we have seen, FDR, despite his wealth, had found money a problem throughout the 1920s. Now he needed more than his private income could provide. Early backers were his old friend and neighbour Henry Morgenthau, Frank Walker, a New York lawyer, and William Woodin, a leading manufacturer, who each gave personal contributions of $5,000 to the Friends of Roosevelt. Other early backers included Edward Flynn, Herbert Lehman, Joseph E. Davies and Joseph Kennedy. Col. Edward House, Wilson's *éminence grise*, was a key link with the last Democratic presidency and Western progressives like Burton

K. Wheeler and Clarence Dill were early contributors, although Wheeler later changed his mind. Howe greatly admired Cordell Hull of Tennessee, who was a spokesman for the South and would have been an appropriate running mate for Smith in 1928.

Now they had money and a team, Howe and Farley set up headquarters on Madison Avenue early in March 1931. In June the annual governors conference gave FDR a chance to speak on national issues. He seized it to offer views on the depression starkly different from not just Hoover but the Raskob conservative wing of the Democratic party. People were rightly asking, he told the governors, 'why government cannot and should not act to protect its citizens from disaster' and undertake 'the better planning of our social and economic life'[22] through sickness and unemployment insurance, taxation, the tariff, land utilization and planned population redistribution.

Meantime, as this call for positive government sharpened the ideological conflict within the Democratic party, Farley was taking soundings to gauge support for Roosevelt across the nation. When he went to the annual grand lodge convention of fraternal Elks in Seattle, FDR and Howe worked out a railway route which took him to 18 states in 19 days. In a whirl of lunches, dinners, meetings, sleeping-car changes at night, new hands to shake, new names to remember, Farley met a thousand local Democratic leaders. In the next few weeks he sent each a personal letter. That autumn Farley's incessant activity continued. He met Congressional progressives like Cordell Hull and Burton K. Wheeler in Washington, talked to national committeemen and established a network of long-distance telephone contacts across the nation. Eleanor and her friend Molly Dewson, a leading light in the Consumers' League, who had worked in Smith's campaigns for governor and president, organized the women's vote. So began Farley's legendary network: thousands of contacts nationwide which made him the best analyst of American voter intentions in the 1930s.

Yet organization alone could not make Roosevelt president. He needed a policy to end the depression. In search of this he displayed a country squire's scorn for the rich who lacked social responsibility. His Hudson river neighbour Claiborne Pell had no use for those businessmen who had taken over after the war. 'The destinies of the world were handed them on a plate in 1920,' Pell put it memorably. 'The piglike rush for immediate profits knocked over the whole feast in nine years. These are the people who, with an ignorance equalled only by their impudence, set themselves up as the proper leaders of the country.'[23] Pell's words were too biting for a politician like FDR to utter. But he shared the thought behind them. Where Pell thought the rich were villains and Smith was in awe of them, Roosevelt knew they were like him, but usually more foolish and ignorant. Yet for the moment he knew that he was no better prepared to deal with the depression than they. 'If you were to be nominated tomorrow,' Rosenman shrewdly pointed out in March 1932, 'and had to start a campaign trip within ten days, we'd be in an awful fix.'[24]

For policy, Rosenman asked Raymond Moley, a 44-year-old political scientist from Columbia University in New York City, to recruit academic consultants. This was a key appointment. Roosevelt's 'Vibrant aliveness, his warmth, his sympathy, his activism' was what attracted him, Moley wrote, not any policy ideas he might have had.[25] Indeed, Moley's job was to devise policy. Accordingly, he asked two Columbia colleagues: Rexford Tugwell for agricultural economics; and for corporate problems Adolf Berle. With Gardiner Means, Berle had recently written *The Modern Corporation and Private Property*, which reinforced Theodore Roosevelt's thesis that the concentration of industrial wealth and power into fewer and fewer hands was irreversible but could be managed by the US government.

The book became a modern classic. Tugwell, brilliantly intuitive, accepted Berle's analysis, while struggling to find a solution to the vicious downward spiral of agricultural prices which had ruined millions of farmers. Tugwell liked to shock. Berle, a child prodigy, had got his Harvard A.B. degree at 18. Enemies said he had ceased to be a prodigy but was still a child. Politically, Tugwell was on the left with Berle on the right. Moley chaired regular meetings of the 'brains trust' (as Howe, to FDR's delight, dubbed it), which Rosenman and Basil O'Connor also attended. FDR was not an intellectual, but enjoyed their company and was in his element at the free-wheeling discussions which hammered out the New Deal. Indeed, the very phrase 'New Deal' may have been coined by Moley at such meetings and nothing was more important than educating FDR in how to use political power to end the depression.

Yet to win power he had first to see off other strong Democratic candidates. Roosevelt's later dominance of the American and world stage can blind us to the fact that there was nothing inevitable about his victory in 1932. Other men might easily have been chosen by the Democrats. First of these was Al Smith. He had said he had given up politics. Yet despite encountering severe bigotry in 1928 he had shown where the emerging Democratic majority was located, a fact of which both Howe and Farley were fully aware. When Ed Flynn approached Smith in 1931 to ask his intentions for 1932 Smith was frank: the party owed him the nomination and he did not want to have to campaign for it. Flynn told him equally frankly that this time he was backing FDR. 'Flynn betrayed me,' Smith said later. 'Wait and see him betray Roosevelt.'[26] By all the rules of the political game Smith was entitled to the nomination: in a just world that would have happened.

Yet what everyone – even Smith – thought they had learned in 1928 was that a Roman Catholic could not win. In that sense, Smith was yesterday's man. Worse, the hero of the cities was now president of the Empire State Building, director of banks and insurance companies, friend of rich men like Raskob and the Du Ponts and spokesman for northern business. In stark contrast to FDR, the bulk of Smith's political pronouncements in 1931 and 1932 were for rigid government economy, a balanced budget, tax cuts for the wealthy and a sales tax. In the judgement of H.L. Mencken, mordant reporter of the 1920s, 'The Al Smith of today is no longer a politician of the first chop. His association with the rich has apparently wobbled him and changed him ... It is a sad spectacle.'[27]

As 1932 opened Smith remained a strong candidate, increasingly exasperated by FDR, the man bent on usurping him. Yet Smith was not Roosevelt's only opponent. The old Bryan–McAdoo wing of the party – nativist, isolationist and implacably opposed to Smith – had found a new candidate. McAdoo was now backing John Nance Garner, a Texas Congressman since 1903 and currently Democratic leader in the House, now seen by some as the new Champ Clark, a politician's politician.

Fearful that other candidates were too internationalist, the unscrupulous tycoon William Randolph Hearst was putting his newspapers and his millions behind Garner. So with at least three strong contenders, the most likely outcome in 1932 seemed deadlock. In that case Newton D. Baker of Ohio was the obvious compromise. He had something for every camp. As Schlesinger summarizes, progressives remembered the reform mayor of Cleveland; idealists admired Baker's long fight for the League of Nations; realists recalled Woodrow Wilson's secretary of war; conservatives knew him as a rich corporation lawyer. Articulate, scholarly and high-principled, Baker was in the tradition of Wilson and John W. Davis.

Yet support for the League made Baker anathema to Hearst. So to widen his appeal he reversed his view that America should join. This left FDR exposed as the most internationalist of the candidates. So he too moved to propitiate Hearst. Though he had supported League membership, FDR explained, 'the fact remains that we did not join'. In present circumstances, 'I do not favor American participation.'[28] When the domestic chips were down FDR could abandon long-held principles in foreign affairs. Yet even apart from Smith, Garner and Baker, several strong favourite sons, such as governors Albert Ritchie of Maryland or the colourful W.H. ('Alfalfa Bill') Murray of Oklahoma, were in the race. As a successful governor since 1920 and a leading non-enforcer of Prohibition, Ritchie had influential support, not least from Mencken, while other favourite sons could block FDR's nomination and then swing their votes to his biggest rivals like Smith. Facing this field, Roosevelt had a clear strategy by February 1932. Keep lines open to the old Bryan–McAdoo wing of the party, now partly backing Garner, and above all stop the Garner group reaching agreement with Smith.

Ancient hatreds which still divided Smith from McAdoo and from Hearst all helped FDR, as did the natural dislike Southern and Western agrarians had for Eastern business. For his own part, FDR's campaign was based on social and economic views he was evolving with the brains trust. He emphasized the importance of planning, public power and public works, although the latter he explained was to be only a stopgap until prosperity returned. A speech in which he urged government to think, as it had done in wartime, of 'the forgotten man at the bottom of the economic pyramid'[29] really angered Smith, who accused FDR of being an unscrupulous class-war demagogue. This was a defining moment. Now Smith was a prisoner of big business, FDR had stolen his role as tribune of the urban working class. In another speech, Roosevelt revealed his means to end economic depression in words Smith could never have uttered, words which moreover became the hallmark of the early New Deal. 'The country needs,' he said, 'and, unless I mistake its temper, the country demands bold, persistent experimentation. It is common sense to take a method and try it. If it fails, admit it frankly and try another. But above all try something.'[30]

## VIII

The first test of Roosevelt's national support came in the 1932 primary elections. In New Hampshire in March Smith was favourite with the press, but Roosevelt won almost 2 to 1. A week later he beat Alfalfa Bill in North Dakota, bursting the Murray boom. In the next few weeks Georgia, Iowa, Maine, Wisconsin, Nebraska, Michigan and Kentucky swept into his camp. But in April in Massachusetts, the first industrial state he had entered, he was badly beaten 3 to 1 by Smith, who won most of the working-class vote. Two days later Smith showed surprising strength in Pennsylvania, another state with a large industrial working class, though fewer Catholics. Yet Roosevelt won a majority of the state's delegates. In May Garner won California, with FDR second and Smith a strong third. FDR might still be in the lead, but his bandwagon had been stopped. Massachusetts, Pennsylvania and California, wrote the progressive journalist Walter Lippmann, three large states, were the only real tests and in all three Roosevelt had made a poor showing. This might be true. But FDR noted shrewdly that if the California and Texas convention delegates could be won over at the convention their support 'would cinch the matter'.[31]

When that convention met at Chicago on 27 June the Roosevelt team, still headed by Howe, knew exactly what they had to do. Two weeks earlier, with depression deepening each month, the Republicans had met listlessly in the same city to renominate Herbert Hoover. Delegates tried to pretend depression was not the issue. Prohibition aroused strong feelings, but even here the resulting resolution was fudged. Clearly the party was doomed. As H.L. Mencken put it, 'I have seen many conventions but this one is the worst. It is both the stupidest and the most dishonest.'[32] The Democrats promised much more. After all they were nominating an almost certain winner. Moreover, the party which had suffered so much civil strife in the 1920s could now resolve its conflicts. Roosevelt was front-runner precisely because he appealed to all sections of the party and promised to appeal to all sections of the American people. But though he had a simple majority of delegates, his campaign manager Farley estimated he was at least 100 votes short of the necessary two-thirds. An ill-prepared procedural motion to scrap the two-thirds rule ended in embarrassing defeat, with New York voting 67–25 to keep the rule, revealing Tammany would go against Roosevelt in a showdown. 'Farley and I took a lesson in national politics,' Flynn explained later.[33] Indeed, their nominating campaign was not notable for its skill.

Next, Smith had a long conference with his old enemy McAdoo, now acting as Garner's manager. As representatives of city and country Smith and McAdoo had fought each other to a standstill and nearly broken the Democratic party eight years earlier. Now they were meeting to stop Roosevelt uniting it. Smith later claimed they had agreed that neither would release delegates without consulting the other. Together they controlled more than the one-third plus one votes needed to stop Roosevelt's nomination. Not surprisingly, the *New York Times* reported, 'Newton Baker loomed tonight as the most probable dark horse.'[34] Faced with this Farley knew he must detach Garner's votes from the anti-Roosevelt line-up. Meanwhile, despite gestures towards the kind of reflationary economic programme Hopkins and Tugwell were urging, which eventually defined the New Deal, the party platform favoured retrenchment and laissez-faire rather than expansion and planning. FDR's conservative supporters, Wilsonians like Cordell Hull, A. Mitchell Palmer and Edward House, had defined the party platform. The convention received it with enthusiasm. 'The resolutions committee has done the best job of any national convention for at least twenty years,' wrote Walter Lippmann,[35] revealing how much the disaster of the depression had outflanked old-style progressivism. The most popular plank in the party programme, however, was ending Prohibition. When this was announced pandemonium broke out and everything stopped for 25 minutes. Finally, the convention moved to a first ballot with states calling out their votes in alphabetical order. Roosevelt had 666 votes – more than one hundred short of two-thirds. Smith received 201, Garner 90 and seven others trailed distantly behind.

With such a big lead, Farley hoped a bandwagon would develop, but none did. He had held a few votes in hand for the second ballot, knowing the importance of making an increase each time. The second round showed Roosevelt up 16 votes, Smith down seven and Garner holding firm. Yet the Roosevelt lines were showing signs of strain. Mississippi, held by a single vote under the unit rule, could slip and if Mississippi went Arkansas would go too. The defection of Arkansas, near the top of the alphabet, might start a stampede away from FDR during the third ballot. Louisiana's Governor Huey Long now intervened decisively by persuading Mississippi to stay loyal to FDR, and as the third ballot began Farley warned, 'Watch this one closely. It will show whether I can ever go back to New York or not.'[36] The line held. Roosevelt had gained another five votes, Smith had lost another four, Garner had gained 11. In the adjournment which followed FDR spoke personally to small groups of delegates via a land line Howe had rigged directly between his hotel suite and the governor's mansion 800 miles away in Albany. Exerting all his famous charm, Roosevelt urged delegates to switch their votes to him, while Farley, Flynn and others like Joseph Kennedy persuaded Hearst that by stopping FDR he was ensuring victory for the man he feared most – the internationalist Newton Baker.

So Garner, who had not come to Chicago simply to stop Roosevelt, agreed to release his votes to him in return for the vice-presidential nomination. When on the fourth ballot McAdoo rose on California's behalf to announce 'California casts 44 votes for Franklin Roosevelt' uproar followed.[37] Before balloting was completed every other candidate had broken to FDR except Smith, who still polled 190 votes at the end. The nomination was never made unanimous. The party's traditional leaders and financial backers – Baruch, Baker, Cox, Davis, McAdoo, Raskob, Smith – had fought FDR up to the fourth ballot. All but Baruch and McAdoo were dismayed, while in particular Smith was soured by his defeat for the rest of his life. Hearing the news in Albany, Roosevelt broke precedent and instead of waiting for the decision to be mailed to him a week or two later flew (still a bold thing to do in 1932) direct to Chicago to deliver his acceptance speech. 'I pledge you – I pledge myself – to a New Deal for the American people.'[38] A powerful phrase had entered the American political vocabulary. The band played 'Happy Days Are Here Again' which thereafter became FDR's signature tune.

He fought the election campaign with his usual delight and energy. The smart advice to Roosevelt was (like Harding in 1920) simply to stay at home and do nothing – he would win anyway. But he was determined to take the vague promise of the New Deal to the people, mainly to show that his physical handicap did not prevent him doing so. At countless whistle stops on the campaign train, his leg braces in place and supported by his son Elliott, Roosevelt looked the very model of a president who would bring back prosperity. Yet his speeches did little to reassure those who thought him an opportunistic politician. Discordant and contradictory ideas gave no hint of what the New Deal would do. The most famous story about FDR is that when advisers gave him one speech advocating free trade and another protection he told them to 'Weave the two together'. He attacked Hoover's high tariff policy but, when Hoover counter-attacked, was by the end offering the same himself. At times he spoke the idiom of New Nationalism, at others the New Freedom. He offered a far-reaching plan to help farmers but one that would not cost any money. At Pittsburgh and elsewhere he promised to cut the cost of government by 25 per cent and attacked Hoover for spending too much.

None of FDR's speeches promised deficit spending, public works, public housing, slum clearance, new rights for labour unions, the National Recovery Administration or the Tennessee Valley Authority. Whatever he offered a bewildered and frightened American electorate it was not what became the agenda of the New Deal. This was not so much because Roosevelt was afraid that if he did so the electorate might reject it, but because that agenda had not yet crystallized in his mind. Nobody, least of all FDR, had any clear idea what the New Deal would mean.

'Given later developments,' an admirer noted, 'the campaign speeches often read like a giant misprint, in which Roosevelt and Hoover speak each other's lines.'[39] Whatever lines he spoke Hoover knew he was doomed. With unemployment rising each month he plunged into the battle against FDR with furious desperation. His campaign, he said, was like riding on

Harding's funeral train. Meetings were no better as, pale and hands shaking, he rose to face glum or sometimes angry audiences. 'In Hoover we trusted; now we are busted' read the banners.[40] On election day, 8 November 1932, the people gave their verdict. Roosevelt, with more than 57 per cent of the popular vote and 472 electoral votes from 42 states, won a huge landslide. This was not just the greatest Democratic victory since the Civil War but one of American history's greatest turnovers in votes.

To understand what this meant we need to set it against FDR's previous political career. He had been a typical progressive. He had entered politics in 1910 because he believed the economy needed regulation and control. During the First World War he had seen this exercised by federal agencies such as the war industries board. So the 1920s were in many ways a triumphant vindication of progressivism, with a managerial elite like Baruch and Hoover in charge. But their bureaucratic solutions suffered from severe limitations. They left the fundamental problems of underconsumption and maldistribution of wealth between agriculture and industry, between sections and between social classes untouched. As the American economy switched from a capital goods to a consumer goods phase this fundamental failure of aggregate demand meant serious trouble. The prosperity of the booming 1920s hid this for a while. The great depression made it plain. As Roosevelt waited to take power in 1932–33 this economic problem loomed over him.

Political developments were equally significant. November 1932 was one of the major realignment elections in American history, comparable with 1860 or 1896, not least because it brought in shoals of new voters and converts. After FDR's victory Democrats would henceforth for a generation replace Republicans as the natural party of government. An era in which an urban agenda of high public spending, welfare and social reform dominated politics had begun. The New Deal beckoned. The most powerful president of the twentieth century was poised to take office. This was a smashing political triumph for the Democratic party, which had seemed on the brink of breaking in two during the 1920s. For Roosevelt himself it was a personal victory over what in 1921 had looked like insurmountable odds. As he told his mother Sara on victory night, 'This is the greatest day of my life.'[41] He had reached the summit of power.

Chapter 6

# Power, Banking, Agriculture and the New Deal

## I

By winning the 1932 presidential election Franklin Roosevelt had achieved his lifetime's ambition. Not only he but Louis Howe and, in her own way, his wife Eleanor had worked relentlessly for twenty years to achieve this goal. Yet the supreme prize of politics was now quite different from what it had been in 1912 or even 1928. Hitherto the pursuit of power had been an exhilarating game for FDR. Elective office in Albany had been fun. Being part of Wilson's progressive administration in peace and war was even more satisfying. Polio had been surmounted in the 1920s largely because he could still play the great game. Even being governor of New York as depression deepened had not prepared him for his national and international burden in the White House. By 1933 economic collapse was so bad that many serious commentators doubted that American capitalism and constitutional democracy would survive. Politics was no longer fun. It was responsibility in a nation facing its most serious crisis since the Civil War. He was fated to suffer the old Chinese curse and become president in interesting times.

Roosevelt had to wait four months before taking office. In 1932–33 presidents were still elected in November but not inaugurated until March. As in 1860–61, when Lincoln stood powerless while Southern slave states seceded, FDR had to watch as, in the nation's second great trauma, the economy ground inexorably down. By March 1933 agricultural and manufacturing output had halved in four years while one-quarter of the workforce was jobless with no federal unemployment pay. Industry was idle, farming had been laid waste, banking, business and finance were at the point of collapse. Purchasing power, the key to recovery, had evaporated. The recent Pecora investigation had revealed that many leading figures in banking, business and finance – the self-styled 'wizards of

American capitalism' – were ignorant tricksters, as wizards usually are. With self-confidence and hope gone it was hard to exaggerate the severity of the crisis. Moreover, this was not just a crisis of American capitalism but of American individualism.

Despite his overwhelming victory in November neither Roosevelt nor his party looked likely to find a solution. The Democrats, out of power for years, were controlled in Congress by reactionary Southerners, while the party programme – apart from the promise to end Prohibition – had been the usual fudge which promised little. Roosevelt himself, who had played the 1920s bull market so unprofitably, did not look like a man who could deal effectively with the collapse of capitalism and was still widely regarded by many serious people as a lightweight. Yet Hoover, triumphantly successful engineer and entrepreneur, personified the prosperity of the 1920s which had now crumbled into dust. Outside every city in America the jobless lived in tar-paper shanty towns known as Hoovervilles. But where FDR was powerless during the interregnum Hoover, though still in office, was a lame-duck president lacking influence, credibility or the will to act.

He lacked ideas too. The very ease of Hoover's success meant he had learned little from it. The things he believed in – efficiency, enterprise, opportunity, individualism, personal success, material welfare – were not only in the dominant American tradition. They were things Roosevelt believed in too. But all had failed. The difference was that Hoover's overriding faith in the system and in laissez-faire made him unable to do anything. He fervently believed that government must not act: the system would right itself. With Hoover passive and Roosevelt powerless in the winter of 1932–33 it became clear that deepening depression was part of a wider picture of collapsing world capitalism. Yet both men disagreed fundamentally about this too. Hoover was convinced that the catastrophe which had struck America had begun abroad. Roosevelt thought the opposite. For while he believed in capitalism and wanted to save it as fervently as Hoover, FDR was equally certain that America was facing a domestic crisis which had spread overseas and could only be solved if the US government acted decisively at home.

While FDR waited to take power these conflicting beliefs came quickly into contention. The depression was revealing something unexpected: those who ran American capitalism in good times were helpless when it broke down. Yet Hoover was still president and the situation so grave that he took the unprecedented step of inviting the man who had defeated him at the polls to discuss policy. Roosevelt had once genuinely admired Hoover. He had wanted him to run for president as a Democrat in 1920 while as late as 1928 refused to criticize him in public because he was 'an old, personal friend'. All that had gone. Whatever greatness FDR thought Hoover possessed in the 1920s he had now clearly lost. In contrast, Roosevelt's relentless battle against polio since 1921 had marked him deeply and taught him a lot. Finally Hoover, convinced economic recovery depended on him personally, could not come to terms with political defeat by a man he despised as an unscrupulous opportunist and demagogue.

Their talks in November–December 1932 revealed the gulf which had opened between them. Hoover was not entirely passive, but his activism was confined to stimulating voluntary and cooperative action. His policies – the gold standard, balanced budgets, repayment of debt and free trade – were supposed to be proof against irresponsible free-spending politicians like FDR. But facing unprecedented crisis he could innovate and did set up the Reconstruction Finance Corporation. The RFC, although ineffective in halting economic decline between 1929 and 1933, became a major bank under Roosevelt and remained so until it was wound up in the 1950s. Though Hoover opposed government intervention at home in 1933 he favoured financial action abroad, where he believed the depression had its origin. European nations owed the United States debts they could not pay. Hoover, certain that he alone knew how to solve the crisis, wanted to call an international conference to discuss this and urged FDR to link debt settlement to strengthening the international gold standard, so giving a world approach priority over pressing domestic problems. FDR strongly took the opposite view. He believed his domestic programme must be given time to work at home before he talked to other nations and resented Hoover's attempt to hog-tie him in advance. Discord deepened, although secretary of state Henry Stimson agreed to continue discussions. 'You won't get anything,' Hoover warned him bitterly. 'You won't get anything. You can't trust him.'[1]

He later told Stimson that they had wasted their time trying to educate a very ignorant if well-meaning young man. 'He didn't get it at all,' Hoover lamented.[2] Further talks simply confirmed Roosevelt's position: he could do nothing before taking office in March but must then give home affairs priority. International debt receded into the background until the London world economic conference opened in summer 1933. The Hoover–Roosevelt interregnum convinced FDR that domestic problems now had clear priority over international ones.

## II

Though he had taken this key decision, just what he would do was far from clear. Raymond Moley, Rex Tugwell and the brains trust were still working, while the 1932 campaign had given no real clue to FDR's bold use of planning, public works and deficit finance in solving the crisis. His advisers were strongly influenced by progressive-style regulation and control of the economy during the war, or by social reform and the New Nationalism. Moreover, far from being a political innocent who had never won elective office until he became president, like Hoover, FDR had won four out of the five elections he had fought.

His main task that winter was to pick his team. The American presidency is an eighteenth-century office: its holder brings his court to Washington; and FDR's broad political experience and wide network of contacts helped him make his choice. First came his personal staff. Steve Early and Marvin McIntyre, two experienced journalists who had been with him on the 1920 campaign, were in charge of the press and his daily appointments. His personal secretary Missy LeHand, another 1920 veteran, held a unique position on his staff. Now 35, tall, slender, attractive with dark hair prematurely grey, she had lived in the Roosevelt household since 1928, would have her own room in the White House and had an intimate but not sexual relationship with Roosevelt. His fondness for her, clear to everyone including Eleanor, was so great he would listen to her as to few others on appointments and even policy.

But Missy's influence on FDR's use of power paled by comparison with Louis Howe's. No one had served FDR longer or played a more important part in making him president. No one equalled Howe in political judgement. He was to have his own suite at the White House and, though Moley may have assumed some of his tasks as chairman of the brains trust, no one could take his place. Eleanor cherished him – indeed, he was the only close friend she and her husband had in common – and he had a unique role as FDR's most candid friend. 'Howe was the only one who dared to talk to him frankly and fearlessly,' Harold Ickes observed. 'He not only could tell him what he believed to be the truth, but he could hang on like a pup to the root until he got results.'[3] Forcing him to canvass all opinions and face unpleasant sides of an issue, Howe skilfully organized campaigns to press his view so that Eleanor, Jim Farley, Ed Flynn and others would suddenly converge on FDR and, as if by accident, all make the same point.

But as FDR took power Howe's limitations were becoming more apparent. Though only just over 60 he had always been wizened but was now frail and in failing health. Moreover, though his political judgement was excellent it was limited. 'Louis knows nothing about economics,' Roosevelt lamented.[4] In fact he knew little about the kind of strategic choices FDR now faced: political tactics was Howe's game. He could save FDR from mistakes in politics but hardly from mistakes in policy, especially as he was only vaguely aware of what the New Deal was all about.

Yet at this stage no one had much idea what the New Deal meant. Moley had written the phrase in FDR's acceptance speech at Chicago in 1932 with little thought as to meaning and none to its significance. The brains trust he chaired, though full of ideas, had no agreed philosophy. Moreover the idea that Democrats in Congress, led for the most part by reactionary Southern racists, might become the party of economic recovery and social reform seemed laughable. That this happened was largely due to the unlikely political coalition FDR put together in the 1930s, starting with his cabinet. His personal staff – Howe, Missy LeHand, Early, McIntyre – were old hands already in place. Members of the brains trust – Moley, Rex Tugwell, Adolf Berle – were key figures expected to spend at least two years working for the president. But the New Deal had to be executed by the Roosevelt administration acting through its departments. So naming his cabinet occupied most of FDR's time after January 1933.

Though historians have paid little attention to the way FDR chose the members of his cabinet, his method revealed much about the style of the New Deal. He ignored advice from Democratic party bosses and senior figures who had been against him at Chicago in 1932. Yet the result conformed to normal political standards – three senators and a governor along with representatives of farmers, businessmen and reformers. Though he told Moley that he would 'more or less' fit his cabinet around his secretary of state this key post presented problems. A year before, FDR had wanted Newton Baker. But Baker's long-held belief that America must join the League of Nations ruled him out now. Moreover suspicion that, had the Democrats been deadlocked in Chicago in November, they would have picked Baker as a compromise candidate also told against him. Other names – Norman Davis, Owen Young – had dubious business connections. But FDR owed Cordell Hull of Tennessee a big political debt from Chicago; Howe favoured him; and so Hull became secretary of state despite his free trade views, holding the post until November 1944.

Roosevelt's first choice for the treasury was Carter Glass of Virginia, the Democratic party's expert on public finance in the Senate. Orthodox views on monetary questions prompted Glass to ask if the new administration planned a policy of inflation. FDR told Moley (in characteristic style), 'So far as inflation goes, you can say we're not going to throw ideas out of the window simply because they're labelled inflation. If you feel the old boy doesn't want to go along, don't press him.'[5] Berle believed FDR wanted Moley to haggle so that Glass would refuse – which he duly did. Moley then suggested William H. Woodin to Howe, who readily agreed.

Despite Woodin's complete lack of political experience, FDR was glad to offer him the treasury. A rich New York businessman, who had contributed generously to his campaigns, Woodin's record reassured Wall Street. Yet crucially he was much more unorthodox on policy than Glass, as his decisive role solving the banking crisis soon showed. The New Deal would by definition mean much new legislation, so selection of an attorney general was of critical importance. FDR's first choice here was Tom Walsh, the progressive Montana senator who had investigated in the Teapot Dome case and chaired the Chicago convention which nominated Roosevelt in 1932. But Walsh was 72 and, returning from honeymoon on the eve of taking office, he died. At the last minute FDR had to replace him with Homer Cummings, who had been Wilson's solicitor general in 1913.

Henry Wallace inherited the family job of secretary of agriculture. His father had held the post under Harding and Coolidge while his grandfather had turned it down when McKinley offered it. Frances Perkins, who had helped shape the landmark 1911 Triangle fire commission, became the first woman to enter a cabinet as secretary of labor. An old associate of FDR, she served in his cabinet for 12 years. By contrast, Harold Ickes, who served equally long at interior, had never met the president. Roosevelt, who really cared about conservation, had wanted a leading Western progressive like Hiram Johnson or Bronson Cutting, but they said no. Yet when he met Ickes, a Chicago lawyer with an outstanding record as progressive and champion of the American Indian, he said they had been talking the same language for years and 'I liked the cut of his jib.'[6]

Given FDR's conservationist beliefs, the ecological damage unregulated free enterprise had brought and the corruption which had tainted the department of the interior since 1910, Ickes's role was important. By hard work and persistence 'the old curmudgeon', as Ickes called himself, became one of the New Deal heavyweights. Jim Farley got the customary campaign manager's job of postmaster-general with its rich patronage. So in summary three members of the new Democratic president's cabinet – Ickes, Wallace and Woodin – were nominally Republicans, even though Wallace and Woodin had voted for Smith in 1928 and Ickes had voted Republican in only one presidential election in the last 25 years. All save

Wallace and Ickes were friends of FDR. Only in Glass's rejection of the treasury had issues been decisive. Viewed another way, the influence of old Wilsonians like Hull and Cummings was striking as was the length of service of Hull, Ickes and Perkins, who remained in office until 1944–45. It was all indicative of FDR's style of government which so alarmed intellectuals like Moley. Yet his cabinet, while not particularly impressive to public or posterity, worked well with him and Congress in delivering the New Deal.

III

Then luck – the Roosevelt luck – intervened. On 15 February, cruising in Florida waters, Roosevelt disembarked at Miami where he survived attempted assassination. A mad gunman missed him but shot Chicago's mayor Anton Cermak, whose dying body FDR cradled as they drove to hospital. Moley, who had been won over by FDR's vibrant activism when they first met in 1930, was even more impressed by his courage now. 'I have never in my life', he later wrote, 'seen anything more magnificent than Roosevelt's calm that night.'[7] To Moley he completely lacked physical fear. Yet on the train to his inauguration in Washington on 4 March he confided in his son James. Only one thing – fire – had ever frightened him. Now he was afraid of failing in his new job. In the next three months – indeed the next 12 years – he routed his secret fears and the fears of the nation. What made him use power with such zest and such effect was not his mind but his personality. 'A second-class intellect,' in Oliver Wendell Holmes's famous distinction, 'but a first-class temperament.' Not a philosophy but a temperament shaped the New Deal. Indeed, FDR's calmness in face of economic crisis made people wonder whether he realized how serious it was. Tugwell was also keenly aware that FDR defined the New Deal in very simple terms as being the search for economic recovery and the greater social security that Europeans enjoyed.

In fact, as Tugwell knew, he faced a stark economic choice: further deflation, urged by all sound opinion; or risking inflation to raise demand and so create jobs. Characteristically, FDR chose inflation not out of conviction but in consequence of a whole series of separate decisions taken for different reasons. At this point the American people were demanding action and FDR understood that his most important task was not only to act but also to use action to boost popular morale. This is a key to understanding the first three months of the New Deal, known as the Hundred Days. In his Inaugural Address Roosevelt boldly asserted that 'The only thing we have to fear is fear itself'. But he warned that if Congress failed to pass appropriate legislation he would seize 'broad executive power', as in time of war, to meet the emergency.[8]

He then revived special wartime legislation to legitimize his emergency measures and called Congress into special session. The precise nature of the emergency was clear. Banking was at the point of collapse. In his inaugural FDR had spoken biblically of driving the money changers from the temple of finance, but most of them had already fled. In 47 of the 48 states banks were either closed or working under tight restrictions. To buy time to seek a solution Roosevelt called a meeting, attended by Will Woodin and his Republican predecessor Ogden Mills, which declared a four-day bank holiday. To those who doubted FDR's power to do this Moley retorted, 'If two secretaries of the treasury and the governor of the federal reserve board couldn't order the closing of the reserve banks who, in God's name, could?'[9] Moreover, it was typical of FDR's method that, while banks closing indicated crisis, the phrase 'bank holiday' seemed festive and liberating. The real point – that account holders could not use their money or get credit – was obscured. Once again appearance masked reality, not this time to make FDR look lame rather than crippled but to restore confidence in a crippled nation.

During the next four days, with US commercial life halted, FDR and his advisers hammered out a policy which saved the banking system and gave a jump start to the whole New Deal. Moley has left a vivid picture of these critical meetings. Progressives like Robert M. La Follette Jr urged Roosevelt to use this opportunity to set up a truly national banking system. Heads of great financial institutions and corporations opposed this. Bankers themselves, red-faced, frightened and angry, had little idea what to do. They favoured suspending bank notes and substituting scrip – essentially IOUs of the kind issued by mining companies in remote camps with no banks or shops. But Moley argued that 'funny money' would destroy public confidence. Then Woodin who, rather improbably for a secretary of the treasury, had written 'Raggedy Ann's Sunny Songs', spent an evening strumming his guitar and arrived at a solution. 'We don't have to issue scrip!' he told Moley at breakfast, crashing his fist down on the table. 'We don't need it. These bankers have hypnotized themselves and us.'

The answer was to open at least one bank in every state by guaranteeing its currency against the assets of the federal reserve – essentially against the value of America's gross domestic product and natural resources. 'It won't look like stage money,' Woodin explained. 'It'll be money that looks like money.'[10] This would immediately restore confidence and put banking on an orderly footing so that soon the assets of those banks which had opened could be used to guarantee others – and so on. Roosevelt was convinced. Capitalism was saved in a week, Moley noted, and a thankful Congress passed the Emergency Banking Act in less than eight hours. Experienced in the use of executive power, Roosevelt delayed thousands of patronage appointments to put political pressure on individual Congressmen and senators. With the spectre of a national system gone, bankers were back in charge. The money changers FDR had threatened to drive from the temple the previous week had returned.

Yet he still had to convince the American people that when the banks reopened their money would be safe. Now he revealed himself to be a master in the use of power. He gave the first of his famous 'fireside chats', as his national radio broadcasts became known. Presidents had hardly used radio before. Coolidge and Hoover had both been hopeless in front of a microphone. No one could forget the dour, uninspiring performances of FDR's predecessors. Dorothy Parker said of Coolidge that he looked as if he had been weaned on a pickle, while another critic said of the doleful Hoover that 'A rose would wilt in his hand'.

Roosevelt, first and foremost a great charmer, now revealed that he was a natural broadcaster. This was partly because he understood the banking problem and could explain it in simple terms. On radio he instinctively tried to address one person, not millions. 'His head would nod and his hands would move in simple, natural comfortable gestures,' said Frances Perkins. 'His face would light up as if he was sitting on the front porch or in the parlour with them.'[11] Speaking slowly and simply in his aristocratic tenor voice he analysed the problem, explained his solution and convinced Americans that their money was safe. 'The president took a complicated subject like banking,' said the folk humorist Will Rogers, 'and made everybody understand it, even the bankers.'[12] The New Deal was on its way.


IV


FDR's first week in office was like his first three months. The 'swift staccato action' Moley recommended led to 15 major bills by June 1933. Agriculture, industry, banking, Wall Street, organized labour, mortgage protection, public power, conservation – every major problem was confronted. Though the New Deal was not the product of a consistent economic or philosophical approach FDR's great political victory gave him a mandate for anything he wished. Despite the cautious conservatism of its Democratic leaders, Congress was Roosevelt's pliant servant. The most astonishing burst of legislation in American history resulted.

Yet in a sense all this hectic activity postponed the fundamental choice he faced between further deflation or inflation. The early New Deal was an attempt to plan the whole economy. To many this was completely alien to the American tradition; but then the whole point was that the American tradition had failed. Yet regulation and control through bureaucracy had always been progressive policy. Though what Roosevelt was doing now looked to opponents like the approach of Hitler or Stalin, Congress was glad to pass his programme. The brains trust for its part agreed on planning but disagreed on emphasis. Where Tugwell thought government should take the initiative over business in planning, Berle believed government and business should be equal partners while Moley urged that business have the upper hand. Yet every member of the brains trust rejected the philosophy of Woodrow Wilson and Louis Brandeis that, as Moley put it, 'If America could once more become a nation of small proprietors, of corner grocers and smithies under spreading chestnut trees, we should have solved the problems of American life.'[13]

New Deal planning began with the Agricultural Adjustment Administration (AAA) which covered farming and continued with the National Recovery Administration (NRA) for industry. Action was urgent in farming because in March new crops were being planted and new livestock born. FDR was working against the sun to save the devastated agricultural sector. Devastation was not too strong a word. Net farm income in 1932 had fallen two-thirds from the already low levels it had reached in 1928. Stripped of all complexity the reason for this could be stated simply: chronic overproduction. Jobless families in the non-agricultural sector could spend little on food and, as prices fell, individual farmers tended to try to make ends meet by producing still more and sending it to market next year. The resulting glut drove prices down still further and the whole process would be repeated. Bad throughout the 1920s, this problem had been merely prolonged under the McNary-Haugen policy by which the federal government bought farm surpluses and then used subsidy to dump them abroad.

So while other sectors of the economy had boomed in the 1920s agriculture languished and then collapsed after 1929 when depression drove down demand. The parity ratio – the ratio of the prices farmers received to the prices they paid – which had been 100 in 1910–14 and 109 in 1919 was 89 in 1929 and 55 in 1932. Corn was 15 cents a bushel, cotton and wool 5 cents a pound, pigs and sugar 3 cents and beef 2.5 cents. Some economists reckoned wheat prices were lower than at any time since Queen Elizabeth I. Ironically, America had the lowest wheat prices and longest bread queues in history. At a time when about one-quarter of the population was directly dependent on farming it cost a farmer a bushel of wheat to buy a plug of chewing tobacco and 16 bushels – the average yield of a whole acre – to buy his child shoes. 'In agriculture,' Henry Wallace explained succinctly, 'supply sets the price. In industry, price sets the supply.' So the burden of agricultural adjustment had fallen not on production but on price.

The figures showed this clearly. Between 1929 and 1934 industrial production fell 42 per cent in volume, 15 per cent in price while agricultural production fell 15 per cent in volume, 40 per cent in price. So one overriding problem of the New Deal was to bring agricultural and industrial prices into better balance, restoring to farm products their prewar power to command industrial goods in exchange. This adjustment was already happening. Desperate Southern cotton farmers were organizing 'cotton holidays': refusing to plant new crops so hoping to drive up prices. Similar 'farmers' holiday' movements grew elsewhere. Yet the most important single restriction on supply stemmed from the coincidental ecological catastrophe of the Dust Bowl.

In Midwestern grain states generations of prodigal farming on dry land had finally destroyed the topsoil, which was now blowing away in black blizzards which piled soil against walls like snow and darkened the sky at noon. Though centred on the Dakotas, the Dust Bowl seared crops and livestock in two dozen states as far south as Texas and as far east as the Alleghenies. At the same time destruction of forests, the natural function of which had been to retain surface water in the Tennessee, Ohio and Mississippi valleys, was causing more frequent devastating floods. As if the worst economic depression in history was not enough, one half of America seemed to be blowing away while the other was being washed into the Gulf of Mexico. Nothing dramatized the rape of the fair continent more starkly, or the importance of FDR's core belief in conservation. The photographs Dorothea Lange took in the 1930s revealed the human cost. Pare Lorentz's pathfinding documentary movies *The Plow That Broke the Plains* and *The River* told a similar story as did John Steinbeck's powerful novel *The Grapes of Wrath* when it was published in 1939.

Roosevelt really cared about and understood the problem of conservation. His efforts to repair the ravages of the Dust Bowl included a personal initiative to plant a 2,000-mile shelter belt of trees to protect the Midwestern plains from wind damage. The ecologist who had planted woods at Hyde Park was now doing the same for the nation. Yet though he liked to be thought of as a farmer his credentials for solving the farm problem were slight. However, no one had a better farming pedigree than his secretary of agriculture Henry Wallace. Born in Iowa in the heart of the corn belt, his grandfather had edited the influential *Wallace's Farmer* during the Populist era while his father had been secretary of agriculture to Harding and Coolidge. Blaming Hoover for blocking his father's efforts to help farmers in the 1920s, Wallace now had, at the age of 44, his chance to put things right. An agricultural economist and geneticist, Wallace had evolved the idea of 'the ever-normal granary' whereby government would buy farm surpluses, store them in good times and then release them in time of scarcity. Intensely practical, Wallace was also deeply interested in mystical Asian religions, which set him apart from his colleagues. Yet in other respects he was a typical New Dealer. Like Roosevelt he believed that no road should remain unexplored to restore farmers to their place in the national economy. Moreover, if it were to be saved, the whole American system might have to be limited, with more paid to workers and farmers. 'I am inclined to think,' he said, 'both the AAA and the NRA will have to insist on a complete look at the books because of the fact that capitalism, as I see it, inevitably takes out too much in the way of profit and does not pay out enough for labour and agriculture.'[14]

To help Wallace achieve this rigorous reappraisal of capitalism Roosevelt appointed Rex Tugwell, the most creative member of his brains trust, assistant secretary of agriculture. Wallace modestly told Tugwell he felt he should have been working for him, for although only 42 no one in government had quite Tugwell's standing. Along with Mordecai Ezekiel and M.L. Wilson he had become not just FDR's leading agricultural economist but his boldest social experimenter. The problem was devising a domestic allotment plan which reduced output. Individual farmers would not do this unless they were sure their neighbours would but they could not be compelled. There had to be an incentive and Tugwell's solution was certainly bold. Pay farmers not to produce and watch comparative scarcity raise prices. This subsidy would be financed by a process tax levied on canneries and mills which prepared food and commodities for consumers. Later abuse after 1950 of agricultural subsidy by farmers and governments in both the United States and Europe should not blind us to the value of Tugwell's insight in the 1930s. Unlike McNary-Haugenism in the 1920s, Tugwell believed that subsidy should be used, not to buy surpluses, but to reduce production, control farm output and raise prices. Unorthodox then, it was also in a sense regressive since, in the words of historian Richard Hofstadter, it solved the paradox of poverty in the midst of plenty only by doing away with the plenty. Yet it proved a real turning point. It was a significant step in achieving balance between agriculture and industry.

Subsidy remained central to US agricultural economics. 'Under this plan,' Tugwell explained, 'it will pay farmers, for the first time, to be social-minded, to do something for all instead of himself alone. We thus succeed, we think, in harnessing a selfish motive for the social good.'[15] Here was a middle way between self-interest, which might mean anarchy, and coercion, which might mean tyranny. Tugwell's idea was to plan by incentive rather than by command. 'We can go further than this,' Tugwell concluded. 'We can make [the farmer] contribute towards a long-run program in this way. We can plan for him and with him.'[16] His creative insight provided the basis on which, for good or ill, agricultural policy was to develop for a generation. After 1933 it remained central to American farming.

## V

When the draft AAA bill was ready, Tugwell and Wallace took it to the White House with a draft message to Congress. But Roosevelt had already scrawled his own message in longhand. 'I tell you frankly,' he warned Congress in words which summed up the New Deal, 'that this is a new and untrod path, but I will tell you with equal frankness that an unprecedented condition calls for the trial of new means.'[17] Conservative reactions to the bill were summed up in the phrase, 'We are on our way to Moscow.'[18] But FDR himself was more alarmed by radical inflationists. A silver amendment, which had received a mere 18 Senate votes in January, got 33 in April. Could the White House stop this drift? Elbert Thomas, professor of government at the university of Utah, was only a freshman senator. Yet his omnibus amendment, which partially accepted the old 1890s Populist demand for free silver, would unite all inflationists and almost certainly pass. Faced with the choice between inflation which was mandatory and that which was merely permissive, FDR chose to accept the Thomas amendment which gave the president power to expand the money supply by reducing the gold content of the dollar by up to 50 per cent, re-monetizing silver and issuing greenbacks. Thus without really intending it FDR had provided the crucial opening to such overall economic recovery as occurred during the New Deal.

The Act he signed on 12 May, which passed the Senate by 64 votes to 20, had three parts. Title I was the Agricultural Adjustment Act; Title II was the Emergency Farm Mortgage Act, which refinanced farmers' mortgages; and Title III concerned monetary issues, including the Thomas amendment. The Roosevelt revolution in agricultural economics now gained powerful support from Jerome Frank. Felix Frankfurter, of Harvard Law School, Roosevelt's influential adviser on law and economics, had strongly recommended Frank as legal counsel to the Agricultural Adjustment Administration (AAA), the agency set up to enforce the new Act. A successful lawyer in Chicago, where he had been special counsel in protracted traction litigation in the early 1920s, Frank moved to more lucrative work as a corporation lawyer in New York in 1930. He was now 44 and brought not only a fine mind but also the ability to staff AAA with lawyers – brilliant young men with brains and imagination – who would make New Deal legislation work. Thurman Arnold, Abe Fortas and Adlai Stevenson, all later luminaries of American liberalism, were hired by Frank, as was a group of Harvard lawyers, Lee Pressman, Nathan Witt, John Abt and Alger Hiss, who were all secretly Communists.

There was nothing sinister about this. Under the US Constitution, Communists had the same right as Democrats or Republicans to work in government, though had they revealed their membership, even in the 1930s, they would have ruined their careers. As Pressman later explained, 'The future looked black for my generation . . . [and] in my desire to see the destruction of Hitlerism and an improvement in economic conditions here at home, I joined a Communist group.'[19] Fears in the 1940s and 1950s that they were seeking to advance Communism in the federal government has distorted what was really going on then. Agriculture, where Communist solutions looked less plausible than in industry, would have been the last place to try. Moreover, viewed objectively with hindsight, what Hiss and others who fell under suspicion (like Harry Dexter White and Lauchlin Currie) actually did was make American capitalism work better. Their presence in the federal government in 1933–34 revealed another important point: the New Deal coalition embraced almost everyone on the political left. Only in the 1950s, after Hiss had been jailed for perjury in denying contacts with the Soviet Union, were anti-Communist demagogues like Joe McCarthy able to denounce Roosevelt and the New Deal for '20 years of treason'.

George Peek, appointed head of the AAA by Roosevelt, was dismissive of these sharp legal minds of his staff. 'A plague of young lawyers settled on Washington,' Peek wrote later. 'They all claimed to be friends of Felix Frankfurter or Jerome Frank. They floated airily into offices, took desks, asked for papers and found no end of things to be busy about. I never found out why they came, what they did or why they left.'[20] Peek came from an older generation. He had been an outstanding figure in the agricultural politics of the 1910s and 1920s. Now 60, he had worked with Bernard Baruch and Hugh Johnson on the 1917–18 war industries board, that precursor of New Deal economic planning. FDR and Wallace had wanted Baruch to head AAA because he would have won confidence in Congress and among farm capitalists. But Baruch shrewdly dodged, recommending instead his wartime colleague Peek who, after the war, had gone to Illinois with Johnson to put Moline Plow Company on its feet. 'That is what I was doing in 1920 when the rest of the country started putting the screws on agriculture,' Peek recalled. 'Then I got mad and came out of my hole to fight.'[21]

Fighting George Peek, the farmer's champion, had approved McNary-Haugenism's use of subsidy to buy farm surpluses at home and then dump them abroad. But Tugwell now rejected it because it simply disguised chronic overproduction and did not solve it. Moreover, Tugwell and Frank shared both big city background and urban liberalism, which made them worry about the price of food to consumers. Peek was concerned solely with the income of farmers. 'The job is simple,' he told them. 'It's just to put up farm prices.'[22]

The next few months were to reveal that in trying to put up farm prices Peek had not changed his spots. Jealous that his old colleague Hugh Johnson, now executive head of industrial planning at the NRA, had direct access to FDR he insisted on the same, hoping to use the president as umpire in any dispute he had with Wallace. Such disputes were frequent. Peek was deeply suspicious of Jerome Frank, who had been one of the lawyers who had liquidated Peek's Moline Plow Company in the 1920s. Yet local production control committees, of which there were more than 4,000 by 1934, were key to raising prices. Peek was not against marketing agreements in principle and indeed favoured them instead of production control; but he did object to reform of the processors which Frank and others had managed to insert. So he reluctantly accepted marketing agreements for corn and pigs, wheat and cotton. Cotton prices were critical and Roosevelt further helped cotton growers by telling Jesse Jones at the RFC, 'Jess, I want you to lend 10 cents a pound on cotton.'[23]

This was a typical Roosevelt solution. Keeping the cotton as security would stop the surplus from further depressing the market. If prices rose above the loan, then the grower could redeem the cotton; if not, then it remained in the possession of the government. Jones set up the Commodity Credit Corporation to operate the new programme and by the end of 1934 cotton prices had risen from close to 5 cents a pound to nearly 20. Despite such success Peek resisted more marketing agreements, was unhappy at slaughtering livestock and ploughing crops under to raise prices and still thought the real solution to the farm problem was to dump surpluses abroad. In the end this brought him down. When Wallace stopped Peek using process tax revenues to subsidize American butter in Europe, Tugwell suggested that if Peek cared so much about foreign markets he might be better employed in that field. 'Lordy, Lordy,' Roosevelt exclaimed. 'How Cordell Hull will love that!'[24]

So FDR persuaded Peek that there was important work to be done in foreign trade and by November 1933 he had resigned. His successor Chester Davis, an AAA department head, who had also worked with Peek on the war industries board, was another McNary-Haugen veteran. Peek warned Davis, 'Get rid of Jerome Frank and the rest of the crowd as a condition to your acceptance'[25] but he ignored this bitter advice. Moreover, unlike Peek, Davis fully accepted that McNary-Haugenism was dead and worked with Tugwell and Frank to the end of 1935 when, in Moley's words, AAA had become 'The most successful and generally popular feature of the New Deal'.[26]

Recovery in wheat prices which followed reduction of output did seem to vindicate AAA economics. Yet in reality, the natural catastrophe of the Dust Bowl far surpassed the man-made efforts of FDR and his AAA administrators in making scarcity work to push up prices. The wheat crop, which had averaged 864 million bushels over the years 1928–32, sank to an average 567 million bushels for 1933–35. Yet of this reduction only 20 million resulted from AAA: the rest came from the drought. Largely because of the Dust Bowl, US wheat prices rose so much that by 1935–36 the United States was actually importing wheat. Much the same happened to livestock and other crop prices so that all along the agricultural front AAA programmes appeared to be working. Production control, benefit payments, Commodity Credit Corporation loans, purchase of surpluses for distribution in relief purposes and other weapons in the varied AAA arsenal were all combining with the Dust Bowl to reduce output and raise prices.

In corn, as with wheat, both AAA and weather helped, but the results to farmers were clear. Corn was 70 cents a bushel in Iowa in 1935 where it had been 10 cents in 1933. Pigs were selling at 7.40 dollars – 4.50 to 5 dollars better than a year before. In cotton, grown in states unaffected by the Dust Bowl, AAA could claim sole credit for price increases, while overall agricultural recovery was dramatic. Between 1932 and 1936 gross farm income increased 50 per cent and cash receipts from marketing, including government payments, nearly doubled. Most important, the ratio between prices farmers received and prices they paid rose steadily from 55 in 1932 to 70 in 1934 to 90 in 1936 – higher than it had been in 1929. With the prices farmers received rising two-thirds in this period, Roosevelt had every reason to believe he had used power effectively to help both banking and agriculture. The AAA was a qualified success. Yet the price of such agricultural recovery as did occur was rapid rural de-population, while not until 1941 did net farm income exceed returns for 1929, a poor year for farmers.

Nevertheless, as with much of the rest of the economy, most people felt that something was being done. Banking had been saved, public works were in progress, unemployment had stopped rising, homeowners had their mortgages protected, farmers were safe against further foreclos-ure. Yet as the spring turned to summer in 1933 Roosevelt was aware that he still had to tackle the central problem confronting the American economy. He had to do something to revive industry.

---

✤

## Chapter 7

# Power, Industry and the New Deal, 1933–35

I

Saving the banks opened the Hundred Days. The fight to save farmers opened the New Deal proper. But the heart of the American economy was neither finance nor farming but industry. It had almost stopped beating. The manufacturing index had fallen nearly 50 per cent from 110 in 1929 to 57 in 1932. The total value of all finished goods had fallen still more – from 38 billion to 17.5 billion dollars. Private construction – a key indicator of a healthy capitalist economy – had collapsed from 7.5 billion to a dismal 1.5 billion dollars. So a rise in farm prices without corresponding stimulation of industrial activity might be fatal. It would be, Moley warned Roosevelt, like heating an empty boiler.

FDR's answer was the National Industrial Recovery Act (NIRA). Like AAA this was a bureaucratic solution of the kind used in the progressive period, though never on this scale. With NIRA he tried to plan comprehensively for the whole of American industry, much as he was doing with AAA for agriculture. As with farming, the problem with industry was at bottom simple: start creating jobs and paying wages. The scale of the task could be judged from the stark fact that more than 37 per cent of wage and salary earners were unemployed in 1933.

II

NIRA typified the early New Deal, not least because it was born of complex manoeuvring involving the president, his cabinet, advisers and Congress which threw revealing light on FDR's use of power. In March 1933 Hugo Black of Alabama and William P. Connery Jr of Massachusetts introduced a bill in Congress to establish the 30-hour week which the American Federation of Labor (AFL) was demanding to relieve unemployment by spreading work. Secretary of labour Frances Perkins was sceptical of the value of a 30-hour week unless it included provision for maintaining wages for the hourly paid – always a problem when reformers reduced hours. So she suggested amendments to combine minimum wages with reduced hours.

This unprecedented idea of minimum wages naturally provoked a storm of opposition from employers. The reform aspirations of trade associations, particularly in ailing industries, tended to focus on seeking exemption from anti-trust acts. Nor was the minimum wage idea supported too enthusiastically by the AFL, who feared not only that it would undermine the function of unions but that minimum wages might easily become maximum ones. So both camps urged Roosevelt to raise his sights and launch a recovery programme which would tackle the fundamental problem of creating jobs. As scores of such plans began to appear several independent groups of FDR's advisers started working out specific measures. Little real progress was being made, however, so he decided to intervene. He withdrew support for the Black-Connery bill, in which his interest had been lukewarm if not hostile, and urged his advisers to work together until they could agree.

The result was the National Industrial Recovery Act. Title I of NIRA allowed industry to write its own codes of fair competition but at the same time provided special safeguards for labour. Section 7(a) of NIRA, drawing in part on provisions in the 1926 Railway Act, stipulated that workers should have the right to organize and bargain collectively through representatives of their own choosing; that no one seeking work should be forced to join a company union or banned from joining an independent union; and that employers must comply with maximum hours, minimum pay and other conditions approved by Roosevelt.

Employers ratified these codes with the slogan 'We do our part', displayed under a blue eagle logo at huge American-style publicity parades across the country. FDR used this kind of propaganda cleverly to sell the New Deal. Yet despite all this razzmatazz, NIRA codes were not the answer. Section 7(a), which gave workers the right to form unions, was not effectively enforced. Worse, in trying more generally to put a ceiling on prices and a floor on wages NIRA was attempting the impossible in the wrong way and failing to face the fundamental problem. This was to get wages and prices up, thus generating a virtuous circle to replace the vicious downward spiral of depression. More seriously, NIRA codes did nothing to solve the fundamental problem of providing jobs for unemployed millions. The other half of the legislation confronted this. Title II of NIRA, for which Congress appropriated 3.3 billion dollars to be spent on public works, was the first New Deal measure to do something directly to create work.

The National Recovery Administration (NRA) was set up to enforce NIRA, much as the AAA enforced New Deal agricultural legislation. Yet the NRA was a problem from the start. Roosevelt named Hugh Johnson to head it. 'Ironpants' Johnson was an army general who had made his mark during the progressive period. His flamboyant personality and speech masked real administrative ability which Baruch had used at the war industries board in 1917–18. Now Johnson expected to be given control of the whole NRA. But FDR told him at a cabinet meeting that Ickes had charge of Title II with its 3.3 billion dollar public works programme. Hurt and humiliated Johnson stormed out, and FDR had to send Frances Perkins after him so that she could drive with him round Washington in her official car, calm him down and stop him drinking whisky. Once he had accepted his limited role, as FDR had seen, Johnson's dramatic flair was ideal in 'We Do Our Part' campaigns used to sell NRA codes to businessmen and the urban masses. Yet public works was more important to economic recovery than propaganda about the codes; and here Ickes, Johnson's complete opposite, was a cautious administrator who spent money through the new Public Works Administration (PWA) with painful slowness.

Ickes's caution was designed to protect the president. Fearful of previous interior department scandals like Teapot Dome, Ickes knew public works funds could be wasted or stolen by local bosses whose political machines still ran urban America. So he only released federal money when sure it was safe. That no scandals hurt public works during the New Deal was largely thanks to Ickes. Moreover, it was typical of FDR's use of power during the New Deal that Ickes's parsimony was balanced by the free spending of Harry Hopkins, a New York social worker who had administered TERA when FDR was governor of New York. Now aged 43, son of a saddle maker, the untidy, unconventional, tough-talking Hopkins, who frequented race-tracks, disdained religion and showed little patience with conservatives or moralists, had obvious similarities with Howe and ultimately became FDR's chief aide. Indeed, his influence eventually surpassed Howe's when he became a maker and shaper of foreign policy during the Second World War. For the moment Roosevelt made Hopkins head of Civil Works Administration (CWA), set up to run parallel with Ickes's PWA, to reduce unemployment. At CWA Hopkins – instinctive, creative, generous – released five million dollars in his first two hours in office to become the great apostle of public spending.

After a slow start, explained partly by Ickes's caution, NRA spending proved effective. Public works was not a new idea. It had been used in Britain and Europe for a generation. Even Hoover had accepted that a billion dollars might usefully be spent on public projects. In cabinet Hopkins and Perkins urged five billion, while Ickes wrote in his diary that it was typical of FDR to choose a figure halfway between these two amounts. The important point was that the president was asking Congress to spend more on public works alone than the entire cost of federal government in any year between 1922 and 1930. Nor was this all. Civilian Conservation Corps (CCC) camps put millions of young men to work in their seven-year existence; FERA gave grants to states and cities to create jobs; and the Tennessee Valley Authority (TVA) was building gigantic dams which were transforming the ecology of vast regions and generating low-cost hydroelectric power. By all these means FDR was using political power to reflate and revive economic activity.

Hopkins's role in this process would be hard to exaggerate. 'Harry was really a sloppy administrator,' said C.B. ('Beanie') Baldwin, who as Wallace's assistant saw Hopkins operate at first hand. 'Ickes was a really careful guy. Hopkins . . . seldom wrote a letter. He'd just pick up the phone and say, "Send a million dollars to Arkansas and five million to New York. People are hungry."'[1] He was only half joking when he suggested dropping money from airships all over America to raise aggregate demand. Irrespective of what job he actually held, Hopkins was to become a key New Dealer who was active everywhere, notably at CWA and the Federal Emergency Relief Administration. FERA dealt with rural relief and after 1935 CWA merged with Ickes's PWA to form the Works Progress Administration (WPA). All pumped vital funding into the economy to create jobs. Though Ickes moved slowly, so that economic returns on public works at first proved less than hoped, he eventually became, in the phrase of historian W.E. Leuchtenburg, 'a builder to rival Cheops'.[2]

Between 1933 and 1939 public works projects constructed in whole or in part 70 per cent of the nation's new school buildings, 65 per cent of its courthouses, city halls and sewage plants and 35 per cent of its hospitals and public health centres. This legacy also included a generation of roads, bridges and other public projects. It built the Triborough Bridge in New York, linked Key West to Florida and built warships, combat planes and military airports. Moreover, all this was indicative of FDR's working method. He was a firm believer in creative tension – between Johnson, Ickes and Hopkins at NRA or Peek, Davis, Tugwell, Frank and Wallace at AAA. It was characteristic too that throughout the New Deal tension was often as notable as creativity.

III

Despite its political success, many of FDR's advisers worried about the New Deal's lack of economic coherence and its approach to planning. Moley, Tugwell and Berle continued to disagree about this. Moley's problem was how to justify the billions the federal government was spending on relief and public works and what the temporary expedient of inflation, however well intentioned, might do to the value of the dollar in the long term. Yet sharper minds than Moley's or Roosevelt's believed that new thinking was imperative. When the British economist J.M. Keynes met FDR in 1934 he was struggling to find an answer to the problem of mass unemployment in the world's richest nation. His student Richard Kahn had in 1931 made a key contribution to the academic debate by establishing the theoretical basis for what Keynes himself had intuitively grasped – that there was a formal mathematical relationship between the level of government spending and the level of economic activity, which he called 'the multiplier'. This concept of the multiplier was soon to become an essential tax and spending tool with which governments in capitalist countries tuned their economies to balance unemployment against inflation.

Yet in the short term public works was crucial. As Keynes put it, 'The newly employed who supply the increased purchases of those employed on capital works will, in their turn, spend more, thus adding to the employment of others; and so on.'[3] While Keynes was working on his general theory, published in 1936, Roosevelt's old friend and Harvard Law School professor Felix Frankfurter, on sabbatical in London, was acting as conduit for the ideas of British economists urging the president to finance public works as the key to recovery. When Keynes met Roosevelt it was not exactly a meeting of minds. FDR dismissed Keynes as some kind of mathematician who bored him with a long rigmarole of figures, while Keynes said he had 'supposed the president was more literate, economically speaking'.[4] None of this mattered. The important point was that, by trial and error, largely for political reasons, Roosevelt was adopting Keynesian policies, using inflation and public works to kick start the economy into life.

When asked 'Can America spend its way to recovery?' Keynes and Harold Laski gave the answer, 'Why obviously!' An economy produces in response to spending – it was absurd to suppose one could stimulate economic activity by declining to spend. When individuals failed to spend enough to maintain employment, the government must step in and do it for them. 'It might be better if they did it for themselves,' Keynes and

Laski concluded, 'but that is no argument for not having it done at all.'[5] Hoover had been incapable of acting in this way. But where Hoover feared government intervention, FDR's temperament urged him to try something. The result was bold, persistent experiment, much of it contradictory, adopted suddenly and sometimes abruptly abandoned. For where Hoover's greatest handicap in dealing with the depression had been his philosophy, FDR's greatest asset was his lack of one. 'Philosophy?' he once quizzically told a questioner. 'Philosophy? I'm a Christian and a Democrat – that's all.'[6]

In summary, during the first New Deal, between 1933 and 1935, FDR wanted AAA and NRA to revive agriculture and industry by raising prices, pushing up wages, combining this with public works to stimulate economic activity which would create jobs. Like AAA, NRA was a sprawling agency run by young, idealistic lawyers recruited by Donald Richberg, its legal counsel. Yet as early as January 1934 it became clear something was badly wrong with NRA. Poorly planned, it had been wretchedly administered. Its codes were not raising prices or wages. Employers felt they were chafing under such restrictions as NRA did impose, while organized labour was bitterly aware that Section 7(a) had failed to establish the right to organize unions and bargain collectively. This was the most serious failure of NRA. In a capitalist democracy like America, strong, independent unions were the best way of raising wages, purchasing power and thus aggregate demand, as Frances Perkins frequently told FDR.[7] Moreover, from a political perspective the industrial working class could become an important part of the new Democratic political coalition across the nation if given the right to organize as Section 7(a) promised.

FDR had had high hopes of Richberg as NRA's chief counsel. A celebrated labour lawyer, he had been Ickes's law partner in Chicago. Yet his experience, rooted in the 1920s when paternalistic, conservative AFL craft unions had organized labour, became a handicap in the 1930s when rank-and-file insurgents were starting to organize industrial unions. Richberg was not sympathetic to such ideas. Neither was FDR. But since he always knew where the votes were he might embrace working-class demands to win re-election in 1936. In fact (as argued in the next chapter) he was effectively forced to do this when labour unions erupted to transform the political and economic landscape after 1935. Between 1933 and 1935, however, Roosevelt, management and labour were – for different reasons – all being frustrated by the NRA.

Problems with the NRA stemmed partly from lack of what might be called 'state capacity' – the absence both of government experience in this field and of a trained bureaucracy. In contrast to the failure of NRA's codes its public works programme did start to create jobs. Moreover, as we have seen, the decisive choice of inflation over further deflation had been taken not from FDR's personal conviction but from his chaos of improvisation. It was the net result of dozens of other decisions taken for different reasons on their own merits. Inflation flew in the face of the best opinion. Not just Hoover but orthodox economists, bankers, businessmen, financiers, Congress, labour leaders all shared this conventional wisdom. All believed in cutting expenditure to balance the budget, as their testimony to the Senate Finance Committee in February 1933 had revealed. Roosevelt was no different. As far as he was concerned, Mr Micawber had been right: more spending than income, result misery. In his 1932 campaign FDR had accused Hoover of spending too much and in the Pittsburgh speech promised to cut the cost of federal government by a quarter.

His young budget director Lewis Douglas, who believed recovery would only start when a balanced budget restored business confidence, had been appointed precisely in order to achieve this. Some of FDR's first steps – reducing salaries of civil servants and politicians, refusing to pay ex-servicemen their bonus 15 years early – were clearly deflationary. But others – public works, CCC, FERA – were just as clearly inflationary. Consistency was not FDR's long suit. The salient fact was that the money spent was so much more than the money saved. Yet at this stage Roosevelt regarded inflation as a temporary expedient not a long-term solution. Given his background the surprise is not that he opposed the use of deficit spending but that he accepted it in the short term.

IV

Orthodox objections to inflationary solutions to unemployment and debt in America were reinforced by memories of the nightmare experience of inflation in Weimar Germany ten years before, when a cup of coffee had cost millions of marks. The real opening to inflation, moreover, had come as we have seen from outside Roosevelt's administration when the Thomas amendment gave FDR power to expand money supply. This route became more clearly signposted in April 1933 when Roosevelt abandoned the gold standard. Lewis Douglas's famous comment – 'Well this is the end of Western civilization'[8] – was heartfelt because, as budget director, he had lost the decisive policy battle. Yet we can now see that this was the dawn of a generation when controlled inflation became an acceptable solution to mass unemployment.

Leaving the gold standard was crucial because it enabled government to take on more debt, in order to finance budget deficits, without driving up interest rates. It broke all conventional financial rules, as Douglas's reaction and later resignation revealed. Yet as Keynes explained, 'Under the system of laissez-faire and an international gold standard such as was orthodox in the latter half of the nineteenth century, there was no means open to a government whereby to mitigate economic distress at home except through the competitive struggle for markets.'[9] With the economy at the point of collapse in March 1933 the treasury department and the federal reserve were willing to sacrifice financial orthodoxy. By January 1934 the dollar had been devalued by about 40 per cent enabling the United States to reflate out of economic depression.

Most important, the unifying theme behind the New Deal's chaos of improvisation was not economic but political. FDR aimed at giving every-body something. Business had got the NRA codes, labour Section 7(a), farmers AAA, subsidies and refinancing of farm mortgages, home own-ers refinancing of their mortgages, jobless young men public works and CCC work camps, conservationists unified development of the Tennessee river valley and cheap electricity through TVA. Even Wall Street wel-comed effective regulation by the Securities and Exchange Commission (SEC). The new head of SEC was Joseph Kennedy, another of FDR's big financial backers, who had made a huge fortune market-rigging on Wall Street in the 1920s. His success in the 1930s in stopping activities at which he had himself excelled in the 1920s – a classic case of poacher turned gamekeeper – made him many enemies.

As Kennedy took command of SEC, the Emergency Banking Act, which had dealt with immediate financial crisis in March, was followed in June by a more careful measure designed by Carter Glass and Henry Steagall. Roosevelt took no part in devising the landmark Glass-Steagall Act. Amer-ican banking had been chronically weak. Now the federal government, through the Federal Deposit Insurance Corporation (FDIC), guaranteed the money of small depositers up to $10,000. This idea, which Roosevelt had earlier strongly opposed, meant that in times of crisis banks would no longer be brought down by terrified customers clamouring for their cash. The difference FDIC made was dramatic. Even in the prosperous 1920s some 600 banks a year had failed in the United States. Fewer banks than this failed during the whole of the next decade. Yet once again, as with the Thomas amendment which gave the opening for inflation, the Glass-Steagall Act had come from outside FDR's administration.

The difference between the last year of Hoover's administration and the first year of Roosevelt's was not just one of style. Take their use of the Reconstruction Finance Corporation (RFC). Hoover had set up the RFC in 1932 and used it as an instrument for established businessmen, particularly Eastern rentiers who lived off dividends. Roosevelt put the agency under an unorthodox Texas banker, Jesse Jones, who transformed it into a vastly different organization. Instead of lending money to banks, and thus increasing their debt, Jones bought bank preferred stock, bolstered capital structure and thus helped FDIC's new deposit insurance work. More important, under Jones any RFC loans went straight to farmers and employers through such agencies as the Commodity Credit Corporation and the Electric Home and Farm Authority. Thus Roosevelt made the RFC not just the nation's largest bank but its biggest single investor and enabled it to play a central role in the US economy which continued until it was closed in the 1950s.

## V

During the Hundred Days FDR had devoted all his time to America's domestic affairs. But in the summer of 1933 he was forced to turn his attention to global financial problems. Depression was ravaging the economic life not just of the United States but of Britain, France, Germany, the whole capitalist world. The London economic conference, which Hoover had discussed with Roosevelt the previous December, was finally convened in June 1933 to seek a solution. Every nation was represented. As the world's largest economy America had to take the lead. What this meant was clear to European delegates. They wanted the United States to reschedule war debt and lower tariffs while they pegged their currencies to a stabilized dollar.

But FDR had just devalued the dollar and taken America off gold to revive the domestic economy. If he now stabilized the dollar abroad it would block the road to raising American wages and prices, which was the purpose not just of devaluation but his whole domestic programme. The other two topics on the agenda in London – debt and tariffs – were no more promising. Even talk of rescheduling or cancelling war debt was taboo. Congress, which had repeatedly refused to lower tariffs, had just adjourned after passing 15 major laws in three months. Roosevelt, on a sailing holiday, was thus in sole command. Moreover, confusion reigned in London and no delegation was more disorganized than America's. FDR had typically insisted it represent all major opinions, so it was hopelessly split, thus leaving him free to impose policy. The delegation was headed by his secretary of state Cordell Hull, a Southern Democrat who believed in free trade and had orthodox financial views. Key Pittman, chairman of the Senate foreign relations committee, was only concerned about silver, a special interest of his home state of Nevada. When not putting other delegates to sleep talking incessantly about it he embarrassed them with drunken sprees on which he shot out London street lights with a six-shooter or chased a technical adviser, whom he suspected lacked enthusiasm for silver, down the corridors of Claridges with a bowie knife.

After two weeks of deadlocked discussion FDR sent Moley, nominally Hull's deputy at the state department, to London. Moley, who was FDR's chief of staff, had been lionized by the press. 'Moley, Moley, Moley!' sang his enemies, 'Lord God Almighty!' He appeared to be the man of the moment. Yet his moment soon passed. On 5 July came the 'bombshell' when, without a word to Moley, FDR broke the deadlock with a cable refusing to stabilize the dollar. After lamentations the conference adjourned for ever. No act of FDR's has been more universally censured. As war clouds darkened throughout the 1930s joint efforts to solve world financial and economic problems ceased. Yet Keynes immediately approved FDR's action. So long as American price levels (or British interest rates) were determined internationally the United States (or Britain) would be condemned to permanent depression. The whole point of American self-sufficiency, Keynes argued, was to help AAA and NRA raise farm and factory prices and so make planning possible. 'Above all,' Keynes concluded, 'let *finance* be primarily national.'[10]

No one believed this more than Moley. He had chaired all the discussions which decided to seek salvation through inflation. Yet now he paid a personal price for this policy. Before Moley took ship for Britain the president had not told him he would refuse to stabilize the dollar and then did so without warning. 'We've just got to do something about this,' Moley exclaimed to Hull as FDR's cable came through. 'You had better go back home,' Hull replied. 'You had no business over here in the first place.'[11] Everyone thought Hull had ambushed Moley. 'Hull's gaunt figure and downcast eyes are enough to move one to tears,' a newsman explained, 'until one remembers the stiletto protruding from Moley's back.'[12] FDR's genial charm hid his ruthless methods. Howe had learned that lesson when Moley and the brains trust challenged his position as FDR's political adviser in 1931.

Now Moley learned it too. Resigning as chief of staff in August 1933 he continued writing speeches for Roosevelt until 1936 but became increasingly disillusioned with the New Deal. The candidate he had admired so much between 1930 and 1932, deferring to advisers in pursuit of the public interest, now seemed to him arrogant in pursuit of power. Later events confirmed Moley in his fears that FDR was a demagogue. Returning to academic life at Columbia, Moley wrote *After Seven Years*, an intelligent and searching criticism of Roosevelt and the New Deal. Yet it was easy for other nations, like Britain, to blame the United States for the failure of the London economic conference when none of them intended to limit their own freedom of action. In fact, the collapse of the conference was less serious than feared. By December all wartime debts had effectively been cancelled and later in the 1930s the United States negotiated separate arrangements with Britain, France and other powers.

## VI

Despite this, the economic and political transformation which the New Deal had brought by 1934 was only part of a greater transformation in the nation's mood. This had been accomplished largely by Roosevelt himself and was indicative of his use of power at home. In place of the black despair and inaction of Hoover's last days there was by 1934 renewed confidence, hope and hectic activity. In addition to guiding the New Deal through Congress between March and June FDR had delivered ten big speeches, conducted talks with foreign heads of state, sponsored an international conference, made all major decisions in domestic and foreign policy and held cabinet meetings and press conferences twice a week.

FDR's use of the press was even more crucial than fireside chats on radio in setting his stamp on affairs. With three-quarters of the press Republican-owned he knew he could only hope to 'get a good press' by winning newspaper reporters (like Howe, Early and McIntyre) to his side. In this the American newspaper custom of keeping comment and reporting in separate sections of the newspaper, instead of mixing comment and fact as is now common in Britain, made his task easier. But FDR had thought carefully about how to handle the press. Seated at his desk, before a semi-circle of reporters, he did something everyone told him was impossible. He scrapped written questions and placed his answers on a Westminster 'lobby basis' – some for direct quotation, some without direct attribution, some for 'deep background' only. The twice-weekly press conferences were like well-crafted theatre. Calling reporters who questioned him by their first names, FDR was the broad-shouldered, smiling, buoyant optimist whose uplifted head now seemed not arrogant but reassuring. He would strike dramatic poses and play his audience like a fly-fisherman with wit, charm, sarcasm, amazement, curiosity and mock alarm. Flattered that they were being taken into government, reporters responded so well to FDR's fluent and often funny style of fielding questions that these meetings soon became a highlight of his administration and key to generating favourable publicity. No president ever held better press conferences.

The dynamic mood all this generated in the White House was the more remarkable because FDR did not believe in the 16-hour days beloved of some of his successors. He woke about 8 each morning, had breakfast in bed, read the newspapers, kept appointments and held meetings before noon, often working through a light lunch, dictated letters in the afternoon, knocked off about 6 for drinks and dinner, read for relaxation in the evening and went straight to sleep around midnight. A pool was built at the White House so he could swim each day. This routine was established during the crisis months between March and June 1933 and by and large sustained in peace and war throughout his 12 years in power. Later presidents (notably Richard Nixon) often agonized over the grandeur of the office, the greatness of past presidents and how history would judge them. Roosevelt would have none of this. His view of the presidency was simple: himself in office doing it.

In many ways, the most astonishing aspect of the public perception of FDR in his pomp is that it was the complete opposite of a man who was paralysed. Cartoonists constantly showed him running, walking tightropes, in boxing rings – never in a wheelchair. His command astonished many politicians who thought they had taken his measure. Norman Davis, who had been financial adviser to Woodrow Wilson and considered by FDR for secretary of state, told his friend Raymond Fosdick outside the Oval Office, 'Ray, that fellow in there is not the fellow we used to know. There's been a miracle here.'[13] Davis was not alone. 'Many of us who have known him long and well,' wrote veteran editor Oswald Garrison Villard, 'ask ourselves if this is the same man.'[14]

What had become of the progressive Baruch had dismissed as 'wishy-washy'? As recently as 1932 the influential journalist Walter Lippmann had said that Roosevelt was 'A pleasant man who, without any important qualifications for the office, would very much like to be president'.[15] Now his view was quite different. 'At the beginning of March,' Lippmann summed up, 'the country was in such a state of confused desperation that it would have followed almost any leader anywhere he chose to go . . . In one week, the nation, which had lost confidence in everything, gained confidence in the government and in itself . . . We were a congeries of disorderly panic-stricken mobs and factions. In the hundred days from March to June we became again an organized nation confident of our power to provide for our own security and to control our own destiny.'[16]

## VII

The public response to Roosevelt in the White House was quite unprecedented. In the first week he received nearly 500,000 letters, and though the number declined thereafter it was never less than 7,000 a week. The *New York Times* weekly business index, which in 1933 had risen from 60 in March to 99 in June and then fallen to 72 in October, had moved up to 86 by 1934. Further, national income was almost a quarter higher and unemployment two million less than in 1933. Indeed, the most important measure of success for the New Deal is the fact that for the first time in five years unemployment had started falling: to 21.7 per cent in 1934, 20.1 per cent in 1935 and 16.9 per cent in 1936. Yet this success was severely limited. In 1937, when 14.3 per cent were unemployed, some 25 per cent of wage and salary earners were jobless and unemployment was 10 per cent even in 1941, when war spending began stimulating the economy. FDR's political success must be seen against this background. For though historians talk about the New Deal, for those who lived through it this was the great depression. Yet, as we have seen, during his first year in power FDR had reduced unemployment and restored hope. In the short term he could argue convincingly that the New Deal was working. Every major section of the American community – bankers, brokers, businessmen, farmers, homeowners, organized labour, even the unemployed – had gained something. Bold, distributive social justice was the theme.

Equally important, the nation's morale was recovering through clever use of press conferences, radio broadcasts and the sheer force of personality by which FDR had stamped his authority on the nation. This thread links all conflicting elements in the early New Deal. For despite his apparent use of planning in the AAA and NRA no overall plan was in operation for the New Deal as a whole. Bold, distributive justice had been sought through equally bold, persistent experimentation. Moreover, policy had emerged not from Roosevelt or a group of like-minded policy makers but from argument, dispute and the politics of contention. In terms of political power this was the start of a process which transformed the Democratic party into a reform coalition, set the political agenda for a generation and became FDR's most lasting political legacy.

The New Deal had a decisive impact on the role of women in national politics. Government agencies created by FDR cried out for the talents of that generation of women Eleanor had inspired. The New Deal needed their social work skills, social welfare experience and knowledge of consumer affairs, protective legislation, low-wage industries and social security. Moreover, Eleanor gave women, labour leaders and civil rights workers access to the president they could never have dreamed of, while bringing her whole network unrivalled visibility and, above all, jobs as she and Molly Dewson fired a barrage of patronage suggestions at Jim Farley. Chaotic and improvised though it had been, the New Deal had, by the end of 1934, restored confidence which lasted at least until the serious economic downturn of 1937–38. The president took credit for things which worked; others took blame for those which failed. It won mounting support at the ballot box from 1932 until mid-term elections in 1938.

This emerging political transformation became clear in November 1934 when Americans gave their verdict on Roosevelt and the New Deal in the mid-term elections. The results were a dramatic endorsement of Roosevelt's use of power. The earliest political opposition to the New Deal, which historian Arthur Schlesinger defines as 'the revolt of the rentier class', came from the American Liberty League. Wealthy businessmen like the Du Ponts, Alfred P. Sloan and William S. Knudsen were prominent members, but so too was John J. Raskob, Democratic party chairman in 1928 and rich industrial executive, who had invested $200,000 in FDR's business at Warm Springs. John W. Davis and Al Smith, Democratic presidential candidates in 1924 and 1928, were also leading members of the Liberty League. FDR's use of power had opened a chasm between him and those Democrats who had run the party so badly in the 1920s. The anti-Prohibition, anti-statist, pro-business leadership of 1928 was replaced by the party's transformation during the New Deal. That Smith now spoke for the Liberty League was significant because, as Schlesinger concludes, 'At no point on record did the American Liberty League construe "liberty" as meaning anything else but the folding stuff.'[17]

The Liberty League campaign against FDR was crushed at the polls in November 1934 when the Democratic party won its largest Congressional majorities in living memory. Moreover, this success defied a kind of Newtonian law of American politics which says that in mid-term elections the president's party will lose support. In 1934, for one of the few times in history, the president's party picked up seats in Congress – and in large numbers. Democrats, the minority party between 1860 and 1930, now had a staggering majority of 45 in the Senate and 219 in the House. The party swept state assemblies and governorships too. One of the few reverses occurred in California, where the socialist novelist Upton Sinclair had surprisingly won the Democratic primary for governor on a programme to 'End Poverty in California' (EPIC). FDR had been persuaded not to endorse him and red-baiting Republicans combined with conservative Democrats to defeat Sinclair. Though the New Deal had had only limited economic success, FDR's great political achievement had been to persuade millions of Americans that he was leading them to recovery. Moreover, his remarkable success in getting Congress to pass his entire legislative programme was based on more than the fact that his huge personal victory in 1932 had given him a mandate which made Congress his pliant servant. FDR instinctively understood how to persuade Congress to do his bidding, while even Southern Democrats had accepted the need for radical reform. He now had a chance to transform the party into a modern reform coalition and certainly enjoyed political power rare in American history. Yet in the years ahead both Roosevelt and the nation would learn how elusive economic recovery could be.

## Chapter 8

### ❖

# Power and Reform, 1935–37

I

The years between 1933 and the start of 1935 are commonly called the first New Deal. The period from 1935 until the end of 1938, usually known to historians as the second New Deal, was in many ways quite different from the first. Much that was important about the first New Deal continued into the second. Restructuring and regulation of the banking system and Wall Street, subsidy to reduce farm output, spending on public works through PWA and WPA to create jobs, or for other purposes through CCC and FERA, conservation and the generation of cheaper electric power through TVA – all these vital and long-lasting policy initiatives, begun during the Hundred Days, continued throughout the 1930s. Moreover, despite his campaign pledge to cut the cost of government by a quarter, Roosevelt continued to take on debt and run up big budget deficits in order to stimulate the economy, raise aggregate demand and reduce unemployment.

Because he had also left the gold standard FDR could take on these debts without raising interest rates. Moreover, the immediate choice had been made for inflation and against deflation. Yet this did not mean there was not lively debate within his administration about the danger of unbalanced budgets and how best to achieve economic recovery. Though he knew little or nothing about economics, FDR was fascinated for several months by the commodity-dollar theories of Warren Fisher and the idea that the US government buy gold. This he believed would not only win America an increasing share of world trade but, by reducing the gold value of the dollar, achieve the overriding objective of raising commodity prices and restoring the balance between raw materials and consumer goods.

In fact, though it may have helped stop further deflation, gold buying was one of Roosevelt's worst moves. The British economist J.M. Keynes, who was still seeking to influence FDR while writing the book which made him the father of managed capitalism, dismissed it as a 'puerile' theory which would not have been accepted in an undergraduate essay and had wasted money far better spent on accelerated public works. Worse, it had caused the first serious policy breach in his administration. So on 30 January 1934 – his 52nd birthday – Roosevelt halted gold buying and signed the Gold Reserve Act, which he called 'the nicest birthday present I ever had'.[1] Inflationists denounced this concession to conservatives, while conservatives protested against his 'clipping of the national coin in exactly the fashion of the medieval kings'.[2] Fixing the price of gold at \$35 an ounce, he had reduced the gold content of the pre-1933 dollar by about 40 per cent. Such economic recovery as occurred in the 1930s would take place on the back of this devaluation. It freed FDR from inflationist pressure and constant preoccupation with the price of gold. More significant, it enhanced treasury hegemony over credit and currency.

II

Decisive changes in Roosevelt's cabinet and staff further strengthened his hold over the treasury and use of deficit finance. His budget director Lewis Douglas, deeply worried by New Deal financial policies and by growing opposition from big business, had resigned on 30 August 1934, echoing his reaction to FDR leaving the gold standard the year before. 'I hope, and hope most fervently,' he told him in his letter of resignation, 'that you will evidence a real determination to bring the budget into actual balance, for upon this, I think, hangs not only your place in history but conceivably the immediate fate of western civilization.'[3] When Will Woodin, hero of the Emergency Banking Act, became ill and was then accused of having taken part in insider trading in the 1920s, FDR made his old friend and financial backer Henry Morgenthau acting secretary of the treasury. This was a decisive moment. Douglas had gone, and when Woodin died in May 1934 FDR made Morgenthau secretary of the treasury, where, in the words of historian W.E. Leuchtenburg, he 'became the Roland of the balanced budget'.[4]

Tall, heavy-set, diffident, Morgenthau was the son of a wealthy, German-Jewish family whose father, a man of strong social conscience and a political activist, had served as Woodrow Wilson's ambassador to Turkey. Reluctant to involve himself in any of his father's vastly profitable businesses, Morgenthau became a farmer and met FDR in 1915. Sharing similar backgrounds and habits of mind they became close. 'To Henry,'

FDR once inscribed a photograph of himself and Morgenthau, 'from one of two of a kind.'[5] A daily visitor when FDR had been struggling to get back on his feet in the 1920s, Morgenthau was one of FDR's most valued friends who, like Douglas, was also a believer in balanced budgets. Unlike Douglas, however, he opposed regressive tax policies and would tolerate deficits if they were the price of relief and recovery. Morgenthau's political function now was clear. He was the symbol of financial orthodoxy FDR needed while he used deficit spending to restore economic health.

Another of FDR's key appointments in this new approach to public finance was making Marriner Eccles assistant to Morgenthau. Though this young Mormon banker from Utah claimed never to have read Keynes, he had nevertheless jolted Senate finance committee hearings in 1933 by urging that the federal government forget about trying to balance budgets during the depression and instead spend heavily on relief, public works, the domestic allotment plan and refinancing farm mortgages, while cancelling what remained of war debt. Morgenthau was so convinced of the need, at least temporarily, to accept such Keynesian notions that he recommended FDR make Eccles governor of the federal reserve board.

This was a critical appointment in the debate which transformed Roosevelt's approach to public finance between 1935 and 1945. Eccles's first step in February 1935 was to draft a new banking bill to secure radical reform of the central bank for the first time since the federal reserve had been introduced in 1913. He was helped by his influential adviser Lauchlin Currie who, because he never advocated a position before putting analysis and data together, now did the work which made him famous by documenting the contradictory actions of the federal reserve since 1929. Though the House passed it comfortably, the banking bill was fiercely resisted by conservatives and bankers and ran into determined opposition in the Senate from Carter Glass, the Democratic party's financial expert, who had drafted the 1913 law which set up the federal reserve.

J.P. Warburg, a former Roosevelt adviser, called it 'Curried Keynes' – 'a large, half-cooked lump of J. Maynard Keynes . . . liberally seasoned with a sauce prepared by Professor Lauchlin Currie'.[6] Facing this conservative opposition, the president did nothing to help the bill and Eccles had to fight on alone through the summer until FDR, for no clear reason, suddenly decided to make it 'must' legislation. With strong support in the House and from California bankers eager to throw off New York dominance of national banking, the bill, heavily amended, became the 1935 Banking Act. Glass boasted that he had nullified Eccles's intentions; but the board's governors, appointed by the president for 14-year terms, now

had far greater control over policy, currency, credit and reserve require-
ments, which Currie said should be doubled. It was, in Walter Lippmann's
words, victory for Eccles 'dressed up as a defeat'.[7]

From now on policy at the treasury and federal reserve was increasingly influenced by three men. Eccles, Currie and Harry Dexter White
all agreed that the federal reserve bore major blame for the depression
because it had restricted money supply. This meant that during the 1930s,
in a period of unparalleled economic crisis, government was starting to
set interest rates and tax and spend in a way which was new and designed to maximize employment. In that sense managed capitalism, which
became commonplace in the 1960s, began with FDR in the 1930s and
was one of the most significant consequences of his use of power. Yet to
see Roosevelt as the conscious agent of this kind of change is wrong. In
1935 he was no Keynesian – indeed, Keynes did not publish his momentous *General Theory* until 1936. FDR's fundamental beliefs were still quite
orthodox although the political opportunist in him was prepared to
unbalance the budget in the interests of economic recovery. Yet, as we
shall see, he was on a steep learning curve in the 1930s so that in the
1940s he began not only to use but to accept Keynesian notions about
the role of government in economic management.

III

All this was in the future. For the moment the Banking Act was one of
several landmark reforms passed during 'the second Hundred Days' of
1935 which were at the heart of the second New Deal. The Democrats
had won huge majorities in Congress in 1934. Supported by these votes
FDR, who had acted so boldly in the dire emergency of 1933, now had to
seek more permanent political solutions. Typically, his method was in-
consistent and often contradictory. Interestingly, too, in the second New
Deal between 1935 and 1938 he was never so clearly in control as he had
been in his first two years in power. Reform initiative passed increasingly to Congress, where conservatives in the Democratic party were
struggling to resist radical reformers taking control. More important,
from 1935 the US Supreme Court began striking down much New Deal
legislation as unconstitutional. Though still dominating politics more completely than any other twentieth-century president, Roosevelt began after
1935 to react to events rather than seize the initiative as he had in 1933.

Yet in this period of crisis and transformation certain points are clear.
Where the first New Deal had been about saving capitalism, the second

was primarily about reform of a kind which aimed at making the New Deal more like European social democracy than American progressivism. Moreover, where FDR had tried in 1933 to plan agriculture and industry through AAA and NRA and generate cheap electricity through TVA, the second New Deal after 1935 was about specific pieces of legislation designed to deal with specific problems. Finally, legislative initiative increasingly began in Congress rather than in the White House.

The Supreme Court provided the catalyst for the second Hundred Days of New Deal reform. On Black Monday, 27 May 1935, in a 9–0 decision, the Court tore the heart out of the first New Deal by declaring NIRA unconstitutional. A Brooklyn poultry firm run by the Schechter brothers was, the Court ruled, commerce within a state and thus, within the US federal system, immune from regulation by the president. That a Court so deeply divided between liberals, moderates and conservatives should reach this unanimous conclusion indicated there could be no argument, despite the fact that New Deal lawyers like Cummings and Corcoran had expedited the test case so that the Court could rule authoritatively. Some even argued that Roosevelt was secretly relieved that the Schechter decision removed an albatross from round his neck. In fact, he was really angry not just out of loyalty to NRA and its administrator Hugh Johnson, or even because it ruined his industrial recovery programme, but because its 'horse-and-buggy' definition of interstate commerce threatened the whole New Deal.

In reaction FDR threw himself behind all the reforms then before Congress. Apart from Eccles's Banking Act the most important were tax reform, social security and the right of workers to organize unions. Despite the radical nature of the 1934 elections Roosevelt still sought a coalition of all interests including big business. Yet big businessmen like Du Pont and Raskob were now backing the American Liberty League. Then in May the US Chamber of Commerce denounced the New Deal. 'The interesting thing to me,' FDR commented, 'is that in all these speeches made, I don't believe there was a single speech which took the human side, the old-age side, the unemployment side.'[8] Moreover, the Louisiana senator Huey Long, with his promises of root-and-branch redistributive taxation to 'Share Our Wealth', was just one of several demagogues like the anti-Semitic radio priest Charles Coughlin, Dr Francis Townsend, advocate of generous old-age pensions, or the revivalist orator Gerald L.K. Smith urging more radical action.

Of these Huey Long was the greatest political threat. Polls conducted by Jim Farley for FDR indicated that, if he ran for president in 1936, Long could take enough votes from Roosevelt to throw the election to a

Republican. Under pressure from the treasury to raise taxes and resentful of business criticism, FDR decided to 'steal Huey's thunder' by sending his own 'soak the rich' tax bill to Congress which aimed at redistributing wealth and power. By reaching for the first time into the pockets of the rich, this measure raised more outcry from big business and the press than anything FDR had done. Moreover, where the New Deal had hitherto rejected attacks on monopoly, this aimed at the goal of progressives like Louis Brandeis: to break up monopoly but this time by attempting to use taxation. Since Brandeis was on the Supreme Court he could influence the outcome of legislation. The bill also proposed increased taxes on inheritance, gift taxes, graduated levies on 'very great individual net incomes' and finally progressive corporation tax scaled according to the size of corporation income.

The newspaper magnate William Randolph Hearst instructed his editors to use the phrase 'Soak the Successful' and the words 'Raw Deal' instead of 'New Deal' in all references to the tax measure. Yet though Roosevelt was buoyed up by this political conflict he appeared less committed to quick action on some of its more radical provisions. It was typical of his method that, just as with the Eccles banking bill, he wanted to carry conservatives with him and seemed fearful that liberal support would scare them off. Progressives like Senator Robert La Follette wanted to move quickly not just because they saw it as a social weapon but because, as leading advocates of spending, they wanted to use the Wealth Tax to reduce the budget deficit. Yet when Morgenthau asked FDR if he really wanted the inheritance levy passed that session he replied, 'Strictly between the two of us I do not know. I am on an hourly basis and the situation changes momentarily.'[9] He threatened to keep Congress in session throughout the intolerable Washington summer heat until it passed the bill. In the end levellers like La Follette were defeated by Congressmen denouncing class legislation and by irate big businessmen. Congress eliminated the inheritance tax and reduced the graduated income levy to symbolic importance.

In final form the Wealth Tax Act of 1935 destroyed the distinction between big and small business, and did little to redistribute wealth and still less to raise revenue. However, it did step up estate, gift and capital stock taxes, levied an excess profits tax Roosevelt had not asked for and raised surtax rates to the highest level in history. It had great symbolic significance and created deeper business resentment than any other New Deal measure. Yet upper-income groups' share of wealth remained much the same throughout the 1930s, while the share of the top one per cent even increased. What the wealth tax revealed was that FDR had no appetite for genuine redistribution of wealth if that meant taxing the middle class more heavily. Only the insatiable demands of the war economy imposed heavier taxes on the middle and upper classes. Not until the war years did income distribution substantially change and, even then, partly because the booming war economy increased the annual earnings of the poorest Americans. What the outcry from opponents of the Wealth Tax obscured was that much of Roosevelt's tax programme remained sharply regressive. His emphasis on local responsibility for the unemployed encouraged spread of the regressive sales tax, while his insistence on payroll levies to help finance social security hit low earners hardest.

The next reform – the Social Security Act – showed this clearly. As we have seen, Roosevelt had not favoured unemployment insurance of the kind common in Europe. Then catastrophic unemployment after 1929 had taught him two unwelcome lessons. First, American capitalism was not a self-righting system but was as prone to be capsized by economic storms as capitalism in other countries. Second, and politically more significant, the United States alone among industrial democracies had no national system of social security. Cheap and inadequate schemes provided by financial institutions, individual states or by employers as part of the much-trumpeted 'welfare capitalism' of the 1920s had all collapsed when depression struck. Welfare capitalism had been found wanting when most needed.

So, with more than 10 million still unemployed in 1935 FDR launched the Emergency Relief Appropriation Act (ERA). This authorized 5 billion dollars, the largest single appropriation in the history of America or any other nation, to be spent on programmes to provide jobs for all who could work. Yet the relief they brought fell pitifully short of this goal. Roosevelt divided the billions Congress had provided among so many different agencies that Harry Hopkins had only 1.4 billion dollars to spend on the whole WPA. Workers received a disguised dole not a job; their security wage in the South was a mere $19 a month; while unemployables – the aged, the crippled, the sick – were denied a place on federal programmes and thrown on the mercy of state governments. The depth of suffering endured by millions meant that for the first time Americans like FDR were forced to face the fact that social security only made sense if it insured all workers against mass unemployment, sickness and old age. The cabinet committee he had set up in June 1934 under Frances Perkins, to tackle some of the objections to his relief programme and draft a workable social insurance system, was now ready to report. It quickly devised a national system of contributory old-age and survivors' insurance but had more trouble reaching agreement on the vexed question of unemployment benefit.

Tugwell and Wallace favoured a national system, which would guarantee uniform standards to workers who moved from state to state where state government was notoriously mismanaged. Yet since social security plans of different types already existed in Ohio and Wisconsin FDR and others argued that Congress wait until it could see how these worked out before acting. This won the committee's support because it would permit experiment in a new area where so much was unknown. Moreover, it would gain the backing of Brandeisians who favoured local solutions and so be more likely to win blessing from the Supreme Court, where Brandeis was a justice.

As it went through Congress in 1935 social security legislation was in the hands of reformers who knew about social insecurity at first hand. Senator Robert Wagner, who had begun his political career like FDR in the New York legislature, was a German immigrant and son of a janitor who had sold papers on the streets of New York and later worked his way through law school at night. Deeply marked by his experience with Perkins and Smith on the 1911 Triangle fire hearings, he was now America's leading social democratic reformer. David Lewis, who piloted the bill through the House, had become a coalminer at the age of nine. Their conception of social security greatly transcended FDR's. They argued that the dole would not simply prevent suffering but, by raising aggregate demand, help end the depression. Yet to conservatives it violated traditional American assumptions about self-help, self-denial and individual responsibility. However, in the depths of the depression such objections fell by the wayside. Germany had had social security for half a century and other Western industrial nations like France and Britain for a generation or more. Big business had long resisted the whole idea and Alfred Sloan of General Motors, the National Association of Manufacturers and others issued dire warnings. But real opposition now came not from conservatives but from those who believed the bill too mean. Townsend supporters proposed a monthly old-age pension of $200 and though this was voted down it impressed Congress with the need to pass a law which would quiet such demands. With John Taber and James Wadsworth prominent opponents, on a crucial test every Republican but one voted in the House to send the bill back to committee. However, opposition had collapsed by April when the House passed it 371–33. In June the Senate approved 76–6 and in August Roosevelt signed it.

The Social Security Act was a major landmark of the New Deal, though FDR had not advocated it strongly himself and had been converted late to the need for it. Moreover, it was in many ways not simply conservative but inept. While it provided, for the first time, a comprehensive system of federal social security against unemployment and old age, which would take effect in 1940, levels of compensation were low. The federal government shared with the states care of the over-65 destitute unable to take part in the new system and the care of certain categories: dependent mothers, children, the crippled, the blind. Yet it excluded large categories of workers – domestic servants and agricultural workers, for example – most in need of social security. Funded by contributions from both employers and employed, it was a regressive tax for the lowest paid because it bore most heavily on their pockets. It further excluded compensation for sickness, which was the commonest cause of loss of work. It failed both to provide a truly national system of unemployment compensation and to set adequate national standards. Finally, despite the provision of categorical assistance, the American system, unlike any other, essentially shirked government responsibility for poverty in old age and took funds from workers' current earnings.

Yet for all its defects the Social Security Act was a real break with the past. It established the basic principle that the entire community, through the federal government, had some responsibility for mass welfare. Though this never grew into the kind of comprehensive system common in Europe after 1945 it remained the basis on which the American model, expanded to include Medicare and Medicaid, was built for the rest of the century. It gave individual Americans clear-cut social rights which neither courts nor Congress could take away. 'I guess you're right on the economics,' FDR conceded when told employee contributions were a mistake, 'but those taxes were never a problem of economics. They are politics all the way through. We put those payroll contributions there so as to give the contributors a legal, moral and political right to collect their pensions and their unemployment benefits. With those taxes in there, no damn politician can ever scrap my social security program.'[10]

## IV

Senator Wagner had been key to passing social security legislation. He was so important in drafting the National Labor Relations Act that it was known as the Wagner Act. Like social security this was a landmark which could not have been passed at any other time. For its supporters it was like watching a rank outsider romp home in a horse race. As we have seen, Wagner had persuaded FDR and many others that social security would sustain demand during economic decline, enabling the old and unemployed to buy goods, so speeding recovery. Strong labour unions, by bidding up pay when the economy was thriving, would do even more to sustain prosperity. Others in FDR's circle, like Hopkins, Perkins and Tugwell, shared this belief in salvation through high wages which was to become a feature of American capitalism when the depression ended.

Wagner was a firm friend of labour. FDR's relationship with the organized working class, by contrast, had always been ambivalent. An acquaintance rather than a friend, FDR's progressive mind opposed monopoly and feared the power union leaders had to monopolize labour supplies. Despite this, FDR came to understand that the Wagner Act went straight to the heart of US economic problems. Wagner had seen more clearly than he that a crucial cause of the depression had been that working-class purchasing power, uneven and sluggish even in the prosperous 1920s, had failed to keep up with productivity and had then simply collapsed when nearly 40 per cent of wage and salary earners were thrown out of work between 1929 and 1933. Wagner believed that the industrial working class was America's great reservoir of purchasing power and that, in a capitalist democracy like America, the best way to replenish that reservoir was for strong unions, bargaining collectively with employers, to bid up wages and so raise aggregate demand which would start to restore prosperity.

FDR had no instinctive sympathy for this view. His attitude towards labour in 1935 had none of Wagner's strategic economic perspective but was paternalistic and progressive. His dealings with labour leaders lacked that instinctive rapport he had with farmers. Unions, led by the American Federation of Labor, were for the most part dominated by conservative crafts like carpenters, engineers and plumbers. Seduced by the prosperity of welfare capitalism in the 1920s they had lost members and then been virtually destroyed by mass unemployment after 1929. Yet Section 7(a) of the NIRA codes had failed unions mainly because Donald Richberg, FDR's trusted labour adviser, opposed the creation of single unions for all automobile or steel workers. Under the Wagner Act millions of semi-skilled and unskilled workers in mass-production, the great untapped source of union membership, were to transform organized labour in the 1930s. Between 1935 and 1940 industrial unions erupted like a force of nature, tripling the number of organized workers from under three to more than nine million and so giving them a chance, for the first time, to organize effectively in the same way that manufacturers, farmers and the middle class had done for at least fifty years.

The Wagner Act was significant because it fully enacted Section 7(a) of the NIRA codes. For the first time it threw the weight of government behind the right of workers to organize and bargain collectively, forcing employers to accept unions on the shopfloor while asking nothing of unions in return. What gave the law teeth was that it set up a National Labor Relations Board (NLRB), with effective powers, to enforce the right to organize. The NLRB, whose three members were to be selected with union agreement, was to become a supreme court of industrial relations. It could order elections to see if unions had majority support in the workplace; define and prohibit employer interference or coercion in this process; define and punish unfair labour practices, including the use of employer-dominated company unions which had been illegal since the 1932 Norris-La Guardia Act; and define and punish unfair labour dismissals.

These new powers alarmed and angered corporate America. Even FDR was cool towards the bill. Sharing the opposition of his chief aid on labour, Richberg, he 'never lifted a finger' to help it, his secretary of labour Frances Perkins recalled. 'Certainly I never lifted a finger ... I, myself, had very little sympathy with the bill.'[11] Despite this it passed the Senate and when the House voted it out on 20 May 1935 FDR asked Wagner to work out differences with his administration. Then he suddenly announced that he not only favoured the bill but that it was 'must' legislation. The reasons for this are not wholly clear, but the Supreme Court's decision striking down the NIRA codes, including Section 7(a), on 27 May must have played an important part. Moreover, Roosevelt was the greatest political opportunist and vote-winner of his generation. He was keenly aware that the American working class was the largest in the world; that they all had votes; and that if he identified with their struggle to organize unions the dividend would be large and longlasting – as indeed it was. Not the least of the many ironies in FDR's career was that he outshone Al Smith as hero of the working class largely because Robert Wagner was such an effective law maker.

Moreover, FDR's whole attitude to the second Hundred Days was now transformed. After months of temporizing he finally used his influence in favour of reform, calling House leaders to a White House conference where he thumped his desk to emphasize that they would have to pass the whole reform programme before he would let them go home. Yet Perkins and the department of labour still resented the NLRB's new powers; the AFL feared shopfloor elections would favour industrial unions at the expense of craft ones; and farm workers wished the bill to be extended to them. African Americans believed that closed shop unions which discriminated against them, as many craft unions did, could legally bar them from membership and so employment. Newspaper editors argued that unions in their industry might breach the First Amendment; and so on. Business hotly protested that the Wagner Act was unconstitutional while American Liberty League lawyers agreed. Southern Democrats only voted for it because they believed the Supreme Court would strike it down and so save them the risk of opposing organized labour. The automobile and steel industries vowed they would ignore it.

Yet it was in steel and cars that the Wagner Act passed its crucial test. The United Mineworkers (UMW) was the one big industrial union affiliated to the AFL. Its powerful president John L. Lewis had led some disastrous coal strikes in the 1920s and seen UMW membership fall. For years Lewis had been demanding that the AFL do something to organize steel workers; for years nothing had happened. By custom AFL unions did not endorse Democrats or Republicans at elections, but rewarded friends and punished enemies. The AFL was so conservative it had opposed unemployment insurance in 1932 while Lewis, who came from Republican Iowa, had voted for Hoover (also born in Iowa) and had no friends at FDR's court. Yet though UMW membership had revived to some 400,000 by 1935, steel was still completely unorganized. Matters came to a head in a fist fight at the AFL convention in October 1935. Lewis marched out and, with Sidney Hillman of the clothing workers and others, set up the Committee (later Congress) of Industrial Organizations. The CIO aimed at seizing its new legal rights under the Wagner Act; but by organizing workers in each industry into one industrial union it cut clean across the AFL's craft lines of jurisdiction.

While Roosevelt watched, dramatic events were now transforming organized labour. The CIO by-passed AFL craft conservatism to reach unorganized workers in steel, cars, chemicals, meatpacking, rubber, textiles, everywhere. Lewis, whose coalminers were economically closely linked to the steel industry, took the lead. In February 1936 he pledged 350 paid union organizers, an annual budget of 500,000 dollars and his best lieutenant Philip Murray to set up the Steel Workers' Organizing Committee. SWOC began at United States Steel, the citadel of the open shop, whose 250,000 unorganized workers alone produced more steel than the whole of Germany. First Murray worked with the ethnic groups – African Americans, Czechs and Poles – so vital in the steel workforce. Then he used the slogan 'The president wants you to join a union' to convince workers that FDR and the law were on their side. Finally he cleverly captured company unions, hastily set up by US Steel to make some pretence of complying with Section 7(a) of the NIRA codes, and turned them into independent unions under the Wagner Act.

While throughout 1936 SWOC was organizing US Steel from the top down, rank-and-file members of the United Autoworkers (UAW) were organizing General Motors from the bottom up. Though he had played no direct part, Roosevelt reaped the political benefit of this CIO activity when he ran for re-election in November. One thing he knew better than anyone was where the votes were. Huey Long's demagogic threat had disappeared when a madman shot him in December 1935. But throughout the industrial heartland of the Northeast and Great Lakes region, in New York, Pennsylvania, Massachusetts, Ohio, Indiana, Illinois, Michigan, Wisconsin, union activists provided funds and organizers to re-elect Roosevelt. 'There's one issue in this campaign,' he told Moley. 'It's myself and people must be either for me or against me.'[12]

Moley feared that the modest man he had admired so much when he ran for office in 1932 had now become a dangerous demagogue. Yet Roosevelt was right – he *was* the dominating issue of the election. He knew that the voters who would re-elect him were the working class of the industrial states who were now using the Wagner Act to form unions. 'The old enemies,' he told a Democratic eve-of-poll rally in Madison Square Garden, 'business and financial monopoly, speculation, reckless banking, class antagonism' were seeking to regain power. 'But we know that government by organized money is as bad as government by organized mob. Never before', he pointed out, 'in all our history have these forces been so united against one candidate as they stand today. They are unanimous in their hate for me – and I welcome their hatred.' He concluded, 'I should like to have it said of my first administration that in it the forces of selfishness and lust for power met their match. I should like to have it said', he added to thunderous applause 'of my second administration that in it these forces met their master.'[13]

Moley was 'stunned' by this speech and Richberg 'frankly horrified'.[14] The American people felt differently, however, and on 2 November 1936 Roosevelt enjoyed the most crushing victory in history over the Kansan Republican Alf Landon, winning 61 per cent of the popular vote and every state save Maine and Vermont. 'You are now leaving the United States,' read a handwritten sign on the Vermont border. Democrats won many state legislatures and governorships for the first time in living memory. Support from the industrial working class in urban America was overwhelming. That unnoticed 210,000 majority Al Smith had won in 1928 in the 12 largest cities, which FDR had raised to 1.7 million in 1932, was now an astonishing 3.4 million. A whole generation of working-class Americans, many of recent ethnic origin, women or black, seeking their first job and casting their first vote in the depths of the depression, were voting for Roosevelt and the Democrats.

V

They were organizing their first union too. At Flint, Michigan, on 30 December 1936 the 300,000-strong United Autoworkers began one of the most celebrated strikes in history. When General Motors refused to recognize the UAW as a Wagner Act union, workers at the end of their shift stayed in and sat down, stopping production while preventing GM from putting in strikebreakers. The sit-down strike paralysed production throughout GM, affecting 112,000 of the company's 150,000 workers and transforming American labour history. Fed by women's auxiliary brigades, who radicalized the whole Flint community, the sit-down strikers held out for two months against a freezing winter, tear-gas and violence. GM's attempts to use the courts or persuade Frank Murphy, the governor of Michigan, to evict the strikers failed.

Murphy, elected Democratic governor in November, refused to call out the national guard while Lewis and the CIO put pressure on GM to recognize the UAW and so end the strike. Behind the scenes FDR also urged GM to settle, which they eventually did on 11 February 1937. It was a famous victory not only for Roosevelt but for the CIO and the UAW. The victory for the Wagner Act was more ambivalent. The sit-down strikers had won the right to bargain collectively. But they had not been granted exclusive representation rights and dared not call an election to secure them, supervised by the NLRB under the Wagner Act, for fear of losing. Yet essentially one of the largest multinational corporations in the world had been forced to recognize a union. The knock-on effect of this was astonishing. In March, to general incredulity, the CIO won an even more astonishing victory when US Steel signed a contract with SWOC granting a 10 per cent wage increase, an eight-hour day, a 40-hour week and, most important, recognition of SWOC as the bargaining agent for its members – all without a strike. The nation's two greatest open-shop bastions – GM and US Steel – had fallen. The whole pattern of labour relations in mass production – essentially based on brutal paternalism – was unravelling.

There followed a general CIO assault on mass-production industry. Organizing drives among rubber workers, radio and electrical workers, lumbermen, longshoremen and many others built powerful new unions.

Hillman's skilful leadership of the new Textile Workers' Organizing Committee (TWOC) was especially significant because it reached hitherto unorganizable Southern mill towns. CIO membership gains by the end of 1937 were impressive: 600,000 mineworkers, 400,000 automobile workers, 375,000 steel workers, 300,000 textile workers, 250,000 ladies' garment workers, 177,000 clothing workers, 100,000 agricultural and packing workers. The CIO had built a new base for organized labour among semi-skilled and unskilled workers which cut clean across the exclusive craft unionism of the AFL and embraced immigrants, blacks and women.

But the CIO triumph was far from complete. In steel 1937 was the exception to the rule that where US Steel led the rest of the industry followed. The so-called Little Steel companies like Bethlehem, Republic and Youngstown Sheet and Tube fought bitter and bloody rearguard resistance to unionization. These strikes made 1937 the worst year in history for industrial unrest, with more than 28 million working days lost. The 1937 Memorial Day Massacre in Chicago ended in victory for Republic Steel with 10 strikers shot dead. As SWOC's campaign dragged on to defeat it revealed sharply the limitations of Roosevelt's support. La Follette's Senate investigation committee showed where the blame should be put. Republic Steel executives found it hard to explain why they spied on their own workforce, hired goon squads to beat them up, practised sabotage and spent $50,000 on guns, grenades and explosives stored in their factories. Yet FDR's attitude was 'a plague on both your houses'. Lewis, who had fought for Roosevelt's re-election in November 1936, felt betrayed. 'The economic royalists represented by General Motors and Republic Steel,' Lewis explained, backed every effort to defeat FDR in 1936. 'The same economic royalists now have their fangs in labour' but FDR would not now help labour defeat them.[15]

This was partly because he believed that, despite Lewis's sense of betrayal, he could rely on the labour vote. For perhaps the only time in history union growth had occurred in an era of economic depression and high unemployment. This was mainly because the law had been on the side of the workers. Even then, unionization took place when the economy had been growing in 1933–34 and more dramatically in 1936–37. To crown this achievement, in June 1938 FDR signed the Fair Labor Standards Act. This established a minimum wage (25 cents an hour, to be raised to 40 by 1945) and a maximum 44-hour week (to be lowered to 40 by 1941) and ended employment of children under 16. These standards were minimal and, as with Social Security, farm and domestic workers were excluded. But they provided a basis which would be built on later and from which there could be no retreat.

Organized labour had made dramatic gains. Moreover, its political position had been transformed. Far from standing on the outside of politics, merely rewarding friends and punishing enemies, it was now a central part of the Democratic party's new social democratic reform coalition and was to remain so for a generation. Roosevelt and the Democrats had transformed the balance of power in American politics in a manner which lasted until the end of the 1960s. Organized working-class votes carried the big cities of the populous industrial states and so helped Democratic candidates to win those states for a generation. When combined with the Democratic vote of the solid South it made the party hard to beat in presidential elections. Labour's political strength was such that it was able to withstand schism in 1938 when the AFL expelled the CIO, enabling it to form its own federation of industrial unions. Stung by competition from these new CIO industrial unions, the AFL had revived by 1938 and began to grow faster than the CIO. Nevertheless, the house of labour remained divided until 1955.

Chapter 9

## Power at Home in Peace and War, 1937–45

I

FDR was not concerned about organized labour's schism between AFL and CIO because throughout the violent industrial conflicts of 1937 he had been preoccupied with the greatest political crisis of his presidency. This was his attempt to reform the US Supreme Court. His Second Inaugural on 20 January 1937 (the first on the new date which replaced 4 March) was a benign and lofty address. He had told the American people that there was still much to do and spoken movingly of 'one-third of a nation, ill-housed, ill-clad, ill-nourished'. His huge win in November 1936 had given him command of Congress enjoyed by few presidents, which he might have used to embark upon social reform to help these forgotten Americans. Instead he took a different course unmentioned in his inaugural, astounding the nation, Congress and even friends by making his first action the unveiling in February of a secret plan he had been working on throughout 1936 to enlarge and reform the Supreme Court.

Clearly the Court had become a serious political problem. To start with the nine-man Court was deeply divided. There were four conservatives, three liberals and two floaters, with conservatives usually winning 5–4. During the 1920s the majority of the Court had based its work on social and economic cases on the pro-business ethos of the nation. This had collapsed after 1929. Moreover, as Brandeis pointed out in one of his dissenting judgments in 1932, the majority on the Court should exercise restraint in interposing its view about social and economic law between the people of the United States and the laws passed by Congress elected by the people. Early in 1935 the so-called 'hot oil' decision declared parts of NIRA unconstitutional while the Court handed down other decisions nullifying policies which American voters had endorsed with increasing majorities at every election between 1930 and 1934. In three other separate decisions the Court had upheld and then invalidated measures outlawing minimum wage laws. Then came the *Schechter* decision, unanimously outlawing Title I of NIRA in May 1935, which ended the industrial planning of the first New Deal. As if this were not enough, in the *Butler* case in January 1936 the Court struck down AAA by a vote of 6–3, thus ruining Roosevelt's policy for agriculture as it had earlier done for industry. Congress was able to restore much AAA aid to farming in later legislation. Moreover, in the *Butler* decision the three dissenting judges wrote a powerful opinion arguing that the majority on the Court were subverting the role of Congress and deepening the divide between Court and people.

This gave FDR the opening for his Supreme Court reform bill which caused such outcry when he sent it to Congress in January 1937 after re-election. The problem as he saw it was simple. Four conservative justices faced three liberals with Owen Roberts voting sometimes with one camp and sometimes with the other. So did Chief Justice Charles Evans Hughes in trying to discharge the impossible task of seeking to mass the Court's opinion during a decade of social upheaval and unprecedented demand for New Deal reform.

Conservatives on the Court, led by William McReynolds of Tennessee, feared the direction this New Deal reform was taking. McReynolds and his fellow conservatives – Pierce Butler, George Sutherland and Willis Van Devanter – were voicing strong minority opinion in the 1930s and it was a central function of the Court to protect the interests of minorities. Yet just as Hughes's problem was to mass majority opinion on a divided Court, FDR's as president was to mass the majority of the nation who had voted for New Deal reform. Roosevelt's real political problem was that, although the Court had upheld TVA legislation by 6–3 in the Ashwander case in 1936, it would soon have to rule on the constitutionality of the Wagner Act and on social security. Given its track record in 1935–36 there was every reason for thinking that the Court would strike down both measures and so nullify the second New Deal as it had done the first.

Roosevelt spent much of 1936 wrestling with this problem. How could he make an elitist Court more amenable to social reform passed by large majorities in Congress? Constitutional amendment reforming the Court was one route. Yet this would take years and almost certainly fail to secure the necessary two-thirds majorities, as repeated failure to outlaw child labour through Constitutional amendment had shown. Moreover, Constitutional amendments achieved nothing if Congress and the Court chose to nullify them, as a generation of African Americans could testify about the 14th and 15th Amendments.

So FDR decided to use the huge Congressional majorities Democrats had won in 1936 to pass legislative reform of the Supreme Court. In the greatest secrecy he and his attorney general Homer Cummings drafted their reform bill. Its preamble argued that the Court needed to act more quickly and that the advanced age of the justices – five of them were over 70 and the youngest was 66 – inhibited this. It proposed that at 70 justices should normally retire but if they refused the president would have power to appoint additional judges up to six in number, so enlarging the size of the Court to a possible 15.

The outrage this caused is hard to recapture today. Even FDR's most committed supporters were alarmed by his blatant attempt to pack the Court. William Allen White warned that if a reactionary president as charming and eloquent as FDR were elected he could change the Court and abridge the Bill of Rights. George Norris, the father of TVA, disgusted by FDR's opportunism, asked himself how he would have voted if 'Harding had offered this bill'.[1] Moreover, the objective of speeding up the Court's deliberations was obviously fraudulent. As Hughes argued in a devastating rebuttal, more justices would take longer to convince and decide. The bill's 'ageism' (a term not current in the 1930s) was equally clear. Yet the argument that the Court was conservative because the justices were old men fell down in the case of Louis Brandeis, who at 81 was not only the most respected but also the most progressive voice on the Court. Nevertheless, as Felix Frankfurter, the Harvard law professor and one of the Court's keenest critics, put it, the need for action was imperative. What FDR liked most about the bill that he and Cummings had devised was that it was based on one McReynolds himself had drafted as Woodrow Wilson's attorney general in 1914. The scene was now set for the kind of political conflict which Roosevelt enjoyed more than anything in life.

But he also loved being a winner and in this case he lost. Despite his party's overwhelming majorities he failed to persuade Congress to pass his bill. Conservative Democrats who feared opposing his popular economic and social policies now had the perfect excuse for breaking with him and going to the people. 'Boys, here's where I cash in my chips,' said Hatton Summers, chairman of the House judiciary committee.[2] Vice-president John Garner made no secret of his total opposition while Senate majority leader Joe Robinson, another conservative Southern Democrat, worked himself to death seeking support for a measure he himself had no faith in, suffering a sudden heart attack in July 1937. When Robinson died it was clear FDR was beaten. Yet it was a Pyrrhic victory for conservatives on the Court like McReynolds.

What no one had taken into account was the political pressure the bill would create while it was being debated not only in Congress but on the Court. Before FDR announced his bill the Court had shown it could support the New Deal by upholding TVA 6-3 in the *Ashwander* decision. In March 1937 the moderate judges Hughes and Roberts, the youngest but least predictable member of the Court, made the 5-4 majority in *West Coast Hotel* v. *Parrish* which upheld a Washington minimum-wage law, reversing the decision reached a few months earlier in *Morehead* v. *Tipaldo*. Observers thought Roosevelt's Court message must have been responsible, but they were wrong because the minimum-wage decision was reached before the president sent his message, though not handed down until after.

Whatever the reason, Roberts now began joining consistently with liberal justices to give them a majority. The effect was of critical importance for Roosevelt and the New Deal. In April, in *NLRB v. Jones & Laughlin*, the majority reversed its traditional strict construction of interstate commerce as revealed in the *Schechter*, *Butler* and *Carter* v. *Carter* cases to uphold the Wagner Act 5-4. The next day Hugh Johnson wrote wryly to FDR, 'I was taken for a ride on a chicken truck in Brooklyn two years ago and dumped out on a deserted highway and left for dead. It seems this was all a mistake.'[3] In May, in *Steward Machine Company* v. *Davis*, it upheld the unemployment provisions of the Social Security Act in two decisions, again 5-4, and in *Helvering* v. *Davis* ruled 7-2 that old-age pensions were constitutional.

Nor was this all. In June Van Devanter's sudden resignation gave FDR the chance to appoint Hugo Black, author of the 30-hour bill, to take his place on the Court, which the Senate confirmed in August. As Supreme Court reform moved to inevitable defeat, James Byrnes, a New Deal Democrat from Georgia, pressed for compromise, pointing out that the Court was now firmly 6-3 behind FDR and the New Deal. 'Why run for a train after you've caught it?'[4] Having got what he wanted, FDR accepted substantive defeat in Congress in return for face-saving reform of federal circuit courts. As so often with FDR, appearance masked reality but, uniquely over the Supreme Court, reality was better than the appearance which masked it. By the end of his second term, resignation or death enabled him to name his own Court. Hugo Black was joined by Frank Murphy, friend of the UAW during the Flint sit-down strike, by Felix Frankfurter, recruiter of key Keynesian lawyers to federal agencies, and by other liberals like William O. Douglas and even James Byrnes. Between 1938 and 1946, as a rule, the due process clause of the 14th Amendment was used to sanction state action, the exact opposite of the condition which had prevailed for the previous fifty years. Yet FDR paid a high price for his attempt to reform the Court. Thereafter he never regained the trust of those who feared he was essentially a political opportunist motivated mainly by lust for power.

## II

The period 1937–38 was a crisis for FDR. Louis Howe was dead. With Hopkins working outside Washington on relief, the lawyer Tom Corcoran for a time took over Howe's role. Moley and Tugwell had both returned to academic life, while industrial unrest and the Court conflict coincided with darkening clouds in foreign affairs as war loomed. Roosevelt's campaign to reform the Court had at last given his conservative opponents an issue they could all rally behind which also appealed to other political groups who did not share their views. Painting the president as a potential dictator bent on constitutional revolution fitted the wider picture of dictatorship in Europe. Worst of all the economy, which had been moving up since Roosevelt came to power, suddenly collapsed again even more steeply than before. By 1936–37 the economy had in many ways recovered, yet unemployment still stood at 14.3 per cent though industrial output had reached 1929 levels. Some even feared a runaway boom. Pressed by Morgenthau FDR believed it was time to start to redeem his campaign pledge to cut the cost of government and try to balance the budget. When the federal reserve raised interest rates to put a brake on credit Roosevelt asked Congress for economies. The consequent government cut in spending of 1.5 billion dollars, coinciding with the first impact of regressive social security taxes in millions of small pay packets, had immediate impact, with economic downturn even steeper than after 1929. Production fell by 70 per cent in steel, 50 per cent in automobiles, 40 per cent in rubber and 35 per cent in manufacturing. Unemployment leaped in less than a year to one in five – close to the 1933 figure – and this time people called it 'the Roosevelt recession'.

He was hoist with his own petard. Public spending was no longer a temporary economic expedient but a key tool in managing a modern economy. The United States was now experiencing what Britain had experienced since 1921. Even with the economy performing in high gear more than 10 per cent of the workforce was idle and at other times far more. Roosevelt's reaction was twofold. He returned to large-scale spending and revived the attack on monopoly. Before either could take effect the 1938 mid-term elections took their toll. The combined effect of depression, industrial unrest and the Supreme Court crisis swung the political pendulum for the first time against FDR. His efforts to defeat conservative opponents in Democratic primaries failed, and in November national results showed that the Democrats had lost seven seats in the Senate and 70 in the House.

This 1938 mid-term election was a real landmark. Thereafter Southern conservatives combined with Republicans to form the Dixiecrat–Republican coalition to limit further substantial social reform for a generation. Thus the session of Congress just before this election became with hindsight the last in which New Deal reform was possible. Yet there was still much for FDR to do. Unemployment never fell below 14 per cent while there were major omissions in welfare reform. Social security never included child allowances, which all other countries saw as the most significant single step to end poverty. Moreover, Roosevelt had no real interest in public housing which would have further raised living standards. His belated endorsement of Wagner's 1937 Housing Act, with capital of only one million dollars and borrowing capacity of 500 million dollars (later raised to 1.6 billion), meant that low-cost housing never developed in the United States as it did in Europe.

Roosevelt's reform interests were moving away from welfare to old-style progressive goals. Even before the second Hundred Days Roosevelt had backed a Brandeisian bill which broke up monopoly even more directly than the Wealth Tax. Sharing popular outrage against holding companies which in electric power had fleeced consumers, corrupted legislatures and evaded state regulation, FDR persuaded Tom Corcoran and Ben Cohen to draft the so-called 'death sentence' provision which empowered the SEC to dissolve any utility holding company after 1 January 1940 which could not justify its existence.

Under severe pressure from the utility companies Congress narrowly rejected the death sentence, replacing it, as the *Boston Globe* put it, 'with a chance for life imprisonment'.[5] As Brandeis told a friend, 'F.D. is making a gallant fight and seems to appreciate fully the evils of bigness. He should have more support than his party is giving him; and the social worker-progressive crowd seems as blind as in 1912', when they had backed Theodore Roosevelt, advocate of NRA-style government, rather than Wilson, the opponent of bigness.[6] Nevertheless, veteran Montana progressive Burton K. Wheeler and young Sam Rayburn from Texas managed to restore most of what had been removed. The Wheeler-Rayburn law empowered the SEC to wind up all utility holding companies more than twice removed from the operating companies and eliminate companies beyond the first degree which were not in the public interest. This crushing blow against bigness was the most important triumph for the Brandeisian viewpoint in two decades.

Yet the Holding Company Act was the last hurrah of anti-monopoly. Roosevelt's reforms were moving in other directions. He had long believed both in conservation and in the generation of public power. TVA both checked private monopoly and encouraged decentralization through the popular local transmission of electricity. But in the mind of Arthur E. Morgan, one of its three-man board, TVA was meant to have much wider objectives: to control flooding in the Tennessee, Ohio and Mississippi rivers, conserve the environment of an area as big as France and provide sustainable employment in model communities. FDR had once shared these idealistic views but now saw A.E. Morgan as an inept administrator who was preventing TVA securing its overriding goal of cheap electricity. So now he helped TVA's chairman David Lilienthal prevent Morgan from achieving his wider objectives and then sacked him in 1938 so that Lilienthal could concentrate on the provision of electric power.

Lilienthal was bringing public power to a valley where, in 1932, only one farm in a hundred had electricity. The same was true in Mississippi and much of the South. Nothing changed the daily lives of ordinary people more than FDR's creation of the Rural Electrification Administration (REA). In those many American farms which had no electricity life and labour was endless drudgery by kerosene lamp. Farmers toiled without machinery or proper light. Their wives, lacking the vacuum cleaners, washing machines and refrigerators city women took for granted, did backbreaking chores like peasants.

Then FDR helped set up a string of dams like TVA. The mighty Bonneville on the Columbia river was dwarfed by the Grand Coulee project in Washington state, then the greatest man-made structure in the world. This held back water in a lake 150 miles long, generated power to help industrialize the Pacific Northwest and reclaimed more than a million acres of land. Others like the Wheeler Dam on the Missouri and the Hoover Dam on Lake Meade were all helping the electrification of America. Private enterprise had been unable to do this. It could not undertake such massive projects, generate electricity, charge rates the poorest could afford and make a profit. But the REA set rates so low everyone could afford them and forced private corporations like Commonwealth and Southern, in direct competition with Lilienthal's TVA, to cut its rates. With everyone using electricity low rates soon proved profitable.

In January 1939 in *Tennessee Electric Power Co.* v. *TVA* the US Supreme Court ruled government competition against private power companies legitimate, greatly enhancing the 1936 *Ashwander* decision on the constitutionality of TVA. In August Wendell Willkie, head of Commonwealth and Southern, who had led the fight against Roosevelt and TVA, sold Tennessee Electric Power to the TVA for 79 million dollars, personally taking the cheque from Lilienthal. By 1940 four out of ten American farms had electricity; by 1950 nine out of ten. Economic prosperity based on widespread use of consumer durables was only possible once this had happened.

While this campaign for public power was in progress, FDR renewed the old progressive attack on monopoly in the late 1930s by setting up the Temporary National Economic Committee (TNEC). The TNEC investigations cast revealing light on the way the economy actually worked in the 1930s and bore fruit in one of the most remarkable economic documents ever to come from the White House. 'The power of the few to manage the economic life of the nation', FDR concluded, 'must be diffused among the many or be transferred to the public and its democratically responsible government.'[7]

Yet this Brandeisian attack on monopoly coincided with the Roosevelt recession. Roosevelt responded by reviving Keynesian public spending which tended to eclipse the attack on monopoly. Facing economic downturn as steep as in 1932, Congress readily appropriated new funds, the economy revived quickly and the Roosevelt recession was soon liquidated. Big business had to judge the work of the TNEC against this deficit spending and the debate which took place revealed the extent to which Keynesian ideas were winning acceptance. Big business had always opposed unbalanced budgets but by 1938 accepted that if business could not provide work then government spending should. More significant, if it was a choice between deficit finance, socialist-style planning or government attack on monopoly through TNEC then deficit finance was the least of three evils. Taxes on profits were reduced and TNEC quietly wound down while Roosevelt spent to stimulate the economy and reduce unemployment. If, as historian Arthur Schlesinger puts it, the New Deal after 1935 was a coalition of lawyers in the school of Brandeis and economists in the school of Keynes then by 1938 the Keynesians were winning the argument.

As government spending revived economic activity between 1938 and 1940, opponents of unbalanced budgets, who had argued that they saddled posterity with debt, began to see that, if this debt served to increase national output and was geared to this, it could be carried without damaging the economy. Indeed, the whole purpose of FDR's spending was to grow the economy. The problem was to spend money in ways which did this effectively. Moreover, as Eccles pointed out, counter-cyclical spending was really a conservative option which implied 'Sustaining government contributions to general purchasing power while the obstacles to private spending are cleared away'.[8] The basic structure and values of capitalism, the ownership and control of the system, would not be disturbed in the long run. Spending rather than attack on monopoly or further social reform would get priority. In his annual message to Congress in January 1939 Roosevelt rang the death knell of the New Deal. 'We have now passed the period of internal conflict,' he explained, 'in the launching of our program of social reform. Our full energies may now be released to invigorate the processes of recovery in order to preserve our reforms.'[9]

III

Yet America's full energies were never successfully released in peace-time. Roosevelt revealed the problem in an off-the-cuff comment in March 1939. 'We have the choice', FDR told a press conference, 'of following the policy recommended in the annual message or adopting the policy which has been advanced by perfectly well-meaning people; that is, cutting down on certain expenditures by government . . . They include: relief for the unemployed, all forms of public works, social security for the aged, slum clearance and other items which today give work in large volume – all of those being predicated on the guess – again the guess – of so many well-meaning people that thereby, taking away employment from several million workers, business will automatically pick up and employ the entire slack plus the other large number of people who are out of work but not in any way helped by the government. If there was some guarantee that this would happen, it would be worth considering. I doubt, however, whether this would meet with popular approval if it were tried and the results were not attained. There is the answer. It is purely extemporaneous but I think I said a mouthful.'[10]

Congress not only went along with deficit finance but agreed that the president needed help and voted funds in April 1939 for the Administrative Reorganization Act. Acting under this, in September FDR issued executive order 8248 expanding his staff. The long-term effect of ARA was the modern expansion in the size and grasp of the presidential office; but its short-term effect was to make Lauchlin Currie the first full-time White House economist. Here he shaped Roosevelt's policy on Keynesian lines. 'I know that you will be pleased to learn', Currie told FDR in February 1940, 'that secretary Morgenthau and Mr Eccles have had a long talk and, in the words of Mr Eccles, have "a complete and

thorough understanding that they will co-operate closely . . . and acknow-
ledge the perfect right of the other to differ as to method." '[11]

Thereafter FDR took it for granted that the economy could not operate
without the stimulus of government funds. In his 1940 budget he accepted
in theory what he had been doing in fact, blamed Hoover's retrenchment
for the recession, credited recovery to government spending and discussed the problem of the federal budget in Keynesian terms. Yet as far
as Keynes himself was concerned Roosevelt was not doing enough. 'It
seems politically impossible', Keynes wrote in July 1940, 'for a capital-
istic democracy to organize expenditure on the scale necessary to
make the grand experiment which would prove my case – except in war
conditions.'[12]

Hitler's lightning conquests in Europe in 1939–40 brought these conditions into being. Although FDR had now accepted a Keynesian approach
to the economy, that year was another crisis in his career. Domestic
politics was dominated by fear of war. Isolationism was strong, especially in the Midwest and among German-, Irish- and Italian-American
voters. Many who had voted for FDR in the 1930s were afraid he was
now trying to manoeuvre America into hostilities. Urged by Eleanor he
had thought of leaving office, retiring to Hyde Park and seeking that
elusive cure for polio at Warm Springs. But there was no obvious Democratic successor, and those seeking to succeed him, like his former campaign manager Jim Farley, vice-president John Garner or secretary of
state Cordell Hull, were conservative or inadequate or both. His attempts
to promote New Deal Democrats like Harry Hopkins or William O. Douglas got nowhere. An old-style Democrat or a Republican president elected
in 1940 would, he feared, undo the New Deal while his failure to purge
his party's Southern wing meant that the Dixiecrat–Republican coalition
was still strong in Congress.

Moreover, foreign danger loomed larger every month. Hitler's blitzkrieg in the spring and summer of 1940 not only conquered Western
Europe but also outflanked all other US presidential candidates and made
FDR's experience a priceless asset. When the Republicans met in June to
choose a candidate three strong contenders, Thomas Dewey of New York,
Robert Taft of Ohio and Arthur Vandenberg of Michigan, cancelled each
other out. With France falling, Dewey's youthful inexperience and the
relentless isolationism of Taft and Vandenberg made them look unlikely
national leaders. After three inconclusive ballots delegates began shouting, 'We want Willkie!' and on the sixth nominated the head of Commonwealth and Southern, who had made his name fighting Roosevelt
over TVA. Wendell Willkie was a real dark horse, a lifelong Democrat

from Indiana who had voted for Roosevelt in 1932. Party regulars resented him. 'I don't mind the church converting a whore,' explained Indiana's Jim Watson, 'but I don't like her to lead the choir on the first night!'[13] Few had heard of this 'Simple, barefoot Wall Street lawyer' as Ickes mordantly described him.[14] Moreover, he faced a problem in his campaign. When he had been merely a spokesman for big business he had been free to lambast FDR. But the New Deal was so popular with middle America that he and the Republican party had now implicitly to accept much of it.

A Republican party divided in face of the unprecedented peril of the depression partly explains FDR's power over Congress. Moreover, conservative Southern Democrats had been prepared to back his welfare and social reform so long as they continued to benefit from policies which helped farmers and – most important – so long as nothing was done to give African Americans civil rights, which Eleanor always championed. Despite his lack of interest in civil rights and other reforms FDR had been trying since 1937 to purge Southern reactionaries from the party and form a new kind of national party which would include liberal Republicans. This again became apparent as the Democratic convention approached in July 1940 and the Rubicon of a third term loomed for FDR.

He did nothing to try to win the nomination. He hoped to tackle the third-term issue and perhaps his own lingering indecision by being drafted, ostensibly against his will, by a spontaneous uprising of delegates rather like those who had just nominated Willkie. This outcome was helped by the fact that he had picked Chicago, where Ed Kelly's machine ruled politics with an iron rod, to host the convention. 'I am not overlooking the fact that Kelly could pack the galleries for us,' FDR explained. Shouts of 'We want Roosevelt!' were transformed by men on Kelly's payroll into 'The world wants Roosevelt!'[15] Many delegates were embittered by such chicanery. To memories of the demagogic campaign in 1936 and the attempt to pack the Supreme Court in 1937 was now added the third term in 1940. 'You know,' wrote Thomas Gore, former Democratic senator from Oklahoma, 'I have never doubted for one moment since he was nominated in 1932 that he would seek a third term ... Caesar thrice refused the kingly crown – but this Caesar never.'[16]

They made an issue of his choice of running mate. He had long fallen out with Garner and selected Henry Wallace, a deeply anti-fascist New Dealer whose record as secretary of agriculture would appeal to the Corn Belt. As with Willkie, party regulars were aghast. Not only was Wallace a mystic but also a former Republican. Old-time Democrats displaced by New Dealers like Hopkins ran a campaign to nominate the conservative

House speaker William Bankhead from Alabama instead. Listening to proceedings from Chicago on radio, FDR scribbled out his refusal to run. 'For God's sake,' Jimmy Byrnes asked, moving from delegation to delegation, 'do you want a president or a vice-president?'[17] Bullied by threats that Roosevelt might not run, the convention gave Wallace 628 votes to Bankhead's 329. Though the attempt to purge the party's Southern conservatives in 1938 had failed, New Dealers now demonstrated convincingly that they controlled the party.

As the Battle of Britain raged in the skies, Roosevelt ran another powerful campaign. Hoover, accused of extravagance in 1932, was now criticized for not having spent enough to fight the depression. Though some Republican campaign buttons read 'Third International, Third Reich – Third Term?' Willkie started with a bipartisan approach in foreign affairs. Yet in September he found his attacks on Roosevelt's domestic record were making little headway and began branding him a warmonger, predicting that his election in November would mean war by April 1941. FDR counter-attacked vigorously. Though opinion polls showed that some 40 per cent of the country felt it more important to stay out of war than aid Britain, FDR argued that the United States could only keep out of war by helping Britain defeat the aggressors. Still Willkie seemed to be cutting into his lead: polls in the last week of the campaign put him within 4 per cent of the president. FDR could not of course guarantee that Germany or Japan would not attack the United States; but he pledged many times that he would not send Americans to fight abroad unless this happened. Yet, pressured by party chiefs, fearful of polls which showed Willkie could win, Roosevelt declared in Boston in early November, 'I have said it again and again and again: Your boys are not going to be sent to fight in any foreign wars' – omitting the vital proviso about attack. At Buffalo three days later he simply announced, 'Your president says this country is not going to war.'[18]

The legendary Jim Farley had broken with FDR and was replaced by Ed Flynn over his third-term decision. The remaining campaign advisers failed to see the war issue's more subtle effect. Though they feared its impact on German-, Italian- and Irish-American voters, so important to the Democrats, closer examination of opinion poll data would have reassured them. Asked how they would vote if there were no war voters favoured Willkie by 5.5 per cent – 48.7 to 43.2. But facing the possibility of involvement in war they preferred Roosevelt by a margin of 18.2 per cent – 54.6 to 36.4. Where FDR was able to blunt Willkie's war warnings with peace declarations, the actual conflict in Europe may have given him an advantage Willkie could not overcome. On these (uncertain) figures, 11 per cent of FDR's supporters voted for him chiefly because of the international crisis, while only 2 per cent of Willkie voters backed him principally because he would keep America out of war. On 7 November strong isolationism cost FDR the Corn Belt and made 1940 the closest presidential election in popular vote for 24 years; but with strong support in the cities, more than 54 per cent of the popular vote and 38 states he beat Willkie easily. He had broken the 'George Washington precedent' and been elected for a third term.

Had he left office in January 1941 Roosevelt's reputation would have been quite different. He would have been judged to have only partly ended the depression and perhaps to have left the nation unprepared for war when it came. Instead he became the man who led America to victory in peace and war. In fact he did not get into the war until the end of 1941 although earlier that year his Four Freedoms speech – freedom of speech and religion, freedom from want and fear – defined potential war aims much more effectively for a world audience than Churchill's eloquent speeches. Meantime Hitler's sweeping victories in Europe brought change. In June 1940 FDR had startled the nation – and wrong-footed Republicans – by appointing Henry Stimson secretary of war and Frank Knox secretary of the Navy. These two Republicans greatly strengthened the hawks in his cabinet, since both had taken tougher positions on the war than FDR himself, with Knox even advocating that the US Navy convoy munitions to Britain.

In September Congress agreed to give Britain 50 ageing destroyers in return for 99-year leases on bases in the Caribbean and Newfoundland. Congress further accepted FDR's demands to bring in conscription and, through generous aid for embattled Britain, place the American economy on a war footing. With Lend-Lease he bamboozled Congress into lending the British arms which they were expected to return when the war was over and the arms presumably obsolete or destroyed. Because Britain was close to going broke the United States was giving her the means to fight Hitler. Yet again appearance masked reality. The main point was that the United States at last began to rearm seriously. Congress, which in early spring 1940 had talked of slashing War Department appropriations, now voted more than 27 billion dollars for defence. Roosevelt could at last spend in a way to make the grand experiment which would prove Keynes's economic case. As events developed a momentum of their own, spending rose exponentially. In June 1941 Hitler invaded the Soviet Union. In December the Japanese attack on Pearl Harbor finally brought the United States into the war. Public spending was now not simply acceptable but a patriotic imperative.

Having spent 62 billion dollars during the depression, winning the war cost 321 billion – more in current dollars than the US government spent on everything between 1790 and 1940. Put another way, government spent 70 cents for every tax dollar collected in 1926–27, two dollars in 1935–36 and 1939–40 and three dollars in 1942–43. Conscription of 12 million young men, who would otherwise have been seeking work, ended unemployment. Soldiers were also paid a minimum wage, which took care of both demand and supply problems. The insatiable appetite of the war economy for military hardware, built to be destroyed and replaced as rapidly as possible, also took care of supply. With good management both sides of the economic equation would move into balance. War not the New Deal defeated the great depression.

The war transformed economic priorities. Inflation replaced unemployment as the major problem. FDR had to control wages, prices and profits to maintain domestic harmony and in this he was only partially successful. He was more successful in his determination that war should not undo all the gains of the New Deal. As France was falling in May 1940 he had set up a seven-man Advisory Defense Commission, with Sidney Hillman of the CIO in charge of employment. But he refused to give it real executive power. Instead, he kept industrial mobilization largely in his own hands where he could protect the New Deal. 'Government policy [is] in no way to weaken the social gains that have been made in the last few years,' he told the press.[19] 'That is very, very important.' In a fireside chat broadcast on 21 May he told the nation, 'There is nothing in the present emergency to justify making the workers of our nation toil for longer hours than now limited by statute . . . There is nothing in our present emergency to justify a lowering of the standards of employment . . . There is nothing . . . to justify a breaking down of old age pensions or of unemployment insurance . . . There is nothing . . . to justify a retreat from any of our social objectives.'[20]

The contrasting fate of New Deal agencies during the war was instructive. Some like TVA and RFC (the latter actually created by Hoover) were able to adapt and establish a place in the war economy, expanding and surviving well into the postwar period. Others like WPA and FSA tried but failed to sustain their relevance in a changed situation where skilled workers rather than work was scarce. Despite this, war did enable Roosevelt to weave together two major themes of the New Deal: more influence for organized labour and more importance for public spending. After Pearl Harbor his first step was to get AFL and CIO to make a No Strike pledge and then join management and government in a tripartite partnership to manage the war economy. The War Labor Board was a typically progressive bureaucratic approach to war planning which did an unprecedented job. It imposed settlements in nearly 18,000 wartime industrial disputes involving more than 12 million workers and in 95 per cent of these cases averted further threats to production. It also approved 415,000 voluntary wage agreements covering 20 million workers.

This was a gigantic and time-consuming task. Yet FDR's experience with the Navy department during the Great War served him in good stead when it came to labour relations, profiteering and strikes. The Office of Production Management, the Office of Price Administration and many similar agencies, often staffed by young Keynesian economists like J.K. Galbraith, controlled production, prices, inflation, scarce raw materials, limited rationing and all the problems of a war economy. With labour, especially skilled labour, suddenly scarce, unions gained greatly in power and influence. Wages, hours and conditions were set with union agreement. FDR only gave Ford Motors lucrative government war contracts if it would recognize the UAW. More important, under these war contracts employers agreed to 'maintenance of union membership' which effectively imposed a closed shop. As a result by the end of the war some 80 per cent of manufacturing industry had been unionized.

In return unions agreed to enforce contracts on their side. Employers who had fought unions so vigorously in the 1930s now welcomed them. With the old pattern of shopfloor relations collapsing during the war, unions now disciplined the workforce. Much labour deskilling took place as apprenticeships and training were shortened. There was great mobility of labour as peacetime plants converted to war production, while war industries were started in new regions like California and the Pacific Northwest. Millions of women who moved in to take the jobs of men called to arms found themselves earning good wages for the first time in a way which Eleanor Roosevelt thoroughly approved. Similarly, African-American workers, so badly hit during the depression, now enjoyed much greater job opportunities.

In contrast to Eleanor, FDR's record on civil rights had never been good. He had constantly refused to back anti-lynching bills in the 1930s for fear of losing crucial support among Southern Democrats who ran the party in Congress. Yet when the black railway unionist A. Philip Randolph organized a March on Washington in 1941 and threatened industrial action, FDR moved at last against racial discrimination. Fighting the racist doctrines of Hitler and the Nazis, Roosevelt was forced to do something. Executive order 8802 outlawed racial discrimination in war industries and set up the Fair Employment Practice Committee (FEPC) to enforce it. Backed by the indefatigable Eleanor and the so-called 'Black

Cabinet', led by Robert Weaver, Roosevelt's FEPC was an important pre-cursor of the postwar civil rights movement, although the 1943 race riot in Detroit which killed 24 blacks and nine whites showed how inflam-mable the issue was.

By contrast, his treatment of Japanese-Americans was a great blot on his record in civil rights. In the panic after Pearl Harbor in February 1942 he ordered the rounding up and arrest of some 118,000 Japanese-Americans, many born in the United States, in California and the West Coast. In April about 100,000 were sent to concentration camps while others were offered resettlement on farm camps in the Midwest or East. All lost their jobs, property and businesses, but by the end of 1944 the Supreme Court, in *Korematsu* v. *United States*, upheld the action as constitutional under the 'clear and present danger' of war. In his lone dissent Frank Murphy, who as governor of Michigan had refused to order the national guard to evict sit-down strikers at Flint in 1937 and been appointed to the Court by FDR in 1940, described the decision as 'the legalization of racism'.

The American Civil Liberties Union went further, calling the whole episode 'The worst single wholesale violation of civil rights in our history'.[21] Though represented as a 'military necessity' the action in fact had no sound military justification, especially as nothing similar was done against German- or Italian-Americans, two of the nation's largest ethnic groups. Moreover, it prevented the United States from making full use of the language skills of Japanese-Americans in intelligence or code break-ing. By 1944 all victims of this internment had received compensation from the federal government.

Yet, as FDR's biographer James MacGregor Burns points out, 'Roosevelt was not a strong civil libertarian and the wartime White House was not dependably a source of strong and sustained support for civil liberties in specific situations.' In the midst of war FDR had little patience with traditional rights that in any way jeopardized the war effort. 'That de-lightful god "The Freedom of the Press"', he told Churchill in March 1942, was one of the 'additional burdens' by which they were both men-aced in time of war.[22] 'I am perfectly willing to mislead and tell untruths,' he told Morgenthau in May 1942, 'if it will help win the war.'[23]

His hypocrisy in these matters is striking. At the very time when he was contrasting Nazi 'barbarism' with the great upsurge of human liberty embodied in the Bill of Rights and the American conception of individual freedom, so making the Four Freedoms the basis of the Allied struggle, he was breaking constitutional guarantees by interning American-born Japanese, urging limitations on the freedom of the press and sanction-ing invasions of individual privacy by the FBI. Ickes, who had such an outstanding record on rights for American Indians, recorded the cabinet meeting which took the decision on Japanese internment. 'There was practically no discussion of the plan,' he recorded in his diary, 'and I interjected nothing. However, I feel it both stupid and cruel.'[24] It was, as we shall see in the next chapter, of a piece with his policies towards the Spanish civil war and Jewish refugees from Nazi persecution. As Robert Dallek puts it, 'Each of these issues required FDR to take a stand on principle against prevailing political, military and/or foreign opinion. But this he would not do.'[25]

Other developments were equally dramatic. On the eve of the Second World War, on 2 August 1939, Albert Einstein wrote to Roosevelt warning him of the danger that German scientists could devise an atomic bomb. He reacted at once by setting up the top-secret Manhattan Project. For reasons of security the cost was completely hidden from Congress, but the greatest array of scientific talent ever assembled in one place, including many foreigners, had by 1945 secretly developed the devastating weapon which, when dropped by the United States on Hiroshima and Nagasaki in August 1945, ended the war.

Hiding the Manhattan Project was only one of FDR's wartime domestic problems. Maintaining industrial harmony became harder because of his failure to control inflation or profiteering. He had seen this from the start. 'If we get like what happened in the [first] world war,' he told business leaders at a secret meeting at the end of 1941, 'you almost inevitably get labor trouble. I can hold labor to the present level if I can say to them "You [industry] won't profiteer, the cost of living hasn't gone up." I think I can avoid the most dangerous spiral.'[26] But spectacular profits did occur, the cost of living rose steeply and led to 'the tragic race between wages and prices' caused by wartime inflation. Though FDR helped devise 'the Little Steel formula' to contain pay increases, strikes became more frequent each year during the war, especially on the railways and in coal mining where the colliers had serious grievances and where Lewis, the UMW leader, now held FDR in contempt.

Though the War Labor Board by and large kept control, workdays lost to strikes rose steadily to reach 1937 levels by 1945. Wartime inflation and industrial unrest clearly helped Republicans as the 1942 mid-term elections approached. Recalling that Democrats had suffered a serious political reverse when Woodrow Wilson led a partisan mid-term campaign in 1918, FDR now decided to stand aloof. But his failure to campaign resulted in general apathy, low voter turnout and big Republican gains. In its best showing since the 1920s the GOP gained 77 seats in the House, only seven short of a majority, while capturing several governorships, including California and New York. In short, Democrats in 1942 lost twice as many seats as they had in 1918.

Following this impressive increase in support, Republicans in Congress naturally reacted to mounting industrial unrest with greater anti-labour sentiment which led directly to the 1943 Smith-Connally Act. Liberal Democrats were able to remove some of its punitive provisions. Nevertheless, this somewhat limited anti-union measure was important not so much for what it did but because it anticipated the Taft-Hartley Act, passed in 1947 after FDR's death, which attempted root-and-branch repeal of the Wagner Act and restored the initiative in labour relations firmly to employers. Despite this the class conflict of the 1930s was a thing of the past. Organized labour was now a partner with industry and government to win the war – a precursor of 'the military-industrial complex' which emerged after 1945 during the Cold War.

Labour's political importance to FDR increased as the 1944 presidential election approached. By the end of 1943 he believed he would need a fourth term to conclude the war and design the peace. 'God knows I don't want to but I may find it necessary,' he said. 'I just hate to run again for election.'[27] By February 1944 he was 62, tired and in poor health. Nine years of depression and war had taken its toll, as had heavy smoking – expansive waves of his cigarette holder, combined with his confident, uptilted head, were a personality trademark. A number of physical illnesses and problems – the flu, bronchitis, occasional inability to concentrate and a blackout once while signing a letter – prompted a full medical examination at Bethesda, Maryland, Naval Hospital. Doctors were shocked at their findings – hypertension, hypertensive heart disease (or an enlarged heart) and evidence of cardiac failure.

FDR was supremely uninterested in the results of these tests and there is no evidence that his doctors ever passed them on to him. They prescribed more rest, fewer cigarettes, reduced weight and various medications, including digitalis, which he took without asking their name or purpose. Unquestioningly accepting their advice, he recovered, regained much of his strength and believed he could serve a fourth term if he cut down his work load. Organized labour played a key role at the Democratic convention in July. Sidney Hillman, who had set up the CIO with Lewis in 1935, was now not only FDR's key labour adviser but also ran the party's Political Action Committees vital in organizing the labour vote. FDR had decided to drop Wallace from the ticket ('Henry's passed it' he said) but delegates seeking to nominate Harry S. Truman as Roosevelt's running mate were warned by FDR 'to clear everything with Sidney'.[28]

The issue of his health dogged FDR during the 1944 campaign. Having lost about 20 pounds in weight since the start of the year he appeared haggard and gaunt. Speechwriter Robert Sherwood, who had not seen the president in eight months, was shocked by his almost ravaged appearance in September. A photograph snapped in July, widely used during the campaign, showed an emaciated face with a slack, open mouth and encouraged rumours that the president was a dying man. Carefully staged appearances were designed to scotch these rumours. But a speech broadcast nationwide from the destroyer *Bremerton* in August added to the fears. An attack of angina, painful leg braces he had not worn in a year and strong winds combined with a slanted deck all upset his balance and made the president's delivery halting and ineffective.

Characteristically, he bounced back with a series of outings in September and October culminating with 'The greatest campaign speech of his career' which refuted the idea that he was a feeble old man and threw Dewey on the defensive. 'These Republican leaders have not been content with attacks on me, or my wife, or on my sons,' he said in his most memorable passage. 'No, not content with that, they now include my little dog, Fala.' Recounting with mock seriousness Republican allegations that he had sent a destroyer back to the Aleutians at a cost of millions of dollars to find Fala, he concluded, 'Well, of course, I don't resent attacks, and my family doesn't resent attacks, but Fala *does* resent them.'[29]

The second problem FDR faced after his health in 1944 was to win the backing of millions of independent voters, especially the Willkie internationalists and independent Republicans. He believed they embraced 20 per cent of the electorate and would decide the election. Since losing in 1940 Willkie had toured the Middle East, the Soviet Union and China and published *One World*, a plea for US intervention to preserve the postwar peace which, in only three months, became the third non-fiction book in US history to sell a million copies. Yet Willkie's decisive defeat in the Wisconsin primary in April, where he finished last in every district despite being the only candidate to campaign in the state, knocked him out of the contest and left his backers up for grabs. Dropping Wallace from the ticket seemed unlikely to win FDR support from liberal internationalists, though he hoped a reliable party man like Truman would not offend either liberals or conservatives.

Typically, FDR dealt with this difficulty by seeking to enlist Willkie's support. He asked Sam Rosenman to talk to him about joining a post-election effort to set up a liberal party composed of both Democrats and Republicans, a counterweight to the Dixiecrat–Republican coalition. This bold initiative was all of a piece with his repeated efforts in 1938, 1940 and 1942 to purge his party's conservatives and launch a new liberal-democratic party which would include Republicans like Willkie and for that matter Ickes, Wallace or the Republican mayor of New York City, Fiorello La Guardia. Willkie was guarded and, when news of this approach leaked out, urged all independents to support the candidate who espoused the most advanced view on a postwar international organization. Then on 8 October, before he could decide who this was, Willkie suddenly died. A month later, on election day, FDR's close advisers like Hopkins were confident of victory over the Republican governor Thomas E. Dewey. 'We are going to lick that lying bastard,' said Roosevelt's appointments secretary Edwin 'Pa' Watson.[30] In fact Dewey did better than Willkie in share of the popular vote, making this the closest election since Wilson's narrow wartime victory in 1916. Yet FDR's popular majority of 3.6 million gave him a wide electoral margin of 432 to 99 while his 53.5 per cent of the popular vote was similar to the share McKinley had won in 1896, establishing Republicans as the natural governing party for a generation. Now roles were reversed: between 1932 and 1968 only one Republican, the Second World War hero Dwight Eisenhower, would win the White House. In the short term too Democrats strengthened their position in Congress, re-establishing solid majorities in both Houses. Even more important, most Congressional isolationists, including Congressman Hamilton Fish of New York and Senator Gerald P. Nye of North Dakota, had lost their seats. Roosevelt's political position in 1944 for the postwar period was far stronger than Wilson's had been in 1918.

In 1943 FDR had explained that 'Dr Win-the-War' had temporarily replaced 'Dr New Deal'. But he was always at pains to defend New Deal gains against wartime attack and in January 1944 made a speech which his biographer James MacGregor Burns calls the 'most radical of his life'.[31] This combined unstinting war measures with a promise of radical reform. With victory over Germany in sight FDR could now paint a picture of postwar America. Returning war veterans were to be rewarded with great generosity. In June 1944 he signed the Servicemen's Readjustment Act, or GI bill of rights as it was known. Expenditure on this rose from 828 million dollars in 1944 to 10 billion dollars in 1950. More than 13.5 billion dollars was spent on education and training alone while a further 16.5 billion dollars went on loans for houses, farms and businesses and a chain of 150 veterans' hospitals. Though the GI bill transformed the lives of millions, its real significance was that it was restricted to ex-servicemen not, as liberals had hoped, open to everybody. FDR's economic bill of rights, proposed in a Chicago campaign speech, went much further. It was a piece of propaganda couched in Keynesian terms which envisaged huge government investment in industry. Yet such planning was not socialist – indeed, as he was at pains to point out, its whole purpose was to head off any possible socialist challenge.

'All the measures proposed in this program', he said at Soldier Field on 28 October 1944, 'are designed to make American capitalism and private enterprise work in the same great manner in peace as in war.' War in fact had revealed how to make capitalism successful in the second half of the century. 'Greater output is not the only benefit from this plant expansion. In fact our benefits also include the wages paid to the labor employed in building these plants, in constructing the machinery to be used in these plants and in operating the plants after they are erected. These payments in wages all contribute to the nation's buying power so that as a nation we will have the money to buy the goods produced in these expanded plants . . . Why just the job of *building* these plants and the machinery for them would give America five million more jobs a year than we had in this work before the war. And this does not include the workers who would be needed to operate these plants after they are built.'[32]

Roosevelt's real problem during the 1944 campaign was, as we have seen, not how to communicate this Keynesian vision but how to hide the fact that he was no longer the vigorous candidate of 1936 and 1940. The campaign largely succeeded in disguising this as, for the last time in his career, he used appearance to mask reality. Only two weeks after his fourth inauguration FDR had to travel 15,000 miles to meet Churchill and Stalin at the crucial Yalta conference which shaped the postwar world. The myth of Yalta, powerful in the postwar years, is that Roosevelt, sick and full of liberal illusions, sold out to Stalin. The reality is that the overwhelming might of the Red Army made it impossible to prevent Stalin determining postwar politics in Poland, eastern and central Europe. As he told Berle, who was fearful of Soviet intentions, 'Adolf, I didn't say the result was good. I said it was the best I could do.'[33] Reporting back to Congress on 1 March he broke all precedent and spoke sitting down, admitting in public, for the only time in his life, that he was paralysed.

His death at Warm Springs in April 1945, on the eve of victory, robbed him of the chance to lead the political fight for his postwar programme at home and abroad. During the war the Republicans, as we have seen, had grown much stronger in Congress and in the postwar years the Dixiecrat–Republican coalition in Congress was not only able to pass the Taft-Hartley Act but also put a cap on the economic bill of rights and much social reform. Yet Roosevelt's use of power in dealing with both depression and war made him the greatest president of the twentieth century. War had given him a new theatre in which to exercise leadership and we must now examine the foreign policy he pursued in peace and war between 1933 and 1945.

Chapter 10

# Power Abroad in Peace and War, 1933–45

I

Throughout the 1930s Roosevelt, like most Americans, was preoccupied with domestic problems. Yet the most serious challenges confronting the United States in that decade came from abroad. During the 1930s fascist dictators in Germany and Italy and military imperialists in Japan were seeking to redraw the world map by force. The danger this posed to capitalist democracies like Britain and France as well as the United States became increasingly clear as the decade progressed. The German challenge led to war in 1939, and although America did not enter hostilities until the end of 1941, the critical period of the twentieth century, from 1929 until 1945, coincided precisely with FDR's tenure of power as New York governor and US president. His reputation rests above all on how he used power in both peace and war during this crisis.

The domestic policy of the New Deal can be understood without knowing much about Roosevelt's thinking. He was a man of warm human sympathies and uncanny intuition who, despite his wealth, could readily identify with the poor and who also had a healthy scepticism for economic ideas. But to understand his foreign policy we must penetrate his mind. FDR was better equipped to deal with foreign affairs than most presidents. He had lived abroad every year when growing up, could speak and read some French and German and had served in the Navy department throughout the Great War. He also had a strategic view of world politics, shaped partly by writers like A.T. Mahan, who influenced many twentieth-century politicians. He was a realist like cousin Teddy, who had nevertheless been deeply impressed by the impact Wilson's idealistic internationalism had had on the world in 1918–19 and also by its tragic failure. He had wanted the United States to join the League of Nations, and though he did not share Herbert Hoover's belief that the American depression began abroad he understood the interaction of domestic and foreign affairs and realized that modern air power, military strategy and complex financial and economic links bound the United States to the world economy in a way which made isolationism obsolete.

Nevertheless, the foreign challenges he faced in the 1930s made those articles he had written about foreign affairs in the 1920 seem empty and complacent. By the mid-1930s he came to understand that Japanese militarism and German Nazism were not simply barbaric but the most dangerous threat possible to the kind of progressive capitalism he personified. But devising a policy to resist this challenge proved all but impossible. First came the problem of rousing the American people to the danger. Second came the search for reliable allies, when the League of Nations had no army, Britain and France were weak and divided and the Soviet Union, though anti-Nazi, was in its own way as big a threat to capitalist democracy as Nazism. Finally, Roosevelt failed to solve the dilemma which faced all liberal democracies in the 1930s. He fervently wanted to resist aggression but feared even more that if he did so he would find himself at war. This fundamental conflict in his thinking was at the heart of Roosevelt's foreign policy.

II

The first serious challenge to confront US foreign policy makers came the year before FDR was elected when, on 19 September 1931, Japanese forces occupied Manchuria. This was technically part of China, who appealed to the League of Nations for redress. The Manchurian problem was not an easy one. The Japanese had a good case. China had been in terminal disintegration since at least 1900. The authority of its central government – nowhere strong – did not run to Manchuria, which had for years been in lawless confusion. Japanese economic and trading interests suffered and there were many precedents for foreign powers acting independently in China in defence of their interests – the last being a British landing in Shanghai in 1926. Britain indeed was the only European power with any real stake in the Far East; but in the depths of the world depression no one welcomed cutting trade links with Japan.

So the League was powerless. Manchuria was far away. Britain, though a Far Eastern naval power, had no means of action in landlocked Manchuria. America, though very much a Far Eastern power, was not a League member. American policy was essentially impossible to achieve because the Anglo-Japanese treaty was not being enforced. The United States also set great store by the Open Door which had in theory given Western nations equal access to China since the 1890s. Was Japan, who had fought on the same side as Britain and the United States in the Great War, a Western nation? Moreover, the 1922 Washington naval treaty gave Japan local supremacy in the Far East. What would be gained if the League condemned Japan? Hoover's secretary of state Henry L. Stimson (Taft's secretary of war when FDR started his career) proposed non-recognition of any territorial change made by force but no curtailment of trade with Japan. This did not deter the Japanese and brought little comfort to China or Britain.

The League set up the Lytton commission to investigate and while it did so Japan invaded Shanghai, in retaliation for the Chinese boycott, killing thousands. Stimson appealed in vain for Britain to act, adding that the United States would insist on its treaty rights. When the Lytton commission reported it did not reach a simple verdict. It found most Japanese grievances justified and condemned Japan not as an aggressor but for resorting to force before all peaceful remedies had been exhausted. The League nevertheless refused to recognize Japanese conquests, and when Japan set up the puppet state of Manchukuo, ruled by the last emperor of China, in September 1932, called on her to return it to China. Japan's reply, less than a month after Roosevelt became president in March 1933, was to withdraw from the League and later in the year make peace with China.

While all this was going on FDR had been waiting to take office. Top advisers like Moley and Tugwell had not been invited to his meetings with Hoover and Stimson about international debt or consulted when he endorsed Stimson's Manchurian policy. Confused, they believed wrongly that he was about to support Hoover's internationalist approach. He was not. But neither was he willing simply to follow the Moley–Tugwell nationalist line. He was giving his advisers a taste of how he would operate as president. When he collapsed the London economic conference in July 1933 he was choosing nationalist rather than internationalist policy. But he would not allow himself to become captive to one set of advisers or one approach to problems. He wished to keep his options open and make his own decisions.

This meant during the 1930s pursuing a passive policy towards Japan in East Asia. Sanctioning this Far Eastern policy of inaction and non-provocation, Roosevelt was content to leave its execution – or rather non-execution – to secretary of state Cordell Hull and S.K. Hornbeck, Hull's chief of the Far Eastern division. They translated this into more specific terms. The Manchurian crisis had shown that the 1920s Washington and Kellogg-Briand agreements were unworkable and that the League would give American leadership little support. Accordingly, Hull declared that the United States would not 'Assume the role of mentor to the League and accept a responsibility which initially lies with and belongs to the League'.[1] Britain and France, whose interests were more acutely menaced, should take the lead. 'The United States', Hornbeck explained, 'has not much to lose' from further Japanese aggression in China. 'The principles of our Far Eastern policy and our ideals with regard to world peace may be further scratched and dented . . . and our trade prospects may be somewhat further impaired; but from the point of view of our material interests there is nothing there that is vital to us.'[2]

For his first few years in office FDR was quite prepared to follow this approach. Later during FDR's presidency the Manchurian crisis was seen as a significant milestone on the road to war: the first decisive betrayal of the League, especially by the British, fatally combined with US appeasement of aggression. In a sense this was true. Yet at the same time the League, under British leadership, had simply done what the British thought it should do by limiting conflict and bringing it, however unsatisfactorily, to an end. Moreover, far from weakening the League's coercive powers, it actually brought into being, again at British prompting, those economic sanctions which were to be used when the next crisis occurred in Abyssinia in 1935.

III

While the Manchurian affair unfolded Roosevelt and Hull were busy with the Soviet Union and Latin America. Since 1917 the United States had refused to recognize the Communist government which had seized power in Russia. Though fascism had not yet revealed its full menace to capitalist democracy the threat posed by Communism was plain: it had abolished private property and outlawed religion. Yet FDR was pragmatic in all things and saw that the Soviet Union could counterbalance Japan in the Far East. Typically, his main concern was not with the international repercussions of diplomatic recognition but squaring public opinion at home. When polls conducted by Jim Farley revealed comfortable majorities among both press and public he began charming opponents in the business community and Catholic church, while using Hull, Morgenthau and his old Republican friend William Bullitt, long an expert on Soviet affairs, to set up negotiations. Talks with Maxim Litvinov, a skilled Soviet diplomat of whom it was said he could 'come out dry from the water', failed to resolve such problems as outstanding debts or guarantees of religious and political freedom in the Soviet Union. Yet on 16 November 1933 the United States extended diplomatic recognition.

This seemed like a momentous step. Public reaction was all FDR could have asked. Most interested Americans, including business leaders, welcomed the move. It promised prosperity and peace by reviving US–Soviet trade and inhibiting Japanese aggression. In fact it did neither. US refusal to seek effective Soviet support to resist aggression was as marked as the similar failure of Britain and France and was based on the same thing: deep-seated hatred of Bolshevism. As the historian W.E. Leuchtenburg concludes, US diplomatic recognition of the Soviet Union 'was an event of monumental unimportance'.[3] Relations with Latin America, however, were much more significant and personally important to FDR. He was eager to make good the gross historical deficiencies of US foreign policy in Latin America. Here the problem was not too little contact, as with the Soviet Union, but too much. The United States dominated the Caribbean, Central and South America, controlling trade and often intervening militarily to quell local revolutions, collect debts or impose regime change. The Monroe doctrine, the basis of US foreign policy since 1823, had been modified by the Roosevelt corollary, announced by cousin Teddy in 1904, which said that, since Monroe enjoined European intervention in the region, the United States was justified in intervening first to forestall outsiders. Interventions reached record levels in the following two decades of 'dollar diplomacy' when FDR made the notorious, but false, claim to have written the Haitian constitution.

Now he claimed to be reversing all this, renouncing the Roosevelt corollary and embarking on a Good Neighbour policy towards South America. Much of this was handled by Hull, who, since the London economic conference failed, had emerged as what W.E. Leuchtenburg calls 'the Galahad of internationalism in a nationalist administration'.[4] He was no such thing. A hard-bitten, hot-tempered Tennessee mountain politician, Hull was throughout the 1930s stronger in word than deed on collective security and on some crucial issues the most powerful appeaser of later German, Italian and Japanese demands. But on the single issue of the tariff his reputation as an internationalist was rock solid. A disciple of 'Locke, Milton, Pitt, Burke, Gladstone and Lloyd George', his economic thinking was a blend of Adam Smith and the cotton South.[5]

Hull now put FDR's Good Neighbour policy into effect. At a special hemispheric conference in Montevideo in December 1933 he voted that no state had the right to intervene in the affairs of another. A few days later Roosevelt renounced armed intervention even more unequivocally. Latin Americans were delighted. In May 1934 the United States and

Cuba signed a treaty abrogating the 1901 Platt amendment, which had empowered America to invade Cuba at will, while in August the last US marines left Haiti. In 1935 the state department concluded reciprocal trade agreements with Brazil, Colombia, Haiti and Honduras, which brought modest benefits to all, and began trade negotiations with nine other Latin American countries. The following year the United States relinquished the right to intervene in Panama. When FDR toured the continent he was greeted as 'The Man' whose New Deal was a model for the kind of reform Latin America needed – 'The fearless and generous man who is accomplishing and living the most thrilling political experience of modern times.'[6] In Rio demonstrators shouting 'Viva la democracia! Viva Roosevelt!' embarrassed Brazil's president Getulio Vargas. 'Perhaps you've heard I'm a dictator,' he whispered to FDR. 'Perhaps you've heard I am one, too,' Roosevelt replied.[7]

The Good Neighbour policy was typical of Roosevelt in that appearance masked reality. It did not make life better for most Latin Americans or change the brutal paternalism of US relationships with them. Yet it was important in winning support in Latin America because influential groups, especially in Argentina and Brazil, had strong pro-fascist sympathies. What this might mean became plain after October 1933, when Nazi Germany withdrew from the Geneva disarmament conference and Adolf Hitler announced he would quit the League two years hence. When Germany did so, in March 1935, Hitler denounced all provisions of the 1919 Versailles treaty, launched an expensive rearmament programme and introduced conscription. Britain, France and Italy – the powers responsible for enforcing treaty compliance – contented themselves with verbal protests, thus anticipating their weak response to further challenges throughout the 1930s. Yet FDR was equally ineffective.

## IV

Abyssinia (now known as Ethiopia) was a case in point. In December 1934 Benito Mussolini, Italy's fascist dictator, used a skirmish between Italian and African troops to pick a quarrel with Emperor Haile Selassie of Abyssinia, one of the few independent African states. Though he had been in power since 1922 and was thus Europe's senior fascist, Mussolini was fearful of being dwarfed by Hitler and his Nazis. He was also eager to establish an African empire and expunge the shame of Adowa in 1896, when spear-carrying African tribesmen had defeated Italian troops. Diplomacy rumbled on throughout 1935 but Mussolini was unimpressed: he wanted a short, victorious war. In October 1935 the war began.

This crisis embarrassed FDR at home. He wanted Congress to pass his 1935 reforms and faced re-election in 1936. Abyssinia was far away; Italian-Americans were a large ethnic group, important to Democrats. Yet African Americans who, thanks to the New Deal, were now voting Democratic in large numbers for the first time, identified passionately with Abyssinia. Between 1933 and 1938 Haile Selassie was second only to the legendary boxer Joe Louis on the front page of the *Chicago Defender*, a leading black paper. Most important, Abyssinia, like Italy, was a member of the League of Nations and once again, as in Manchuria, war was being used to change the map. The United States was not a League member, and though FDR deplored Italy's actions he feared that anything he did might anger isolationists in Congress and endanger the New Deal. Worse, resistance might lead to the very war he and all democratic leaders were desperate to avoid. At this stage he still believed that the best way to defend democracy was not by fighting for it abroad but by asserting it in America.

Most significant, public opinion in the mid-1930s was not ready for the United States to act. Americans generally thought that involvement in the Great War had been a mistake; that Woodrow Wilson's policy of taking unneutral steps had pushed the country into fighting; and that only strict limitations on presidential discretion could keep this from happening again. Accordingly, on 31 August 1935 Congress passed the first Neutrality Act which forbade the export of arms to all belligerent powers, whether flagrant aggressor or defenceless victim. As time went by Neutrality law gave FDR great trouble, involving him in a long, elaborate tango with Congress over foreign policy. But at first it had little effect. Since the United States sent no arms to Abyssinia it meant outlawing arms to Italy.

Other powers were equally embarrassed by the Italo-Abyssinian war. Britain and France, who wanted Italy to join them against German expansion, were reluctant to do anything which might anger Mussolini. The League turned to economic sanctions, put in place after the Manchurian incident, but found France and other powers unwilling to embargo coal and oil. Then in December Britain secretly urged that Abyssinia give in to Italy and be compensated with access to the sea through British Somaliland – what *The Times* called 'a corridor for camels'. Britain and France even persuaded the League to side with aggressor against victim by imposing this settlement on Abyssinia. But when news of this Hoare-Laval plan leaked an explosion of public anger in London destroyed it and drove its advocates, Samuel Hoare and Pierre Laval, from office. By May 1936 Italy had won the war.

This was a deathblow not just to Abyssinia but to the League of Nations. Its 52 members had combined to resist aggression but all they had achieved was that Haile Selassie lost all his country instead of half. The League further offended Italy when it allowed the emperor to address the general assembly and then expelled him for a speech which took the League covenant seriously. America and the Soviet Union had never joined the League; Germany and Japan had left; Italy followed suit in December 1937. As A.J.P. Taylor argues, the League continued only by averting its eyes to everything. When the Spanish government protested about German and Italian intervention in its civil war, the League regretted events but only helped by housing paintings from the Prado in Geneva. It met in September 1938 and in March 1939 without mentioning the Munich crisis and dismemberment of Czechoslovakia. In September 1939 no one bothered to inform the League that European war had begun.

Roosevelt felt sucked into this worldwide tide of war from 1936 onwards. But while the League was disintegrating he knew America was just as powerless and her people as unwilling to act. 'Nearly all the political leaders in Europe and even here', Norman Davis wrote from London, 'are now thinking of how best to prepare for the war they think Germany is going to force upon them.' 'We are back where we were before 1914,' Bullitt reported from Moscow. 'The whole European panorama', FDR responded, 'is fundamentally blacker than at any time in your life ... or mine. These may be the last days of ... peace before the long chaos.'[8] Events in the Rhineland on 7 March 1936 were a decisive and dramatic demonstration of Hitler's strong nerve. For him German reoccupation of the Rhineland (demilitarized in 1919) was vital to his policy of destroying the Versailles treaty.

This treaty was supposed to be enforced by Britain, France and Italy. Had they put up military resistance, Hitler had ordered German troops to withdraw. But, as with German rearmament and conscription the year before, they did nothing. Italy, busy defying the League over Abyssinia, was on the brink of war with Britain and France. France bordered the Rhineland; but the defensive strategy of the Maginot Line meant response was not an option without British backing. Even had Britain's navy and small professional army been able to do anything effective, public opinion, which widely approved Germans liberating their own territory, would have prevented it. Following Manchuria and concurrent with Abyssinia, Rhineland reoccupation was a significant step on the road to war, a road increasingly lit by Anglo-French appeasement.

## V

The Rhineland crisis was the most serious step to war so far but was over so quickly that it confirmed Roosevelt in his detached approach. American sentiment for strict neutrality was being clearly expressed in Congress. Yet events now came so thick and fast that detachment was hard to sustain. Just before the Rhineland crisis storm clouds loomed in Japan when junior officers mutinied on 26 February 1936. In this *Nini roku jiken*, or 2.26 incident, junior army officers murdered a handful of senior politicians. Though this coup failed, 2.26 was decisive in pushing Japan into a more aggressive foreign policy, as became plain in July 1937 when she launched a full-scale invasion of China. Meanwhile, the Spanish civil war added a further twist to the European crisis. In 1931 Spain had become a republic. The 1936 general election gave power, as in France, to a Popular Front coalition of radicals, socialists and Communists who pursued left-wing and largely anti-clerical policies. In opposition to this, a group of generals attempted a coup which, though it failed, precipitated a bitter struggle in which General Francisco Franco led the forces of the army, the Catholic church and big business against the legitimate government, the Basques, Catalans, anarchists, liberals, socialists and Communists generally.

The Spanish civil war raged until the United States recognized Franco's fascist government in April 1939, sharpening the struggle in America between isolationists and internationalists. In September 1936 27 nations formed a non-intervention committee and established a naval blockade. But German and Italian troops openly fought for Franco while the Soviet Union rather less reliably helped Loyalists. While small American Communist and socialist groups, centred largely in Roosevelt's New York, sent volunteers to fight for the Republic, Roosevelt himself was far more worried by American big business and Catholic support for Franco. Moreover, greater worries loomed abroad. In October Germany and Italy formed the Rome–Berlin axis and in November Germany and Japan signed the Anti-Comintern pact. The stage was set for them to overthrow the existing balance of power. Yet after his sweeping re-election in November 1936 FDR's second inaugural on 20 January 1937 had entirely ignored foreign policy, which Donald Richberg, who helped write it, described as 'ticklish stuff to mix into just now'.[9] Spain in fact strengthened the hand of those who opposed US involvement in Europe and, at Roosevelt's request, Congress hastily passed a joint resolution which, with only one dissenting vote, extended existing Neutrality law to the Spanish civil war.

This was a temporary measure which would need renewing within a year. Accordingly, in May 1937, after careful work by Hull (who at this stage had much more control of foreign policy than FDR), Congress adopted a new Neutrality Act. This conceded FDR's constant demand that he be allowed to exercise more discretion in determining when a state of war existed and when a civil war, like that in Spain, endangered world peace. Roosevelt readily signed this 'permanent' neutrality legislation. In July, after full-scale invasion of China, he condemned Japan's attempt to conquer northern provinces and sent 1,200 American marines to Shanghai to reinforce the 2,000 soldiers already on duty in China. However, he explained this was part of an 'inherited situation', and when opinion polls showed 44 per cent favoured withdrawal he began evacuating Americans. The Neutrality Act presented an even bigger problem. The war was undeclared; China was in greater need of arms and loans than Japan; and applying the Act would mainly hurt China so putting Americans in China at risk from antagonized Chinese. Facing conflicting isolationist and internationalist pressure at home, FDR hoped to apply the Act to help China while turning down British overtures for joint mediation of the conflict.

Though the New Deal was largely complete by autumn 1937, FDR was worried about the Roosevelt recession, which had wiped out most of the economic gains made since 1935. Yet foreign affairs now began to dominate his mind. From now on he began diminishing the importance of the state department and Hull's independent role to shape foreign policy himself. On 5 October 1937 he made his 'quarantine the aggressors' speech. This address, one of the most famous he ever delivered, sprang from a proposal by Hull and Norman Davis that he counter growing isolationist sentiment by making 'a speech on international cooperation ... in a large city where isolation[ism] was entrenched'. So in Chicago FDR pointed out that 'the present reign of terror and international lawlessness' threatened civilized values and warned Americans that they could also be attacked. He proposed to all countries, except 'the three bandit nations' of Germany, Italy and Japan, that 'if any nation should invade the rights or threaten the liberties of any other nations, the peace-loving nations would isolate it'. He did not intend to apply this to Spain and China 'because what has happened in those countries has happened'. His central thrust was 'a warning to the nations that are today running amuck'.[10]

Contemporaries assumed that FDR had some specific plan in mind but it was characteristic of him that he did not. 'His plan does not contemplate either military or naval action against the unjust aggressor nation,'

Cardinal Mundelein of Chicago recorded after talking to FDR, 'nor does it involve "sanctions" as generally understood.'[11] When a newspaper correspondent observed that foreign newspapers were describing his speech as an attitude without a programme, Roosevelt retorted, 'It is an attitude and it does not outline a program but it says we are looking for a program.'[12] To help him find one he made Sumner Welles under-secretary of state. Welles was a typical FDR appointment. He found this gifted and creative homosexual foreign policy maker a more congenial adviser than Hull and allowed him to bypass his superior, the whole point being to create division in the state department so that FDR could rule. But the basic contradictions in his foreign policy – fear of aggression but fear that resisting it would lead to war – remained. Moreover, the United States was still completely unprepared for war. Rearmament would have ended the Roosevelt recession in 1937–38 as it had ended unemployment in Nazi Germany. But neither Congress nor the American people were remotely ready for this. In this situation Sumner Welles argued that the world's specific security problems required preliminary general agreements and proposed that FDR ask other nations to join him in establishing 'standards of international conduct'. Roosevelt was enthusiastic. But Hull dismissed this as an 'illogical and impossible' idea: it would lull democratic nations into devising worthless agreements, which the dictators would then repudiate when it suited them. Roosevelt accepted this argument and shelved Welles's plan. Nothing more clearly revealed the fundamental futility of his foreign policy.

## VI

For in reality quarantining the aggressors amounted to little. It neither created a coalition of democratic nations to resist aggression nor made Americans aware that isolationism would not protect them from attack and might actually invite it. Its weakness was all the more apparent when compared with the strength of forces it opposed. For as 1938 began the curtain rose on the last act of the international tragedy. Japan's dismemberment of China continued, while in Spain Franco had cut Loyalist forces in half. Then attention suddenly switched to Austria when, in March, Hitler sent a brutal ultimatum to the Austrian chancellor Kurt von Schuschnigg who was promptly forced from office by pro-Nazi forces. On the pretext of restoring order Hitler sent his newly formed army into Austria, took complete possession and merged it with the Reich. The Anschluss gave Hitler great satisfaction as Austria was his birthplace.

Mussolini, who had stopped Germany's first attempt in 1934, did not act. Neither did Britain and France.

Roosevelt watched aghast. Though the Austrian Republic had only existed since 1919, it was an independent state, with hundreds of years of history, which had disappeared overnight. Deeply disappointed by the passive British response he still refused to endanger their policy of appeasement by strong objection of his own. Instead he limited Hull to restating US opposition to anything that endangered world peace; ended Austria's most-favoured nation status in trade; and set up a committee to help political refugees from Austria and Germany. Pointing out how ineffective the Neutrality laws had been in meeting aggression in China and Spain, he now renewed his campaign to get Congress to give him greater discretion in using embargoes against the aggressors. Though in April he went along with British recognition of Italy's conquest of Abyssinia he found it highly distasteful. Anthony Eden, the British foreign secretary, resigned over it and forced a Commons debate on appeasement. Later, Eden called his memoirs of this period *Facing the Dictators*; but, as A.J.P. Taylor remarks, neither Eden nor FDR was doing much more than making faces at them.

Hitler now created an even more serious crisis in neighbouring Czechoslovakia. German occupation of Austria had made Czechoslovakian frontiers impossible to defend as Hitler now insisted that the three-million German minority in Sudetenland also be joined to greater Germany. As with Austria, there was strong Pan-German sentiment behind this demand, orchestrated by Henlein's pro-Nazi Czech Sudeten party. But strategic motives were more important. It would give Hitler command of the mountains and mineral wealth in Bohemia, destroying not only an outpost vital to the French security system but also the main obstacle to German expansion eastward. Facing torrential German diplomatic and press abuse France, Britain and to a lesser extent America had to decide their attitude. They began by putting pressure on the Czechs to come to terms with Hitler. Yet when German troops massed on the border on 20 May the Czech government mobilized part of its army. In a show of solidarity which surprised Hitler, the French and Soviets reaffirmed their obligations to the Czechs, while London told Berlin that they 'could not guarantee that they would not be forced by circumstances to become involved also'. Facing a credible threat of resistance Hitler was obliged to retreat.[13] This was a moment of truth from which everyone drew different lessons. Hitler, determined never to give way again, wanted military victory. Britain and France, fearful how close they had come to war, agreed to appease him. Yet there was an alternative to appeasement.

France had a pact with the Soviet Union, ratification of which in February 1936 had been Hitler's pretext for reoccupying the Rhineland. Yet to resist Nazi threats the Red Army wanted the right to move defensively into neighbouring states, which those states would not permit and Britain and France could not condone. More important, their fear of Communism was such that the option of using Soviet pressure on Germany's eastern flank was ignored. Even had it been used, Stalin's purges made the Red Army of doubtful strength in 1937–38, while the United States for its part was not even a player. Yet Roosevelt's reaction throughout the crisis was always to urge peaceful settlement, which in reality meant Czechoslovakia giving way.

So as Britain's Neville Chamberlain flew to Germany in September 1938 to talk with Hitler, FDR cabled, 'Good man.' When Chamberlain became prime minister in 1937 FDR had seen him as the 'ablest and most forceful' of Baldwin's ministers who would spare no effort for peace. It took him three visits to complete the final act of appeasement. Czechoslovakia was excluded from discussions but Hitler's demands were so outrageous that Britain and France felt driven to war, which might have suited Hitler: like Mussolini in Abyssinia in 1935 he craved military rather than diplomatic victory. Then Mussolini, the only negotiator who spoke a little of the others' languages, succeeded in moderating Hitler's tone so that the Munich agreement of 30 September gave him the Sudetenland and virtually everything else he wanted – a fine example, like the Hoare-Laval plan for Abyssinia, of the machinery of peace being used against the victim of aggression. Chamberlain claimed to have brought 'Peace for our Time' back from Munich. Those who believed this were rudely awakened on 14 March 1939 when Hitler invaded the rest of Czechoslovakia, transforming Bohemia and Moravia into a protectorate and leaving Slovakia nominally independent. Hitler had now taken land to which Germany had no historic or linguistic claim. Outraged earlier by the plight of the German minority in Czechoslovakia, Germany now had a Czech minority three times as large. More important, Hitler had the Czech airforce, military equipment, the vital Skoda munitions factories as well as German Memelland from Lithuania and a clear road east towards the Soviet Union. Appeasement was dead and world war merely months away.

VII

Though complicit in these events Roosevelt had watched from the other side of the Atlantic with frustration which turned to despair in March. At first opinion polls had shown a large majority of Americans approved the Munich agreement; but the change of mood was such that in January FDR asked Congress to raise defence spending by 1.3 billion dollars to a record 9 billion dollars, which in April they duly did. During the next five months, as Europe moved like a sleepwalker into war, FDR acted as someone who fears the danger of waking sleepwalkers. Joseph Kennedy, his ambassador in London, watched the increasing strength of Nazi Germany with alarm as, on 30 March, Chamberlain gave Warsaw a guarantee that if Poland were attacked Britain would fight in her defence. On 1 April the United States recognized Franco's fascist government in Spain while a week later Italy invaded Albania. With fascist aggression rampant, Roosevelt made a final effort to save the peace. On 14 April he wrote an open letter to Hitler and Mussolini demanding that they promise not to invade any country in Europe or the Middle East in return for an American pledge to cooperate over disarmament and world trade. Hitler waited until the end of the month and then, in one of the most devastating speeches of his life, treated FDR's proposal with scorn and derision which had the Reichstag roaring with laughter.

Hitler's speech struck a chord with American isolationists. They accepted his assertion that he was merely righting past wrongs; that his actions were no more self-interested than those of Britain and France; and that he had no intention of starting a war. If war came they believed it would be a traditional European power struggle in which the United States had no interest. Hiram Johnson, a leading Western progressive, took satisfaction from FDR's humiliation. 'Hitler had all the better of the argument,' he wrote. 'Roosevelt put his chin out and got a resounding whack. I have reached the conclusion there will be no war. Roosevelt wants to fight for any little thing. He wants . . . to knock down two dictators in Europe, so that one may be firmly implanted in America.'[14]

Such self-fulfilling prophecies were not shared by Britain and France, who now turned in desperation to the once-spurned option of talks with the Soviet Union. These dragged on all summer with little chance of success. Quite apart from his deep anti-Bolshevism, Chamberlain could not accept Soviet demands that the Red Army be given the right to march into Poland, Finland and the Baltic states. Even had they accepted this strategic need Britain and France could never have persuaded those countries to agree, for once they let Soviet troops in it was believed they would never leave. Then Hitler and Stalin finally destroyed the fragile peace when the Nazi–Soviet pact astonished the world on 23 August. Bitter ideological enmity between Communism and fascism was forgotten as Stalin agreed to let Hitler invade western Poland if he could take a slice from the east and control the Baltic states, Romania and south-east Europe. Hitler had laid the ghost of fighting on two fronts which had cost Germany the Great War. Stalin, who needed time to repair the serious damage his own purges had done to the Red Army, reckoned on another lengthy war in the west like that of 1914–18. Moreover he resented the fact that, by abandoning the Czechs, Britain and France had driven Germany eastward towards him and, tired of pointless negotiations with London and Paris, sold out to the Nazis. Roosevelt watched such cynical *realpolitik* powerless; Britain quickly made its alliance with Poland formal, extending similar guarantees to Romania and Greece; and when Hitler invaded Poland on 3 September 1939 Britain and France declared war.

Roosevelt could not prevent Germany's brutal air and tank blitzkrieg defeating Poland in three weeks. After Stalin invaded eastern Poland, Hitler offered Britain and France peace, since the issue which had brought them into war was now settled. Anglo-French policy was no longer to appease but to resist; yet until April 1940 this resistance was quite passive. Early in this 'phoney war' as it was known, FDR turned down suggestions from Berlin and Brussels that he initiate peace talks. King Leopold of the Belgians saw Roosevelt as 'the only person in the world' who could keep the conflict from hardening into 'an irrevocable, bitter, real, long and horrible war', but FDR (unlike Hitler) always had a clear grasp of the limits of his power and replied that an American peace initiative should only occur when it was plain that it would succeed.[15] For his part Hitler now turned his attention to the United States. Though he despised American 'mongrel' society (the Roosevelts in particular for their Jewish or African-American backers) and had discounted US military strength, he was anxious to keep it from playing a part in the war. Roosevelt, however, was becoming increasingly convinced that sooner or later America would be forced into it. Grappling with this problem between 1939 and 1941, alerting Congress and the American people to the danger, winning their support for his policies and getting re-elected made this the supreme crisis of his presidency, one which he handled with more skill than any other.

Soviet invasion of Finland on 30 November 1939 threw light on his problem. When his initial admiration for Finland's plucky resistance was replaced by what FDR called 'an isolationist period of second thoughts' he rejected an urgent Finnish plea for help. Such loans, he reasoned, would fan isolationist fears that he meant to involve the United States in war by stealth, thus undermining his ability to secure his real goal of giving guarded aid to Britain and France and winning re-election in 1940, should he decide to run again. So he began to alert moderate isolationists to reality. Few newspaper editors were more influential than William Allen White, a Republican progressive and instinctive isolationist, who had backed cousin Teddy in 1912. 'What worries me, especially,' he told White in mid-December 1939, 'is that public opinion over here is patting itself on the head every morning and thanking God for the Atlantic Ocean (and the Pacific Ocean). We greatly underestimate the serious implications to our own future and ... it really is essential to us ... to warn the American people that they ... should think of possible ultimate results in Europe and the Far East. Therefore, my sage old friend, my problem is to get the American people to think of conceivable consequences without scaring the American people into thinking that they are going to be dragged into another war.' In summary, 'The country as a whole does not yet have any deep sense of world crisis.'[16]

In March the Soviets forced Finland to cede territory near Leningrad before ending the war. Congress, reacting to small but significant movements of voter opinion against extreme isolationism, passed a fresh Neutrality Act which repealed the general embargo on arms contained in previous laws, enabling FDR at last to do what he had repeatedly urged Congress to allow and sell arms to belligerents on a cash-and-carry basis. Now he could choose which nations to help, get payment up front and not risk American merchant ships. This at last gave him what he wanted: the chance to help Britain and France defeat Nazi Germany. Yet they placed surprisingly few orders in the first few months of 1940. After Poland's defeat there had been a standstill in the fighting which encouraged belief that the war would last for years while they could produce their own arms.

## VIII

This illusion ended in April 1940 with Hitler's lightning invasion of Denmark and Norway, followed by Holland, Belgium and France in May and June. Fearful of being left out, Italy, which had earlier occupied Albania, also invaded France. By July fascist powers controlled most of central and western continental Europe and the Soviet Union most of the east. France had been forced to sign an armistice which allowed the pro-German Vichy government to rule half the country to the south. Early in July 1940 British ships sank or damaged much of the French navy at Mers-el-Kebir in North Africa before the Germans could use it, while helping Free French sailors reach British ports. Free French soldiers, led by General Charles de Gaulle, also escaped to London. The British, though routed at Dunkirk, managed to repatriate some 330,000 soldiers but lost all their guns, tanks and equipment. Winston Churchill, who had replaced Chamberlain as prime minister in May, had an American mother, and was a friend of Bernard Baruch. Though he had spent the 1930s in the political wilderness he was, like Roosevelt, a formidable operator. The two men had actually met during the Great War, an encounter recalled with distaste by FDR and forgotten by Churchill. But he now began a personal relationship which, though less close than Churchill liked to believe, was remarkable and probably crucial during the dark days between May 1940 and December 1941. Churchill's upper-class attitudes and hard drinking repelled Eleanor, while FDR's aggressive informality and cavalier approach to statecraft struck Churchill's wife Clementine as presumptuous and somehow fraudulent. Yet shared language, interlocked national histories, close similarities of class and education, love of the Navy and other things put them on the same wavelength. Their incomparable correspondence of nearly 2,000 letters and telegrams, laced with greetings, gifts and wisecracks, was uniquely candid, informal and friendly between two heads of government in wartime. 'It is fun to be in the same decade with you,' FDR told Churchill.[17]

In some ways, each man was trying to bluff the other – Roosevelt about how far he could support Britain, Churchill both about his ability to stand alone and about how much help he wanted. Standing alone against the might of the Third Reich in 1940–41, Britain's need for American aid was paramount. Like Stalin FDR had assumed a repeat of the Great War with two mighty armies deadlocked on the Western front for years. Hitler's amazing victories almost certainly convinced him to run for a third term in 1940. Yet though the American people were as astonished as their president by the speed and completeness of Axis victories, polls showed that 40 per cent still feared that such aid would drag them into war. Roosevelt, running for re-election, had to be cautious since both he and Congress needed to take account of such fears.

He met them head on with boldness not yet shown in foreign affairs, arguing that the best way to keep America out of war was to help the British win it. Ambassador Kennedy in London told the president that German victory was certain, but by September Hitler had lost the Battle of Britain. Still London was under nightly bombardment, while the Battle of the Atlantic was about to begin. Britain needed vast convoys of arms, food and munitions from America to stay in the war at a time when invasion still seemed possible. Most urgently, in order to defend her empire via the Mediterranean, Suez canal and the world's oceans, she needed more warships. So in July FDR secretly agreed to give Churchill 50 obsolete destroyers in return for 99-year leases on British air and naval bases in the Caribbean, Bermuda and Newfoundland. Announcing this, he skilfully muffled public alarm by arguing that the bases strengthened the New World against Nazi attack, calling it 'the most important action in the reinforcement of our national defense . . . since the Louisiana Purchase'. Expected outcry from Congress proved no more than a murmur. 'You can't attack a deal like that,' one senator explained. 'If you jump on the destroyer transfer, you're jumping on the acquisition of defense bases in the Western Hemisphere.'[18] Roosevelt's chances of re-election in November 1940 were not reduced by the deal.

Nor were they by the introduction in August of military conscription for men between the ages of 21 and 35. Though conscription was unprecedented in peacetime, FDR's Republican opponent Wendell Willkie had also called for it, since in 1940 the US army ranked numerically 17th in the world on a par with Romania. However, unable in September to convince the electorate that the New Deal had failed, Willkie abandoned this bipartisan approach and began warning the people that if they elected FDR in November they would be at war in April 1941. FDR counterattacked vigorously, stressing maximum aid to Britain short of war, but making it clear that he could not prevent German or Japanese attack. As argued in the previous chapter, the war issue at first did seem to help Willkie, tempting FDR into sweeping statements about not going to war in any circumstance. In the end, however, since it brought political experience into play, it actually helped Roosevelt far more than Willkie. When re-elected on 7 November Churchill told him, 'I prayed for your success 'and . . . I am truly thankful for it.'[19]

Churchill now asked FDR to sell Britain enough equipment for ten divisions and to increase deliveries of planes from 14,000 to 26,000. Such huge orders would put the American economy on a war footing but FDR readily agreed and made the request public, pointing out that they would create jobs for the 14.6 per cent of the workforce still unemployed. The problem was paying for them and shipping them: two years of war had drained Britain's foreign reserves. Moreover, the Johnson Act meant that, because Britain had defaulted on its Great War debt to the United States, Congress could not legally authorize a loan, while Britain could not pay cash down for multibillion dollar orders. 'Well boys,' the British ambassador Lord Lothian told the press on 23 November, 'Britain's broke. It's your money we want.'[20] This remark angered FDR, who could not understand how the British empire could be broke until Morgenthau confirmed it several times. In a letter he called 'one of the most important

I ever wrote', Churchill emphasized the momentous nature of events. Victory in the Battle of Britain meant that danger of invasion had receded. But 'the decision for 1941 lies upon the seas'.[21]

Lend-Lease, characterized by Churchill as the most unsordid act in history, was Roosevelt's answer. His re-election in November meant that between January and March 1941 he could press Congress to spend seven billion dollars on arms that would be lent to Britain and then returned when the war was over. He used the homely analogy of lending a neighbour your garden hose on the understanding that 'I want my garden hose back after the fire is over'.[22] The difference was that when the war was over arms lent would either be destroyed or obsolete. That Congress accepted such transparent argument was a sign of changed priorities. Lend-Lease alone cost more than the entire US defence budget a year before. Congress, which had tried to cut defence spending in 1940, now quadrupled it to 27 billion dollars.

Churchill explained what Lend-Lease meant to the British by telling the American people in a radio broadcast, 'Give us the tools and we will finish the job.' FDR responded in a fireside chat on 29 December, justifying and encouraging support for his policy of all aid short of war. America must become 'the arsenal of democracy', he explained in one of his most successful speeches. White House messages ran 100 to 1 in favour, while polls showed 80 per cent of those who had heard or read the speech approved. Impressed by Churchill's early great speeches as prime minister, FDR had asked, 'Who writes his stuff?' and was stunned when told he wrote his own stuff. Yet his magnificent oratory, dramatizing Britain's lone fight against tyranny, was primarily designed to raise morale at home, while FDR was always aware of Britain's imperial interests lurking like a spectre at the feast. By contrast, in his Message to Congress on 6 January 1941 FDR told the American people that the war was about defence of Four Freedoms – freedom of speech and religion, freedom from want and fear. Simple and direct as this was, certainly lacking Churchill's eloquence, it had more universal resonance.

None of FDR's political successes could stop the war going badly for Britain in the first half of 1941. In North Africa, German and Italian armies threatened her Mediterranean naval routes, the Suez canal and the oil-rich Middle East, while U-boats were sinking British merchant ships in the Atlantic faster than they could be replaced. The mighty British empire may still have been intact, but with the tiny island of Britain itself in acute peril of invasion or starvation, FDR was asking the American people to share his remarkable optimism that Britain could still win the war without US intervention. Churchill for his part was haunted by the fear that the United States would not come to Britain's aid in time. When in May 1941 FDR predicted further German victories in the eastern Mediterranean and appeared willing to write off that whole theatre, Churchill observed bitterly, 'There has been a considerable recession across the Atlantic and, quite unconsciously, we are being left very much to our own fate. At any rate whatever may be the final stages of the war this fearful moment is likely to be lost.'[23] Yet, moving two steps forward, one step back towards intervention in 1940–41, it is impossible to determine whether he genuinely thought America could stay out. When FDR declared western approaches in the North Atlantic a neutral zone, enforcement (which included occupation of Iceland) effectively brought the United States into undeclared war with Germany. Then on 22 June huge German armies invaded the Soviet Union, transforming the world strategic picture. Churchill, a belligerent anti-Bolshevik, unreservedly welcomed this new ally, whose incalculable sacrifices did more than anything to defeat Hitler. FDR, though more guarded, was equally aware of the need to back Stalin, sending his closest aide Harry Hopkins to Moscow in July.

Here the former head of WPA and FERA was in effect extending Lend-Lease to the Red Army. Though only one of FDR's war cabinet, which included Hull, Morgenthau and Stimson, his standing with his boss now surpassed even that of the late Louis Howe. Hopkins 'had an almost extraordinary perception of Roosevelt's moods,' writes FDR's biographer James MacGregor Burns. 'He knew how to give advice in the form of flattery and flattery in the form of advice; he sensed when to press his boss and when to desist, when to talk and when to listen, when to submit and when to argue. Above all, he had a marked ability to plunge directly into the heart of a muddle or mix-up, and then to act. "Lord Root of the Matter" Churchill dubbed him.'[24]

These dramatic events in Europe and North Africa could not shield Roosevelt from other worries in the Far East and Western hemisphere. As Hitler swept through European Russia, Japan was doing much the same in China. FDR hoped diplomatic and economic pressure, combined with support for Chiang Kai-shek's Chinese Nationalists (the Kuomintang), would force Japan to withdraw. The problem was supply: China could not pay cash or ship war material while Japan could. 'Cash-and-carry works all right in the Atlantic,' FDR explained, 'but all wrong in the Pacific.' The colonial possessions of defeated European powers, including French Indo-China and the Dutch East Indies, were now vulnerable to Japanese occupation and were too extensive for FDR to protect – though when Japan occupied French Indo-China in July he seized all Japanese assets in the United States and banned export of oil and other raw materials to Japan. US relations with French and Dutch possessions in the New World were also problematic. Moreover, primary producers in large Latin American countries like Argentina and Brazil feared losing their lucrative European markets, which fuelled fears that the United States might have to purchase much of their surplus in 1940–41. FDR was also alarmed by the fact that Germany's continued military successes only stimulated the pro-Axis sentiments many of Latin America's ruling class cherished.

So Roosevelt had plenty on his mind when he finally met Churchill on the US cruiser *Augusta* off Newfoundland in August 1941. Newsreels of their joint British–US shipboard church service capture the values which fascism threatened and their determination to destroy it. The Atlantic Charter they then signed announced common principles, which could be summarized as the right of all peoples to enjoy FDR's Four Freedoms. Democratic mobilization, economic liberalization and self-determination were all Roosevelt ideals – although Churchill's attitude to the British Empire, especially India, created drafting problems. Excluded and suspicious, Stalin derided the whole episode, while for Churchill a declaration of peace was a poor substitute for a declaration of war. Yet from August 1941 until April 1945 FDR and Churchill met nine times, with gaps of no more than four or five months between. Moreover, Hitler now knew that the United States was effectively a belligerent. Yet when it fell the blow which finally brought the United States into war came not from Germany but Japan. The carrier-based air attack on Pearl Harbor on 7 December – 'a date that will live in infamy' FDR called it – was the most successful in military history. Five of seven US capital ships were sunk or irreparably damaged at anchor, 120 planes destroyed on the ground, 2,500 sailors and marines killed. The same day Japan attacked the Philippines, Hong Kong, Siam and Malaya, plus Wake and Midway islands. On 11 December Germany and Italy, in alliance with Japan, declared war on the United States while Japan sank the only two British battleships in the Pacific off Hong Kong.

## IX

In these dire straits Churchill went to Washington on 23 December. With both the United States and USSR now his allies Churchill sensed that Britain would become junior partner, but he was also confident of victory. For two weeks he lived in the White House, worrying Eleanor by keeping her husband up late drinking, while he planned strategy and drafted memorable speeches. He was the first British prime minister to address Congress, and recalled in the Canadian parliament that shortly after the fall of France in June 1940 a Vichy spokesman had predicted that in three weeks Britain would have her neck wrung like a chicken. 'Some chicken!' he retorted. 'Some neck!' Arguments that Churchill knew about the impending attack on Pearl Harbor, but did not warn FDR in order to get the United States into war, or that Roosevelt knew and did nothing for the same reason, have no merit. US naval intelligence was completely caught out because it was simply overwhelmed by the amount of conflicting incoming traffic. Anyway, attack would more likely have been against British, French or Dutch possessions than American. Finally, battleships at Pearl Harbor were seen not as a tempting target but as a concentration of strength no one would dare attack. The key points were that the Japanese failed to destroy all the petroleum stored at Pearl Harbor and, by chance, that US aircraft carriers were at sea and so spared for decisive naval counter-attack. This came in May and June with the battles of the Coral Sea and of Midway. After Midway, where US carriers forced Japanese carriers and support ships to retreat, Japan never regained naval initiative in the Pacific, despite holding the Philippines, many other islands and Singapore. By the start of 1943 Germany, Italy and Japan all had reason to regret their temerity in bringing the United States into war.

Yet as FDR looked at the war maps his military staff prepared for him during 1942 they brought bad news for Anglo-American capitalist democracy, to say nothing of Soviet Communism. Japan held many strategic points in the Pacific; British troops were retreating towards Suez in North Africa; German forces were destroying Atlantic convoys, besieging Leningrad and driving deep towards Moscow, Stalingrad and the Caucasus. Moreover, in the United States, many Americans found FDR's unlikely wartime alliance with imperialist Britain and Bolshevik Russia hard to accept. 'Some people want the United States to win so long as England loses,' explained the journalist Elmer Davis. 'Some people want the United States to win so long as Russia loses. And some people want the United States to win so long as Roosevelt loses.'[25]

FDR had been outstanding during the New Deal but as wartime leader and commander-in-chief he is beyond compare. Facing the peculiar burden of civil war and other crippling problems, Lincoln had used his powers vigorously but often ineffectively. By contrast Roosevelt, who had no more military experience than Lincoln, used them with confidence in his own judgement and in a manner which revealed that, in certain large matters, he was oblivious to the advice of his military chiefs. This approach, all of a piece with his domestic style, had begun in the mounting crisis of the 1930s. From Munich onwards he pursued a diplomacy of military deterrence in which – again quite characteristically – military appearances, including aid to allies, were no less important and in many ways more important than military realities.

In July 1939, invoking a rarely used presidential power, FDR issued a military order which transformed the joint Army–Navy board, the joint Army–Navy munitions board and several other military procurement agencies from the service departments into the newly created Executive Office of the President. By this little-noticed military order of 1939 he laid the institutional foundations for his powers as commander-in-chief. No president has used these so broadly. Again his approach was typical. 'Roosevelt's normal method of organizing a department was to split it right down the middle,' writes the historian Eliot Janeway.[26] 'He has no system,' his secretary of war Henry Stimson explained. 'He goes haphazard and scatters responsibility among a lot of uncoordinated men and consequently things are never done.'[27] General Marshall complained of his ignorance of strategic realities and of the baleful influence of the state department.

Yet his 'inherently disorderly' system was, as always with FDR, decisive. Its origin was a Rooseveltian device to get round his isolationist secretary of war Henry Woodring, until he replaced him with Stimson in summer 1940. The forces shaping his relations with the military were various but the effect was unmistakable. Estimates and deliberations of military planners were not entirely without influence and undoubtedly shaped the details of US military policy during the prewar period. But they had only a small effect on the basic grand strategic decisions. In almost all cases Roosevelt made these decisions on his own initiative. For example, the decisions to build 10,000 and later 50,000 planes a year, to give all aid short of war and later Lend-Lease to the Allies, to station the Pacific fleet at Pearl Harbor in the Pacific and not at San Diego in California were his own decisions, taken in many instances without consulting his chiefs.

Thus in 1940, when an air force planner produced figures to show that aid to Britain was undermining American air rearmament, FDR cut him off with a breezy, 'Don't let me see that again.'[28] In 1940, as their RAINBOW plans crystallized, the joint board consistently advanced defence of the Western hemisphere and urged that elsewhere, particularly in the Far East, the United States seek time through diplomacy. 'We are not prepared [for war in the Far East] and will not be for several years to come,' they wrote.[29] But whenever the military advice of his chiefs diverged from his own notions Roosevelt did not hesitate to override them. From the very start of the rearmament programme FDR sought not rearmament but the appearance of rearmament. In 1940–42 'all aid short of war' to Britain, China and the Soviet Union was resisted by military strategists because it risked US involvement in a war scattered across the globe which they most feared. Typically FDR simply ignored all their advice: he neither approved nor disapproved but merely let it all fade away while he pursued his own agenda. Aircraft production was shared 50/50 with Britain, slowing growth of the US air force. Full military assistance was extended to Britain in June 1940 and US convoys sent across the Atlantic against the advice of the joint board. In June 1941 Lend-Lease was extended to China and the Soviet Union while in July, in a climactic act, FDR seized all Japanese assets in the United States and imposed a complete embargo on oil to Japan for invading French Indo-China. The 10-point ultimatum Hull finally sent Japan in November 1940 was approved by FDR without reference to his military chiefs or even his secretaries of war and the Navy.

So by December 1941 events in the Pacific and elsewhere had brought about the very situation Roosevelt's military advisers had sought to avoid: war on two fronts and serious dispersion of American forces. Conscious of US weakness – a Navy only partly ready for war and an Army which, as one observer put it, was to a large extent closed for alterations – they had at each stage opposed undertaking new commitments. At each stage Roosevelt, influenced by wider strategic considerations, had chosen other policies.

Once war began, however, the situation changed. The old joint Army–Navy board was re-formed into the Joint Chiefs of Staff, who met for the ARCADIA conference to plan war strategy in Washington in December 1941. Here FDR took the key decision to give defeat of Hitler priority over defeat of Japan, thus confounding Hitler's contrary prediction, which had helped persuade him to declare war on the United States on 11 December. America's dominant soldier, General Douglas MacArthur, and an influential China lobby urged the contrary, pointing out that Japan already controlled much of China and the Pacific, so FDR's decision was brave as well as intelligent. Only when Germany had declared war could FDR commit troops – as opposed to planes and ships – to fight in Europe and North Africa. Thereafter too General MacArthur and Admiral Chester Nimitz operated in the Pacific without interference. Unlike Churchill – or for that matter Hitler and Stalin – FDR never meddled in the operational planning of his theatre commanders. Yet in 1942, as political and military advice on the direction of the war drifted far apart, he gave one final display of independence in military affairs which repeated, under war conditions, the story of the prewar period.

Worried about the demands of the Pacific war and the worldwide dispersion of US forces, war department planners pushed hard for agreement with the British to meet Stalin's urgent demand for a second front: a cross-Channel invasion of France in 1943. Its importance to the military staff cannot be doubted. As General Dwight Eisenhower, chief of operations division, minuted Marshall in March 1942, 'unless this plan is adopted as the eventual aim of all our efforts, we must turn our backs upon the Eastern Atlantic and go full out, *as quickly as possible*, against Japan!'[30] Yet Operation BOLERO, or the 'Marshall Plan' as the British called it, was overthrown by events in 1942 when one Allied defeat followed another. Japanese thrusts into the Indian Ocean, the Philippines and the Solomons, Rommel's crushing victory in North Africa at Tobruk, German advances deep into European Russia and not least the initial slowness of American war production all combined to persuade FDR to rule in favour of Churchill's plan postponing the second front in France for a year. He also ruled out any diversion of US forces to the Pacific, saying it would be like 'taking your dishes and going away'. Instead, he ordered Marshall and Hopkins to London to agree strategy with Churchill, using an imperative tone such as he seldom employed and signing his instruction, 'Franklin D. Roosevelt, Commander-in-Chief'. The agreed strategy was TORCH, the American–British invasion of North Africa in November 1942, which Stimson called FDR's 'great secret baby'.[31] TORCH held together the Anglo-American coalition until the tide of war began to turn against the Axis in 1943.

Once again luck – the Roosevelt luck – had played its part. For geopolitical and strategic reasons FDR had got America into the global war his military planners had dreaded, confident that such a war would unleash America's matchless industrial might and help Britain and the Soviet Union win. He got away with it; but it was a close-run thing. Had the Battle of Midway, which balanced on a knife-edge, been won by Japan in June 1942, or had TORCH been repulsed or got bogged down in North Africa in November, the war would have looked very different at the end of 1942. But FDR was able to use 1942 to bring America's unequalled industrial power to bear. Endless supplies of guns, tanks, planes, munitions, ships – the United States built 25 aircraft carriers during the war – proved decisive and helped make Roosevelt the greatest commander-in-chief in history. But to supply her own forces and those of Britain and the USSR with the sinews of war FDR, student of Mahan's

*Influence of Sea Power upon History*, knew the Nazi U-boat menace must be destroyed.

What is really striking about this story is that it precisely fits the pattern of his peacetime leadership of divide and rule. Unlike Lincoln, who as commander-in-chief had intervened frequently with his generals, FDR did what his career in domestic politics proved he was best at: set the sights and the large strategic objectives. At home he often overrode advice from Hull and military chiefs, playing his familiar game of setting one group against another. Abroad, in later Big Three conferences with Churchill and Stalin, he often did the same, while at other times he played his old game of weaving the two together. By summer 1942 victory at Midway and Lend-Lease to China were checking Japan's advance, so helping the Europe-first approach. Throughout the year Stalin urged Churchill and FDR to open a second front in France to help relieve the Soviet Union's heavy losses.[32] Instead, as we have seen, Anglo-American forces invaded Casablanca, Morocco, Oran and Algiers on 8 November 1942. Frontal assault on France would take at least two years to prepare. Meantime, FDR believed, TORCH made good strategic sense. It struck Axis forces, retreating after October's defeat by the British 8th Army at El Alamein, from the rear. Anglo-American troops could soon squeeze them out of North Africa.

Despite TORCH's strategic sense it gave FDR new diplomatic problems with France. Facing the threat of Allied invasion of Italy, Germany now violated the 1940 armistice and occupied Vichy France; to which French sailors reacted by scuttling the bulk of the remaining French fleet at Toulon on 26 November. In this new situation FDR flew 7,000 miles, an arduous and dangerous journey via Brazil and West Africa, in January 1943 to meet Churchill at Casablanca. Vichy still governed French North Africa; but from London de Gaulle insisted they now hand over to the Free French. Churchill was sympathetic; but FDR bowed to Hull's view that Vichy was still the legitimate government and that the United States should try to woo Vichy into the Allied camp. De Gaulle, who identified himself mystically with saving the soul of France, was finally forced to accept this snub. FDR, who wished to place French Indo-China and Dakar in West Africa under United Nations mandate after the war, despised de Gaulle and in the crunch Churchill was bound to go along with him. The Frenchman's postwar distrust and suspicion of the Anglo-American 'conspiracy', so important in the 1960s, had its origins here.

Churchill's preoccupation with North Africa, the Mediterranean and Italy meant that FDR did not always find it easy to sustain his 'Europe first' strategy against advisers urging priority in the Pacific. Yet FDR did accept Churchill's plan that they invade Sicily and then drive the Axis north through Italy, even though it meant postponing a second front in France until 1944. Stalin believed he had been badly let down, since FDR and Churchill had repeatedly promised to open this in 1943: North Africa and Italy was a sideshow in Soviet eyes. Yet for his part Stalin gladly approved FDR's insistence, over Churchill's doubts, that the war must only end when the Axis surrendered unconditionally. Then on 30 January 1943 – Roosevelt's 61st birthday and the 10th anniversary of Hitler coming to power – the German 6th Army surrendered at Stalingrad with total losses of 330,000 casualties or captured.

## X

This catastrophic defeat gave Stalin and his generals time to prepare a sustained advance in which US weapons and supplies played an increasing part. But what Stalin wanted most was US and British forces to invade France in strength, so forcing the Nazi High Command to withdraw combat troops from Soviet territory. Stalin was kept informed when FDR and Churchill met in Washington in May 1943 for talks codenamed TRIDENT, which promised intensified aerial bombardment of Germany, invasion of Italy that summer and a second front in France in 1944, a year later than FDR had promised throughout 1942. Six weeks after the TRIDENT talks the decisive battle in defeating Germany in the east occurred at Kursk in Ukraine. German armies launched the greatest tank battle in history, counter-attacking to regain the initiative lost at Stalingrad. Dead and wounded on both sides were 750,000 – more than Britain or the United States lost in the entire war – but German defeat put them in retreat through Russia and eastern Europe until they capitulated in 1945. After Italy surrendered in August, Cordell Hull met British and Soviet foreign ministers in Quebec to plan postwar policy for Germany. This seemed premature: German troops were still fiercely fighting US and British forces up the Apennine spine of Italy.

Yet by autumn 1943 the tide of war was moving so strongly against the Axis that FDR began allowing Hull and the state department more say in policy making. In October, Hull, Eden and Molotov met again in Moscow to plan wider postwar aims. For Roosevelt all this was a prelude to two key summit conferences. The first came on 20–24 November, when he and Churchill met Chiang Kai-shek in Cairo. Though Churchill was frankly bored by China's problems, they had an extraordinary grip on American opinion. Untainted by Communism or imperialism, victim rather than practitioner of power politics, China was above all seen as America's natural democratic ally. FDR's dealings with Chiang during the next two years ended any such illusions he might have held. For he faced a dilemma. Nationalist China was riddled with corruption and weakness; but if the Kuomintang collapsed the United States would have to make an alliance of some kind with Mao's Communists against Japan. Moreover, with Japan swept aside after the war the United States would need China to sustain order and the balance of power in the Far East. For its part, the USSR wanted no association with Chinese Nationalists – for fear Japan would use it as a pretext to attack the Soviets – but also held Chinese Communism in contempt. 'They do not want to get mixed up in all this rot about China being a Great Power,' Churchill told FDR, 'any more than I do.'[33]

While the United States supplied China largely by air from India over the Himalayas – 'the Hump' – FDR wanted Stalin to carry the burden of expelling German armies from the Soviet Union and across eastern Europe, thus breaking Germany's will to fight, with a promise that the USSR would then immediately join the United States to defeat Japan. This and the exact date of the second front were the most significant issues raised when the Big Three finally met at Tehran on 23–27 November. Stalin for his part was able to commit FDR to a precise time and place for invasion of France, while the Big Three agreed that postwar partition of Germany would forestall future resurgence. Roosevelt also outlined his plan for creation of a postwar United Nations. Having established a good working relationship with Churchill, he had been keen to meet Stalin since June 1941 and, though he had no illusions about the nature of Soviet tyranny, he liked the man. 'What helps a lot,' he explained, 'is that Stalin is the only man I have to convince. Joe doesn't worry about a Congress or a Parliament. He's the whole works.'[34] He began by treating Stalin like an American political boss and, though quickly finding that his charm for once failed, the prevailing spirit of cordiality at Tehran convinced him that he had laid the basis for peaceful postwar US–Soviet cooperation. 'All my hopes for the future of the world', he wrote, 'are based upon the friendship and cooperation of the western democracies and Soviet Russia.'[35]

By the time of the Tehran conference the Anglo-American alliance had ceased to be an equal partnership and become one dominated by the United States. Moreover, Soviet–American relations had moved centre stage and FDR was eager to meet Stalin alone, without British interference. Churchill, who did meet Stalin alone twice, was equally determined to prevent this. For an underlying diplomatic reality was now emerging.

From Wilson to Roosevelt American foreign policy had been based on a radical critique of international relations as conducted by the European powers. Calls for arms control, the elimination of trade barriers and establishment of governments responsive to the needs and aspirations of their citizens – thus ending colonialism and 'oppressive' spheres of influence – were all based on the American belief that European leadership had failed. Bolshevism, fascism and Nazism were distrusted and feared, but not blamed for the collapse of international order in the 1930s. Most Americans placed responsibility for the world crisis on Britain and, to a lesser extent, on France. It was British greed and power politics, so the argument went, that had prevented the development of effective international cooperation and thus permitted the dictators to run amuck.

Moreover, though preoccupied with Europe and the Pacific, FDR still faced the nagging problem of China. Here General Joseph Stilwell acted as his proconsul throughout 1943–44, dealing directly with Chiang Kai-shek. If Stalin reminded FDR of a brutal American political boss like New Jersey's Frank Hague, the Kuomintang reminded 'Vinegar Joe' Stilwell of a cross between Tammany Hall and the Spanish Inquisition. Chiang – called 'Peanut' by Stilwell – constantly clamoured for more US aid. Yet according to Stilwell he hoarded this, not to fight Japan, but to destroy the Chinese Communists once the United States had won the war. In Stilwell's view Chiang would refuse what FDR wanted – democratic reform, a united front with the Communists or any real fighting – 'until, by delaying tactics, he can throw the entire burden on us'. By summer 1944 FDR had had enough and in September ordered Chiang to give Stilwell command of the Nationalist army and make common cause with the Communists. This message, 'with a firecracker in every sentence', in historian Barbara Tuchman's words, 'accepted Stilwell's view of Chiang as incapable of managing his country's role in the war. It called him Peanut by implication.'[36] Stilwell, who 'leapt at the chance to plunge it into the Peanut's heart', delivered it personally. As he gleefully told his diary, 'The harpoon hit the little bugger right in the solar plexus, and went right through him. It was a clean hit, but beyond turning green and losing the power of speech, he did not bat an eye. He just said to me, "I understand."'[37]

Harpooned or not, Chiang bested both Stilwell and FDR. On 1 October his finance minister wired him from Washington to say that 'Harry Hopkins had told him at a dinner party that ... since it concerned the Sovereign Right of China, the President intended to comply with the Generalissimo's request for the recall of General Stilwell'.[38] In the crunch

Roosevelt could not force Chiang to accept that, since the United States was supplying Nationalist forces in China, a US general should command them. On 21 October 1944 Stilwell left China for Washington via India. In giving in to Chiang FDR accepted General Marshall's advice that no American officer replace Stilwell. Henceforth the best FDR could hope from China was containment of some of Japan's forces on the Asian mainland as the United States fought its way, island by island, across the Pacific while in China Communist forces grew more powerful. His constant fear of Chinese collapse was relieved by news about the development of the atomic bomb and by repeated assurances from Stalin that the USSR would join the war against Japan as soon as Germany surrendered. But just as postwar Soviet suspicions of the West were partly fuelled by delaying the second front in France, or by US refusal to share information about the atomic bomb, so FDR's policy in China foreshadowed Communist victory there in 1949.

Events more tragic than those in the Soviet Union or China were unfolding in central Europe. By 1944 the US government had reliable intelligence reports from Poland, Hungary and other parts of occupied Europe which revealed that Nazi Germany was using the cover of war to liquidate European Jewry. Though the factory process by which millions were murdered in Auschwitz, Sobibor, Treblinka and other extermination camps did not become clear until after his death, FDR was aware of the scale of Nazi persecution. Posthumously he was criticized for failing to do anything effective to help the victims escape, especially as German persecution of Jews was well in train throughout the 1930s. In fact, it was Congress who failed to reform US immigration law to allow refugees from Nazism to escape to America in large numbers; the fate of European Jewry was not a priority in the United States in the 1930s, any more than foreign affairs was until about 1938; and once war had started it was impossible for the United States or Britain to stop the mass murder of millions in the Holocaust. Just as the leaders of democratic nations failed to grasp that Nazi Germany was bent on the conquest of Europe in the 1930s, so they did not take seriously Hitler's public pledge that he would use the war he started in 1939 to make Europe 'Jew free'. Roosevelt was complicit in this failure, but so too was Churchill, while Stalin's anti-Semitism was comparable to that of Hitler.

While the Holocaust absorbed dwindling Nazi manpower and resources in 1944–45, the United States was developing the atomic bomb in New Mexico, while FDR's war strategy in western Europe moved steadily towards victory. On D-Day – 6 June 1944 – Anglo-American forces at last opened the second front in France with Operation OVERLORD. US troops took the heaviest casualties and, despite overwhelming air and naval superiority, met tough resistance in Normandy so that Caen did not fall until July. Had Roosevelt and Churchill opened the second front in 1943 when Stalin wished it would almost certainly have been repulsed. But by September 1944 two million men and three million tons of supplies and equipment had been landed in Normandy. As unconditional surrender neared, two crucial international conferences met. Though FDR attended neither, as president he takes credit for what happened. The first, in July at Bretton Woods, moved the financial agenda of the early New Deal on to the world stage by planning postwar financial and trading arrangements. J.M. Keynes (who had tried to influence FDR during the New Deal) and Harry Dexter White played key roles. Conflict over debt, finance and trade, which had poisoned interwar world politics, was to be avoided. The International Monetary Fund would stabilize national currencies; the World Bank would lend money for postwar reconstruction and investment; while all currencies would take their value from the US dollar.

The second conference, at Dumbarton Oaks from August until October, planned the postwar United Nations, or UN. Everyone wanted to avoid the weakness which had ruined the League; but British, Soviet and US delegates could not agree at this stage on UN voting procedures, a code of international law or effective enforcement of UN policy. FDR was horrified, for example, to learn that Stalin wanted each of the federated Soviet republics to have a vote, which would have given him control of 16 votes. He jokingly responded by arguing that each state of the American Union be granted the same right, which would have given the United States 48 votes. In the end Stalin was satisfied with European Russia, Ukraine and Byelorussia voting. Bretton Woods and Dumbarton Oaks ensured that the United States was determined to prevent a repeat of the economic and diplomatic conflicts which had soured interwar diplomacy. Yet FDR took time off from such postwar problems to beat his Republican opponent Thomas Dewey handily at the polls in November, despite rumours about his failing health. Roosevelt was not 63 until January; but eleven years in office, through depression and war, with exhausting trips to Casablanca and Tehran, had taken their toll so that at times he looked like a much older man. Yet he could still recover quickly and in February he went to Yalta on the Black Sea to agree postwar world political arrangements with Churchill and Stalin.

The myth of Yalta, which haunted the public memory of FDR in the 1950s, was that sick and full of liberal illusions he sold out to Stalin. The reality is quite different. For a start, he was not ill at Yalta and had no illusions about Stalin, liberal or otherwise. Friendly postwar relations between capitalism and Communism, which he had once hoped for, he now realized would be almost impossible to achieve if the Soviets did not relinquish their ideology and their wartime control of central and eastern Europe. This was the reality of the Yalta conference and if he sold out so did Churchill, who, if anything, went further than FDR in agreeing spheres of influence in eastern Europe and the Balkans. What determined Yalta was not just the presence of the Red Army but the enormous sacrifice – amounting at a conservative estimate to 20 million dead – the devastated Soviet Union had made fighting Germany. Hitler could not be beaten without the Red Army; and the political price FDR and Churchill paid was to cede Stalin control of Poland, eastern and central Europe. Germany would also be partitioned and Outer Mongolia fall under USSR control because of the Soviet military presence. Stalin conceded FDR's demand that the Polish government in exile must be allowed to form a coalition with the Communists; but Roosevelt realized that there was every likelihood that they would soon be squeezed out.

As we have seen, he made no great claims for the Yalta agreement, explaining to Berle that the result was not good but the best he could do.[39] Reporting back to Congress on 1 March he broke all precedent and spoke sitting down, admitting for the only time in public that he wore leg braces. The 14,000-mile round trip to Yalta had tired him but he bounced back as usual. Then on Easter holiday at Warm Springs on 12 April, posing for a portrait, he suddenly clutched his temple crying, 'I have a terrific headache' and collapsed. Two hours later he died. 'My Fuhrer,' Joseph Goebbels, who controlled Nazi propaganda, told Hitler. 'I congratulate you. Roosevelt is dead. It is written in the stars that the second half of April will be the turning point for us. This is almost Friday, April 13. It is the turning point!' In Japan Radio Tokyo surprisingly honoured 'the passing of a great man' with a programme of special music.[40] Roosevelt had died on the very brink of victory and people all over the world were shocked and saddened. No one said, as Stanton said of Lincoln, that now he belonged to the ages, but it would have been a fitting epitaph for a president regularly ranked by historians with Lincoln as the greatest in history since Washington established the institution.

Conclusion

_____

❀

# Sex, Money and Power

I

America was still mourning Roosevelt's death when, on 30 April 1945, Hitler took his own life and the Nazi regime collapsed, surrendering unconditionally on 8 May. In July American, British and Soviet leaders met at Potsdam to plan peace in Europe and victory in Asia. This came sooner than the world expected when, on 6 and 9 August, the United States dropped atomic bombs on Hiroshima and Nagasaki forcing Japan into unconditional surrender. Though the most terrible war in history was over, it shaped world events for the rest of the twentieth century. Roosevelt's successor Harry Truman, like every president until the 1990s, had to work in the shadow of FDR.

II

As Eleanor Roosevelt stood by her husband's coffin travelling north to Hyde Park by train she knew that she was burying a great man. But she had only just learned that his former mistress Lucy Mercer had been present at Warm Springs when he died; that in the months since her own husband died Lucy had been secretly seeing Frank in Washington and elsewhere; and that her daughter Anna Roosevelt had been the go-between in this deception. The pain this must have caused her is hard to imagine. Yet it is all of a piece with FDR's private life and indeed with his method as political operator.

He had grown up playing off his doting mother Sara against his father James, whose age was that of a grandfather. After his father died he met Eleanor, failed to tell his mother that they were engaged and then played wife against mother. When his family was growing up he met Louis Howe, began a remarkably close relationship with him, and played Howe against wife and mother. The same pattern continued later with Missy LeHand, Harry Hopkins, Harold Ickes, Henry Wallace, Sumner Welles and many others. A prime feature of Roosevelt's executive method was to play one adviser, one agency, one department against another to keep him in control and effect creative tension.

This was equally important in his private life. But here the central question is about his sexual activity. Eleanor's discovery of his affair with Lucy Mercer in 1918 was a landmark in his life. His daughter Anna believed that they never resumed sexual relations. Eleanor's most recent biographer Blanche Wiesen Cook doubts that Anna was right about this. Whatever the truth, we do know that they had not just separate bedrooms, which was common at that time at their age and social class, but separate homes and essentially separate lives. After polio struck FDR this became useful to him. Eleanor became his ears and eyes, so that he relied heavily on her for political information and propaganda, especially among African Americans. 'My Missus tells me different' was his frequent comment on reports from presidential aides. But she was rarely by his side. Her absences were so well known that when he was president the fact that she spent a night at the White House would make news.

The question of what they did for sex is complicated in Frank's case after 1921 by the even more delicate question of what the disabled do for sex. He had met Missy LeHand, before polio struck him, on the 1920 vice-presidential campaign. She was a strikingly beautiful young woman who, like Lucy, was a Southerner and a Roman Catholic. She made no secret of her love for him, while Eleanor came to regard her as an Indian-style wife No. 2. But despite the amount of time she spent with him, or the opinion of one of his cousins that Missy was the only woman he ever loved, there is no evidence that FDR did anything other than make use of her devotion, or that they had a sexual relationship. Indeed, his other secretary Grace Tully, who was also very close, laughed such an idea to scorn. However, when FDR took out a million-dollar life insurance, largely for political reasons, in 1928 his doctors went out of their way to say that he was potent and we can infer that he was sexually active. The question remains: who with?

As Tony Badger points out, the evidence suggests it is unlikely that Roosevelt had sexual relations with any woman after the polio attack.[1] His intense drive to win political power and his pleasure and matchless skill in using it might in part be explained as compensation for this loss. Equally clearly, he relished the undemanding and relaxing attention of attractive women, especially Missy LeHand, when almost all his other friends and contacts wanted something from him. His cousin Margaret

'Daisy' Suckley was another younger woman whose relaxed company Roosevelt enjoyed. No one knew it at the time but, after she died, Geoffrey Ward edited her diary and letters to reveal an intense, touching and close relationship which lasted from Roosevelt's inauguration in 1933 until his death, at which, like Lucy Mercer, she was present.[2]

Eleanor too had admirers and, up to 1933 at least, a big, handsome young bodyguard, Earl Miller. She even used jokingly to threaten to run away with him, especially when it became clear that Frank's election, for which she had worked so long and hard with Howe, would inevitably end the independent life she had enjoyed in the 1920s. For his part FDR fixed up dates between Missy and Miller to take attention off Missy, himself and Eleanor. Yet Eleanor's love-life only moved centre stage in 1979 when the Roosevelt Library at Hyde Park opened 2,336 letters between her and the journalist Lorena Hickok. These reveal a passionate relationship which began about 1928. Eleanor wished 'I could lie down beside you tonight and take you in my arms.' Hickok remembered 'The feeling of that soft spot just north-east of the corner of your mouth against my lips'.[3]

Blanche Wiesen Cook notes that, apart from these letters, much of the documentary record of her relationship with lesbian friends and with Earl Miller has disappeared or been destroyed and that this represents 'A calculated denial of ER's passionate friendships'. She concludes that Eleanor led a life 'dedicated to passion and experience' and that her relationships with Hickok and Earl Miller were 'erotic and romantic', 'daring and tumultuous'.[4]

As with FDR and Missy LeHand we will probably never know whether Eleanor slept with Lorena Hickok. Moreover, the passionate language they use in their letters is very similar to that in the letters Carroll Smith-Rosenberg discovered in the nineteenth century in which women, very much restricted to a 'separate sphere' of existence at home and assumed to be passionless, felt free to express their full emotional range to female friends. The crucial point, in Eleanor's case, is that her personal life was not created by Louis Howe and others designed simply to keep Frank's name alive while he was incapacitated by polio, but was more a personal assertion of her right to independence after the Mercer affair. Nor was he a purely passive participant in this process. He took women seriously, both respecting the political skills of his wife and growing accustomed through her to working with other talented and forceful women. Finally, as noted above in Chapter 4, the strength and long duration of the unique political partnership of Frank and Eleanor was all the more remarkable since it took place within a context of personal separation.

Not surprisingly, the Roosevelt children wondered whether their parents' relationship with each other and with them made their lives more difficult and unhappy. FDR relied on his sons for physical help and no doubt manipulated them in other ways, as he did everybody in his life. Whatever success he won in politics, he may have failed as a father. Certainly, Eleanor felt guilty that the demands of public life had prevented them playing a proper parental role. Whatever the truth, the fact is that the five surviving children had 17 marriages between them; that two of their spouses committed suicide; and that a third attempted to murder James by stabbing him in the back with a wartime marine knife. Apart from the unusual nature of their parents' private lives discussed above, other odd events must be mentioned. Determined that her beloved grandchildren receive enough fresh air, Sara Delano Roosevelt daily placed Anna and James in a chicken-wire cage outside their bedroom window high above the sidewalks of New York and only stopped when a neighbour threatened to report Eleanor to the Society for the Prevention of Cruelty to Children. One of several English nannies locked Elliott in a cupboard and turned the key so hard it broke. It took hours to release him. But the nanny was only sacked when Eleanor found empty gin and whisky bottles in her room. Elliott later wrote a number of mystery novels but none of that generation of Roosevelts was successful, existing only on the fringes of public life, as their family name and fortune went into eclipse.

FDR's private life is further complicated by the fact that he always had a close, intense relationship with another man – at first with Louis Howe and then, after Howe's death in 1936, with Harry Hopkins. Both lived in the White House and were always on call. Both were so like each other – untidy, even ugly but with beautiful eyes, unconventional, tough-talking, secular frequenters of the race-track – and so unlike FDR that it suggests the psychological importance of these two key relationships. Though there was clearly no overtly homosexual element in them, Harold Ickes's biographers argue that there was a strong homoerotic element in the admiration which Ickes and many other close political colleagues, such as Hopkins, Morgenthau and Wallace, had for FDR which expressed itself in the fierce rivalry they felt for each other and the ruthless way they competed for his attention. Discussing Ickes's secret diary, they comment, 'To call such a warm current of feeling "homosexual" is not for a moment to accuse Harold Ickes of unconventional practices ... Yet though such affections may have become entirely divorced from any bodily aim, they still provide almost as fertile a breeding ground for jealousy and possessiveness as heterosexual ones do.'[5]

183

Take for example an extraordinary entry in Ickes's unpublished manuscript diary for 14 May 1936. He believed passionately that his own PWA was spending wisely to relieve unemployment compared with the way the WPA headed by Hopkins squandered money. But in a confrontation with FDR the president ordered him not to make comparisons which were unfavourable to Hopkins, telling him exactly what to say and adding that if Congress should earmark any money for Ickes's PWA he would veto the bill. 'I was pretty angry by this time,' Ickes concludes. 'It was clear as day that the president was spanking me hard before the full cabinet and I resented that too. All the other members appeared to be embarrassed, but I could see Henry Morgenthau stealing a covert glance at me from time to time. Doubtless he enjoyed the spanking very much.'[6]

We will probably never know the answer to the question of who either Frank or Eleanor slept with. So is the question legitimate? Does the affair with Lucy Mercer matter to the historian? The answer is yes because people are bound to speculate and because the importance of their political lives has to be judged against what we know about their private lives. Moreover, sex is not the only topic. Money is another element which enters the Roosevelt equation. He appeared wealthy and was indeed the first American president to leave more than a million dollars when he died. Yet compared with his Hudson Valley neighbours like the Astors or Vanderbilts, he was not rich. According to the historian Richard Hofstadter, this sense in which the traditional ruling class were being dwarfed by even richer men was what drove progressives like FDR and his cousin Teddy into politics. In any case by the 1920s FDR was living beyond his means, feeling the pinch, borrowing from his mother and seeking, with conspicuous lack of success, to increase his income by speculating on the stock market. After eight years of having to entertain in Washington on an assistant secretary's salary, with five children to bring up in upper-class style, all the extra costs which polio brought and with the additional burden of meeting Louis Howe's salary and many other political expenses, he had to ask his mother Sara for help, while his letters to Eleanor in the 1920s are full of worries about money, bills unpaid for months, allowance cheques for the children missed and so forth.

Then he took the enormous risk of using most of his capital to buy Warm Springs and run it as a health spa. Sara lost no time in blaming Eleanor for all this. Eleanor's consequent need for financial independence was a powerful reason driving her to work as an entrepreneur at Val-Kill, into the education business at Todhunter school and into syndicated journalism. Most of these enterprises were of doubtful financial success; but journalism eventually became so profitable that in the 1930s she could proudly boast that she was earning more than FDR did as president.

### III

In politics FDR's use of power was even more Machiavellian than in his private life. 'Never let your right hand know what your left is doing,' he once told Morgenthau. 'Which hand am I, Mr President?' Morgenthau asked. 'My right hand,' he replied. 'But I keep my left under the table.'[7] Morgenthau (who was very close) called this the frankest expression of the real Roosevelt he ever heard. But it was far from unique and he enjoyed his virtuosity. On another occasion he boasted to Morgenthau about his skill in showing a senatorial delegation that he was willing to accept a bill on silver to which his administration was formally opposed. 'I was good,' he explained. 'With my right arm I said "Not one inch will I give in, not an inch." But with my left hand I said, "Boys, come and get it."'[8] Charles Taussig, waiting in the presidential anteroom, caught a glimpse of FDR after he had succeeded in calming an angry Congressional delegation. Roosevelt, unaware that he was being observed, leaned back, slowly picked out a cigarette, stuck it in his holder, lit a match and took a long puff. 'A smile of complete satisfaction spread over his face.'[9]

'Roosevelt had a love affair with power,' writes Richard Neustadt. 'The White House for him was almost a family seat and like the other Roosevelt he regarded the whole country almost as a family property. Once he became president of the United States that sense of fitness gave him an extraordinary confidence. Roosevelt, almost alone among our presidents, had no conception of the office to live up to; he was it. His image of the office was himself-in-office. The memoirs left by his associates agree on this if nothing else: he saw the job of being president as being FDR.'[10] Distrustful of the state department and the Pentagon, he divided responsibility for foreign affairs and defence from the late 1930s onwards (as he had earlier over the economy) and frequently overrode the advice he received. During the war the diplomat George Kennan disagreed with his bosses over policy towards Portugal and Spain. Recalled to Washington he met Stimson, Knox, Stettinius and the Joint Chiefs but made no headway. Then he succeeded in seeing the president, who endorsed his solution. But what about the people in the Pentagon, who seemed intent on a different course? 'Oh, don't worry', the president told Kennan with a debonair wave of his cigarette holder, 'about all those *people* over there.'[11] 'Those people' were instruments of presidential purpose, expressions of FDR's designs on foreign affairs.

Clearly he was a maestro in the use of power in both private and public life. What guided him and what ends he used it for is more problematic. He believed in God but had a healthy respect for Mammon and was always ready to render unto Caesar – especially when he was Caesar. Yet his record on an issue he really cared about, like conservation – in dam building, flood control, planting shelter belts and reforestation – was impressive. Despite his warm human sympathies and incomparable intuition, he was above all a political pragmatist. But there are some guides to his conduct. Roosevelt's roots were in the progressive period. Conservation, the attack on monopoly, the need for regulation and control in the public interest all stem from his progressive past. Less radical than the La Follettes in Wisconsin or Robert Wagner in New York, he did not follow Western and Midwestern progressive politicians like Burton K. Wheeler and Gerald P. Nye, who became heroes of the isolationist right in the 1930s. Indeed, FDR led the United States on to the international stage. By contrast the progressive Hiram Johnson disgusted Ickes, who had idolized him in the 1920s, when he approved Hitler's notorious April 1939 speech deriding FDR and then backed Willkie, 'a slicker, private utilities man, political corruptionist', in 1940.[12]

Progressivism influenced not only FDR's agenda but also his method. As a progressive he observed the changing nature of city bosses and their political machines at close quarters in New York. As he moved up in politics reformers were becoming more realistic, bosses more responsible and supportive of social reform. This pattern had first emerged in the 1890s, with men like Boss Hazen Pingree in Detroit; but Charles Murphy and Edward Flynn in New York were examples closer to hand. There is every reason to think that FDR was deeply influenced. As president he ran public affairs like a benign boss, distributing services and favours in return for votes, seeing that each major section of society got something, trading interests off against each other, integrating the community again.

His use of Irish-American politicians within the Democratic party was instructive and ruthless. He used Farley to help defeat Smith in 1932 and then Flynn to help defeat Farley in 1940. His political skill also enabled him to work happily with corrupt city bosses like Frank Hague and Tom Pendergast, as well as with progressive reformers like Fiorello La Guardia, whose term of office as mayor of New York City coincided almost precisely with FDR's as president. Indeed, at times he hoped he might help create a new reform leadership in US politics in which progressive Democrats like himself would combine with Republicans like La Guardia, William Allen White and even Wendell Willkie.

New Deal reforms undermined the old boss system Roosevelt understood so well. Yet what he hoped reform would achieve is another question. Rex Tugwell said that what FDR wanted in 1933 was for most Americans to have a better deal and greater social security like European nations. For to understand him we must move beyond American progressive reformism to European models. Clearly he was not a social democrat like Robert Wagner. Yet in searching for what guided him in politics few historians have followed his famous explanation – 'I'm a Christian and a Democrat. That's all' – to its logical conclusion. In European terms it makes sense to see Roosevelt as a Christian Democrat. It is easy to imagine Roosevelt, for example, operating in postwar Italian politics during the 1950s and 1960s, forming coalitions, keeping the Communists from power and marginalizing the socialists by passing social reform. The only difference is that he was Protestant and would have given Italy the kind of strong, executive leadership which in many ways the system craved but which the political class rejected like poison. But much of the American political class rejected it too. Few presidents have been selected because politicians wanted to increase the power of the presidency – indeed, probably none since George Washington, who was selected precisely for that purpose.

But in the depths of the great depression they got it from FDR. The Democratic party was glad because Roosevelt transformed domestic politics and the relative positions of Republican and Democratic parties. The New Deal made the Democrats, who had usually been out of power since the Civil War, the natural party of government. What had been a Southern-based agrarian party became in the 1930s and after a national coalition largely focused on urban social reform. But FDR was always the political realist. He knew what kept this unlikely coalition together. Reform must leave white supremacy in the South intact and do nothing to bring civil rights to African Americans. He was not really interested in this problem anyway, unlike Eleanor, whose efforts for black Americans helped shift their support from the party of Lincoln and emancipation to FDR and the New Deal.

In the 1940s Republicans had recovered sufficiently to combine with Southern Democrats in Congress to limit further New Deal reform. But with the conservative South still voting Democrat after FDR died, Republicans found it hard to recapture the White House. Between 1932 and 1964 the GOP only elected one president, the war hero General Eisenhower, in 1952 and 1956. In the next thirty years, however, they won every presidential election but that of 1976, which followed Nixon's resignation over Watergate. FDR's politics encouraged two competing coalitions which continued until the end of the century. One was of the kind of social welfare and urban reform represented by Harry Hopkins and Robert Wagner. For a time FDR backed some of this, if not powerful labour unions like the UAW, with limited social security, though he failed in public housing. Conservative Southern Democrats went along with this for a while but made it clear that civil rights was off limits. The other tradition was the kind of anti-Prohibition, anti-statist, anti-regulation, pro-business beliefs which had been strong in the Democratic party in the 1920s and emerged again under Raskob and Smith with the Liberty League in the 1930s. The Dixiecrat–Republican coalition included this element.

In the 1948 presidential election Strom Thurmond ran as a Dixiecrat against civil rights, and Henry Wallace as a Progressive seeking rapprochement with the Soviet Union and more social reform. Though Truman won, this three-way split revealed fault lines in the Democratic party, especially the fact that Thurmond carried Alabama, Louisiana, Mississippi and South Carolina. In 1960 those states split between Kennedy and the symbolic candidacy of Harry Byrd while in 1964 they all went Republican for the first time. Lyndon Johnson used his huge victory that year to get Congress to pass his Great Society programme and try to complete the unfinished business of his idol FDR. Welfare reform, the 'war on poverty', even Medicare and Medicaid were not embraced but accepted. Civil rights and voting rights for African Americans were opposed by the white South. This was a defining moment. The white South stopped voting Democratic; the New Deal coalition in the North broke down; and a series of Republican presidents – Nixon, Ford, Reagan and Bush – cut taxes, deregulated, generally undid the legacy of FDR and governed in the interests of corporate America. The Raskob–Smith tradition had been substantially resurrected.

## IV

Such long-term conservatism was encouraged by other factors. Keynesian economics may not have worked so well when first unwittingly tried by FDR in the 1930s. By the 1950s and 1960s they were creating the most sustained prosperity in US history. Similarly, the idea of the 'broker state', with FDR acting as broker between competing national interests, such as bosses, workers and consumers, was the way the political economy functioned in the 1960s. FDR's failure in public housing, discussed above, must be set against his refinancing of homeowners' mortgages during the New Deal. This fostered an era of widespread home ownership and suburban sprawl a generation and more later. Yet FDR had nevertheless revolutionized party politics and set the agenda for a generation in ways which could not be undone. First, he enhanced the power of the presidency. The unprecedented burst of 15 major laws in three months which began the New Deal continued with the second New Deal, the 1938 Fair Labor Standards Act and the 1939 Administrative Reorganization Act. This last measure made the presidential office more efficient, partly through the little-noticed executive order 8248, which expanded the size of the president's staff. FDR's zestful use of power as war president and commander-in-chief, through Lend-Lease and all the other war measures, completed the process. Equally important was his use of radio and newspaper reporters to publicize his policies and himself. Though he was careful to limit the number of radio broadcasts he made, delivering only 12 in his first two terms, their impact was such that with hindsight people came to believe that the fireside chat had been a weekly event.

More than any president Roosevelt understood that the source of his power was the votes of the people. The president alone among members of the federal government is put in office by the vote of the entire nation. No other president was so successful at appealing over the heads of his opponents in Congress, the Supreme Court or elsewhere to the people as a whole. Not only did he win huge victories; he won more of them than any other president. During the international crisis of 1940 he ran for a third term and then for a fourth in 1944. He had become what the Founding Fathers had most feared: an elected king. The 22nd Amendment to the Constitution restricting future presidents to two terms, ratified in 1951, was the direct result. But after FDR the presidential office would never be the same again and would always be more powerful than it had been under Harding and Coolidge, or even Teddy Roosevelt and Woodrow Wilson.

By expanding the president's power FDR inevitably expanded the power of the federal government. Before 1932 Washington was still a small, sleepy Southern town. The federal government counted for much less than it does today. Coolidge's notorious comment as head of government that, if everyone connected with it were to die, months would pass before most Americans noticed was essentially true. The average person's only contact with the federal government in the 1920s was when they visited a federal post office or mailed a letter. They might occasionally see a member of the armed forces. That was about all. By 1940 that had changed for ever. Intervention to save banking and Wall Street, planning agriculture and industry, public works to stimulate employment, TVA to generate public power, flood control and soil conservation, federal regulation of labour relations, social security and a whole host of other measures created a network of federal agencies which the war economy greatly increased. Perhaps for the first time the federal government was seen as a friend of the common man, enhancing his freedom by such measures as the GI Bill, which helped so many ex-servicemen after 1945, not simply as a faceless bureaucracy forever raising taxes. The modern power, reach and scope of the federal government, nationally and internationally, in which both Congress and the Supreme Court came to share, sprang from roots which Roosevelt planted during the New Deal and the Second World War.

How does one explain FDR's successful use of power? Part of the answer is that, although not an ideas man himself, he was so adept at using ideas in government. These ideas came from intellectuals like the brains trust and remarkably high-quality people, like David Lilienthal at TVA, who joined government service during the New Deal. Even more important, he and others like Harry Hopkins were very successful in transforming those ideas into effective policies. This could only work because FDR was so good with Congress. Under the American system the president proposes but Congress disposes; and FDR had more success in getting his bills through Congress, while vetoing Congressional bills he opposed, than any other president. In conclusion, what all this means is that the New Deal executed complex and often conflicting reform programmes with unprecedented efficiency and (despite American tradition and the fears of Harold Ickes) very little corruption.

His critics often charged that all this and FDR's social reforms put the skids under American free enterprise to usher in an era of creeping socialism. Nothing could be further from the truth. Like cousin Teddy before him he used the looming threat posed by socialism to frighten big business into accepting changes which would ward off the challenge. He became, as J.M. Keynes told him in 1933, 'The trustee for those in every country who seek to mend the evils of our condition by reasoned experiment within the framework of the existing social system'. Keynes continued in a manner which places FDR's use of power during the critical period of the twentieth century in dramatic historical perspective. 'If you fail, rational choice will be gravely prejudiced throughout the world, leaving orthodoxy and revolution to fight it out. But, if you succeed, new and bolder methods will be tried everywhere, and we may date the first chapter of a new economic era from your accession to office.'[13]

FDR changed every section of the United States, but none more completely than the South. In 1930 the South was a poor, rural, run-down, agricultural, segregated region where too many people chased too little income and blacks were socially segregated and politically powerless. This was still true in 1940, despite the decline in sharecrop farming. Indeed, with jobs still so scarce in urban America the purpose of FDR's farm policies was to keep too many people from seeking work in cities. But wartime government spending on defence changed all that and kick-started the South into self-sustaining economic growth. Purchasing power gave blacks bargaining power which provided the basis for the civil rights movement in the 1950s and 1960s, while economic diversification ultimately led to the growth of the Sunbelt which transformed politics after the 1970s.

The whole point of his policies, as he made clear in his 1944 Economic Bill of Rights speech, was to make American capitalism work more efficiently. The overriding economic problem of the 1930s was to create jobs, raise prices and wages and raise aggregate demand to convert the vicious economic spiral which had caused so much damage after 1929. In 1933 the Brookings Institution study *America's Capacity to Consume* reckoned that the nation's 631,000 richest families had a much larger income than the 16 million families at the bottom of the economic pyramid. The economy had become dangerously dependent on the spending decisions of a few rich people. The New Deal did little to change this. Wartime taxation did make some difference, but when FDR died distribution of wealth remained largely unchanged. True, skilled workers, and the few farmers fortunate enough to survive, enjoyed greater spending power and postwar prosperity was based on the widespread availability of consumer goods and rising demand. Social and welfare reforms, like the Wagner Act or social security, were also part of an improved picture. But they were a much smaller part than they became in Europe after 1945. The kind of comprehensive welfare state which grew up in Europe after 1945 did not develop in the United States, partly because the Dixiecrat–Republican coalition in Congress stopped it and partly, as discussed above, because FDR put in train certain long-term trends which revived corporate dominance.

One way of seeing the truth of this has received little comment. Some members of Roosevelt's team, like Alger Hiss, Lauchlin Currie and Harry Dexter White, were accused after FDR's death of being Communist spies. They certainly seem, at the very least, to have had irregular relationships with the Soviet government. But, viewed objectively, what they did in government – at the AAA or state department, at the federal reserve or treasury, or at Bretton Woods – was simply to make capitalism work better. Moreover, if America lacked a welfare state a kind of warfare state did develop. As we have seen, the New Deal had been only a limited success. Unemployment was still 14 per cent in 1940. War was what ended the depression. The 1944 Economic Bill of Rights was 'designed to make American capitalism work in the same great manner in peace as in war'.[14] War in fact had shown how to turn the trick in the second half of the twentieth century. Public spending would stimulate demand during downturns in the economic cycle. Moreover, after 1945 the United States would either be fighting a war, in Korea or Vietnam, spending a third of federal budget on defence, or financing huge public projects like the Moon and space races. Roosevelt's presidency laid the foundations for the modern approach to defence, budget deficits and public spending.

## V

All these changes which FDR facilitated helped transform America's place in the world. Just as it is hard to recapture how small a part the federal government played in the everyday life of Americans before 1933, so it is important to grasp that as late as the 1930s the role of the United States in world affairs was severely limited. In 1933 the nation was still embedded in a long history of isolationism and fear of foreign alliances. It had failed to ratify the peace treaty which ended the Great War or join the League of Nations set up to preserve the peace. Its tariff, trade and economic policies helped poison international relations between the wars. It was not a player in the crisis of the 1930s which led to war. But during that war Roosevelt changed all this. He made America the Arsenal of Democracy, pushed through Lend-Lease, signed the Atlantic Charter, placed her at the head of an alliance with Britain and the Soviet Union and determined that this time the United States would play the major part in shaping the peace. These were sweeping changes on the widest political stage.

So he laid the foundations for the postwar world in which a president's greatest influence would be in foreign policy and where America played a dominant role in global affairs. The Bretton Woods and Dumbarton Oaks conferences in 1944, which set up the International Monetary Fund, the World Bank and the United Nations, aimed at avoiding the anarchy of the 1920s and 1930s. Not only would the United States be a leading member but the UN would have its headquarters in New York. Marshall Aid, which rebuilt European capitalism destroyed by war, was something FDR would have fully endorsed. Finally, mindful of how the United States had watched helpless as unchecked aggression led to war in the 1930s, his successor announced the Truman Doctrine. This response to the strategic challenge posed by world Communism, which dominated global politics for the next forty years, had its origins in American isolationism and the failure of appeasement in the 1930s. Moreover, it was a feature of the Cold War that those who pressed for domestic reform to complete the New Deal were often the toughest anti-Communists in foreign affairs. It was politically important for FDR's social-democratic heirs to distance their beliefs from Communism. Yet their tough stance was also based on realization of how much diplomatic and military weakness had undermined FDR's foreign policy in the 1930s.

The Roosevelt presidency left not only a huge legacy but also popular expectations with which every successor had to grapple. Until the 1990s every president worked in the shadow of FDR. Ronald Reagan voted for him four times. George Bush was a war pilot when FDR was commander-in-chief. Bill Clinton, the first president born after Roosevelt's death, was free to redefine the office and also the first Democrat since FDR to win re-election. Above all FDR established that the president must set the sights. The truth of this struck me while writing this profile. But I was also struck by the topicality of many of the issues: concern about conservation, steeply falling stock markets, corporate malfeasance on a grand scale, fears about the economy at home, dangerous threats abroad. However, it is easy to make too much of topicality. In other ways this story came out of the past: another country where they do things differently.

The most striking difference is that media coverage was so much less intrusive in the 1930s and that an open conspiracy existed between FDR and press and newsreels to hide the true extent of his paralysis. He was never shown in a wheelchair, being carried from his car or even walking. In the twenty-first century, with a TV set in every living-room, it is hard to believe Americans would send a man in a wheelchair to the White House. So it is even clearer that this is the profile of a great man. Roosevelt's domestic and foreign achievements were in large part the product of exceptional skill as a political leader. No president of the twentieth century or indeed any period has been more effective. To judge his personal impact on his times one has only to think counterfactually for a moment. What would have happened had the Democrats nominated Al Smith or Newton Baker in 1932, if FDR had been assassinated in 1933 and John Nance Garner became president, or if Wendell Willkie had won in 1940? The New Deal would never have happened; the war would have taken a different course. His leadership during that critical period made the critical difference. He knew that the Roosevelt luck was on his side. Had there been no war in 1940 he would not have had a third term and would be remembered now as a dazzling and demagogic domestic leader who only partially dealt with economic depression. But, as always, he used his luck. As Robert Dallek says, 'Roosevelt's management of his third-term renomination, and victory over Wendell Willkie in 1940, for example, did not simply happen because the country wanted FDR to stay in office and deal with the world crisis.'[15]

Such reservations as exist about him are not that he was too partisan, too socialist or too devious. They are paradoxically that – charming, scintillating and successful though he might have been – he lacked weight or gravitas. Blind to art and deaf to music he was uninterested in literature or philosophy. Of fundamental religious questions he famously told Eleanor once that it was best not to think about them. He completely lacked the theological and philosophical dimension of Lincoln. He could never have written the kind of magnificent private memoranda to himself about the problems of his time which Lincoln left. Yet the record shows that he was a model of what presidents should aspire to and as such his place in the pantheon is with Washington and Lincoln.

# Notes

## Chapter 2

1. FDR, 'The Roosevelt Family in New Amsterdam Before the Revolution', December 1901, MS in Roosevelt Library, quoted in Frank Freidel, *Franklin D. Roosevelt*, vol. 1: *The Apprenticeship* (Boston, 1952), p. 6.
2. Franklin K. Lane to FDR, quoted in Freidel, vol. 1: *Apprenticeship*, p. 3.
3. Quoted in BBC TV documentary *FDR*, 20 April 1996.
4. Quoted in A.M. Schlesinger, *The Age of Roosevelt*, vol. 1: *The Crisis of the Old Order* (Boston, 1957), p. 322.
5. Quoted ibid., p. 324.
6. Quoted in Freidel, vol. 1: *Apprenticeship*, p. 33.
7. Quoted in Schlesinger, vol. 1: *Crisis*, p. 328.
8. Quoted in Freidel, vol. 1: *Apprenticeship*, p. 86 and Schlesinger, vol. 1: *Crisis*, p. 330.
9. Freidel, vol. 1: *Apprenticeship*, pp. 94–5.
10. Ibid., pp. 87–8.
11. Ibid., pp. 89–90.

## Chapter 3

1. Frank Freidel, *Franklin D. Roosevelt*, vol. 1: *The Apprenticeship* (Boston, 1952), pp. 100–1.
2. Quoted ibid., p. 97.
3. Quoted in A.M. Schlesinger, *The Age of Roosevelt*, vol. 1: *The Crisis of the Old Order* (Boston, 1957), p. 333.
4. For a full account, see Freidel, vol. 1: *Apprenticeship*, pp. 87–116 and Schlesinger, vol. 1: *Crisis*, pp. 333–4.
5. Quoted in Schlesinger, vol. 1: *Crisis*, p. 338.
6. Quoted ibid., p. 333.
7. Quoted ibid., pp. 334–34.
8. Freidel, vol. 1: *Apprenticeship*, pp. 112–16.

9. Ibid., p. 120. For a full discussion, see the seminal article by J.J. Huthmacher, 'Urban Liberalism and the Age of Reform', *Mississippi Valley Historical Review*, 49 (1962–63), pp. 231–42.

10. Freidel, vol. 1: *Apprenticeship*, pp. 120–1 and Schlesinger, vol. 1: *Crisis*, p. 96.

11. Freidel, vol. 1: *Apprenticeship*, p. 121 and n. FDR did mention two fields of social service he knew about work for seamen in New York City and for purer milk for poor children.

12. Quoted in Schlesinger, vol. 1: *Crisis*, p. 96.

13. Quoted in Frances Perkins, *The Roosevelt I Knew* (New York, 1964), pp. 24–5.

14. *FDR, Happy Warrior*, p. 6, quoted in Freidel, vol. 1: *Apprenticeship*, p. 120.

15. Huthmacher, 'Urban Liberalism', pp. 231–42.

16. Freidel, vol. 1: *Apprenticeship*, p. 110.

17. *New York World*, 8 June 1911, quoted in Freidel, vol. 1: *Apprenticeship*, p. 119.

18. Quoted in Perkins, *Roosevelt I Knew*, p. 14.

19. Quoted ibid.

20. Quoted ibid., p. 15.

21. Schlesinger, vol. 1: *Crisis*, p. 334.

22. Freidel, vol. 1: *Apprenticeship*, pp. 122–8.

23. Ibid., p. 130.

24. William Allen White, quoted in Richard Hofstadter, *The American Political Tradition and the Men Who Made It* (New York, 1959), p. 234.

25. Quoted in Schlesinger, vol. 1: *Crisis*, pp. 336–7.

26. Quoted ibid., pp. 342–3.

27. Quoted ibid., pp. 340–41.

28. Freidel, vol. 1: *Apprenticeship*, p. 157.

29. Lela Stiles, *The Man Behind Roosevelt: The Story of Louis McHenry Howe* (New York, 1954), p. 39.

30. Quoted in Schlesinger, vol. 1: *Crisis*, p. 341.

31. Quoted in Freidel, vol. 1: *Apprenticeship*, p. 161.

32. Ibid., p. 193.

33. Quoted ibid., p. 156.

34. Ibid., p. 130.

35. Ibid., pp. 183–8.

36. Quoted in Schlesinger, vol. 1: *Crisis*, p. 347.

37. Quoted in Hofstadter, *American Political Tradition*, p. 322.

38. Quoted in Schlesinger, vol. 1: *Crisis*, p. 349.

39. Ibid., pp. 352–3. The Warburg quotation is in James Warburg, Columbia Oral History Project, p. 44.

40. Frank Freidel, *Franklin D. Roosevelt*, vol. 2: *The Ordeal* (Boston, 1954), pp. 46–7.

41. Ibid., pp. 60–1.

42. Hofstadter, *American Political Tradition*, p. 282.

43. *San Francisco Chronicle*, 6 July 1920, quoted in Freidel, vol. 2: *Ordeal*, p. 66.

44. FDR to Ralph Hayes, 16 November 1920, quoted in Freidel, vol. 2: *Ordeal*, p. 91.

45. Ibid., pp. 98–9.

## Chapter 4

1. Frank Freidel, *Franklin D. Roosevelt*, vol. 2: *The Ordeal* (Boston, 1954), p. 99.

2. Ibid., p. 104.

3. Ibid., pp. 186–7.

4. Ibid., pp. 101 and 186.

5. Ibid., pp. 106–7.

6. Ibid., p. 111.

7. FDR to Caroline O'Day, 28 January 1922, quoted in Freidel, vol. 2: *Ordeal*, p. 111.

8. Eleanor Roosevelt, interview in BBC TV documentary, 27 April 1996.

9. For a full discussion of this, see David Burner, *The Politics of Provincialism: The Democratic Party in Transition* (New York, 1968).

10. George A. Palmer, interview with Louis Depew, 5 January 1948, quoted in Freidel, vol. 2: *Ordeal*, p. 113.

11. Richard Hofstadter, *The American Political Tradition and the Men Who Made It* (New York, 1959), p. 325, and Freidel, vol. 2: *Ordeal*, pp. 150–1.

12. A.M. Schlesinger, *The Age of Roosevelt*, vol. 2: *The Coming of the New Deal* (Boston, 1958), p. 437.

13. Hofstadter, *American Political Tradition*, p. 325.

14. Frances Perkins, *The Roosevelt I Knew* (New York, 1964), pp. 28–9.

15. Freidel, vol. 2: *Ordeal*, pp. 189–90.

16. Ibid., p. 191.

17. Ibid., pp. 196–7.

18. Hofstadter, *American Political Tradition*, pp. 202–3, Freidel, vol. 2: *Ordeal*, pp. 170–1, 175–80.

19. Quoted in Freidel, vol. 2: *Ordeal*, p. 181.

20. Quoted ibid., pp. 176–7.

21. For a full discussion, see ibid., pp. 122–37, 199–228.

22. Ibid., pp. 214–18.

23. Ibid., p. 215.

24. Ibid., p. 241.

25. Ibid., p. 243.

26. A.M. Schlesinger, *The Age of Roosevelt*, vol. 1: *The Crisis of the Old Order* (Boston, 1957), p. 381.

27. Quoted in Lela Stiles, *The Man Behind Roosevelt: The Story of Louis McHenry Howe* (New York, 1954), p. 111.

28. See, for example, the question asked Smith by Senator J. Thomas Heflin of Alabama, quoted in D.W. Brogan, *Politics in America* (New York, 1960), p. 425.

29. Quoted in Richard Hofstadter, *The Age of Reform* (London, 1962), p. 298 n.

30. Samuel Lubell, *The Future of American Politics* (New York, 3rd edn, revised, 1965), pp. 43–9.

31. Ibid., p. 49.

32. Freidel, vol. 2: *Ordeal*, p. 268.

# Chapter 5

1. Quoted in A.M. Schlesinger, *The Age of Roosevelt*, vol. 1: *The Crisis of the Old Order* (Boston, 1957), p. 386.

2. Quoted ibid., p. 387.

3. Quoted ibid., p. 386.

4. Frank Freidel, *Franklin D. Roosevelt*, vol. 3: *The Triumph* (Boston, 1956), pp. 11–12.

5. Quoted in Schlesinger, vol. 1: *Crisis*, p. 283.

6. Freidel, vol. 3: *Triumph*, pp. 6–7 and Schlesinger, vol. 1: *Crisis*, p. 383.

7. Quoted in Schlesinger, vol. 1: *Crisis*, p. 389.

8. Quoted ibid., pp. 390–1.

9. Quoted ibid., p. 390.

10. For a full discussion, see J.K. Galbraith, *The Great Crash* (Harmondsworth, 1975).

11. Schlesinger, vol. 1: *Crisis*, pp. 391–2.

12. Quoted ibid., p. 392.

13. Quoted ibid., p. 393.

14. Quoted ibid., p. 422.

15. Ibid., p. 394.

16. Quoted ibid., p. 278.

17. Quoted ibid., pp. 278–9.

18. Quoted in Freidel, vol. 3: *Triumph*, pp. 157–8.

19. Quoted in Schlesinger, vol. 1: *Crisis*, p. 388.

20. Ibid., p. 374.

21. FDR to Farley, 21 November 1930, quoted in Schlesinger, vol. 1: *Crisis*, p. 280.

22. Quoted ibid., pp. 280–1.

23. Quoted ibid., p. 397.

24. Quoted ibid., p. 398.

25. Raymond Moley, *After Seven Years* (New York, 1972), p. 9.

26. Quoted in Schlesinger, vol. 1: *Crisis*, p. 283.

27. Quoted ibid., p. 303.

28. Quoted ibid., p. 289.

29. Quoted ibid., pp. 289–90.

30. Quoted ibid., p. 290.

31. FDR to Josephus Daniels, 5 May 1932, quoted in Schlesinger, vol. 1: *Crisis*, p. 293.

32. Quoted ibid., p. 296.

33. Quoted ibid., p. 300.

34. Quoted ibid.

35. Quoted ibid., p. 302.

36. Quoted ibid., p. 306.

37. Quoted ibid., p. 310.

38. Samuel Rosenman, ed., *The Public Papers and Addresses of Franklin D. Roosevelt*, vol. 1: (New York, 1947), pp. 47–59. The 'call to arms' peroration is on the last page.

39. Marriner Eccles, *Beckoning Frontiers: Public and Personal Recollections* (New York, 1951), p. 95.

40. Quoted in Schlesinger, vol. 1: *Crisis*, p. 432.

41. Quoted in Freidel, vol. 3: *Triumph*, p. 371 and Schlesinger, vol. 1: *Crisis*, p. 439.

## Chapter 6

1. Quoted in A.M. Schlesinger, *The Age of Roosevelt*, vol. 1: *The Crisis of the Old Order* (Boston, 1957), p. 445.

2. Quoted ibid., pp. 443–4.

3. Quoted in A.M. Schlesinger, *The Age of Roosevelt*, vol. 2: *The Coming of the New Deal* (Boston, 1958), p. 515.

4. Quoted ibid., p. 515. According to Lela Stiles, *The Man Behind Roosevelt: The Story of Louis McHenry Howe* (New York, 1954), pp. 39–40, this was a particular comment FDR made about Howe during his 1912 re-election campaign. However, it was also true in a wider sense.

5. Quoted in Schlesinger, vol. 1: *Crisis*, pp. 468–9.

6. Quoted ibid., pp. 471–2.

7. Raymond Moley, *After Seven Years* (New York, 1972), p. 139.

8. First Inaugural Address in Samuel Rosenman, ed., *The Public Papers and Addresses of Franklin D. Roosevelt*, vol. 1 (New York, 1947), pp. 11–16 for the full address. The threat to use executive power is on p. 15.

9. Quoted in Moley, *After Seven Years*, p. 14.

10. Ibid., p. 152.

11. Frances Perkins, *The Roosevelt I Knew* (New York, 1964), p. 72.

12. Quoted in Schlesinger, vol. 2: *Coming*, p. 13.

13. Moley, *After Seven Years*, p. 24.

14. Quoted in Schlesinger, vol. 2: *Coming*, p. 56.

15. Quoted ibid., p. 72.

16. Quoted ibid. (italics in original).

17. Quoted ibid., p. 39.

18. Representative Joseph W. Martin of Massachusetts, quoted ibid., p. 40.

19. Quoted ibid., p. 53.

20. Quoted ibid., p. 16.

21. Quoted ibid., p. 46.

22. Quoted ibid.

23. Quoted ibid., p. 61.

24. Quoted ibid., p. 58.

25. Quoted ibid., p. 59.

26. Quoted ibid., p. 73.

## Chapter 7

1. Studs Terkel, *Hard Times: An Oral History of the Great Depression* (London, 1970), p. 256.

2. W.E. Leuchtenburg, *Franklin D. Roosevelt and the New Deal* (New York, 1963), p. 133.

3. J.M. Keynes, *The Means to Prosperity* (London, 1933), p. 31.

4. Quoted in Frances Perkins, *The Roosevelt I Knew* (New York, 1964), p. 226.

5. Redbook, December 1934, quoted in A.M. Schlesinger, *The Age of Roosevelt*, vol. 3: *The Politics of Upheaval* (Boston, 1960), pp. 400–1.

6. Quoted in Schlesinger, *The Age of Roosevelt*, vol. 2: *The Coming of the New Deal* (Boston, 1958), p. 585.

7. Frances Perkins to FDR, President's Secretary File (hereafter PSF), 77, Labor Department, March 1933, in Roosevelt collection, F.D. Roosevelt Library, Hyde Park, New York.

8. Quoted in Richard Hofstadter, *The American Political Tradition and the Men Who Made It* (New York, 1959), p. 188.

9. J.M. Keynes, *The General Theory of Employment, Interest and Money* (London, 1936), p. 382.

10. Quoted in Schlesinger, vol. 2: *Coming*, p. 186 (italics in original).

11. Quoted ibid., p. 221.

12. Quoted ibid., p. 232.

13. Quoted ibid., p. 21.

14. Quoted ibid.

15. Quoted in A.M. Schlesinger, *The Age of Roosevelt*, vol. 1: *The Crisis of the Old Order* (Boston, 1957), p. 291.

16. Quoted in Schlesinger, vol. 2: *Coming*, pp. 13, 22.

17. Quoted ibid., p. 488.

# Chapter 8

1. Quoted in W.E. Leuchtenburg, *Franklin D. Roosevelt and the New Deal* (New York, 1963), p. 81.

2. Quoted ibid.

3. Quoted ibid., p. 91.

4. Quoted ibid.

5. Quoted in Robert Dallek, *Franklin D. Roosevelt and American Foreign Policy, 1932–1945* (Oxford, 1995), pp. 78–9.

6. Quoted in Leuchtenburg, *FDR*, p. 159.

7. Walter Lippmann, *Interpretations, 1933–35* (New York, 1936), p. 194 and Leuchtenburg, *FDR*, p. 160.

8. Quoted in Leuchtenburg, *FDR*, p. 147.

9. Quoted ibid., p. 153.

10. Quoted ibid., p. 133.

11. Quoted ibid., pp. 150–1 n.

12. Quoted in A.M. Schlesinger, *The Age of Roosevelt*, vol. 3: *The Politics of Upheaval* (Boston, 1960), pp. 577–8.

13. Quoted ibid., pp. 638–9.

14. Quoted ibid., p. 640.

15. Quoted in Patrick Renshaw, *American Labour and Consensus Capitalism, 1935–1990* (Basingstoke, 1991), p. 37.

# Chapter 9

1. George Norris to Francis Heney, 25 April, 6 May 1936, quoted in W.E. Leuchtenburg, *Franklin D. Roosevelt and the New Deal* (New York, 1963), p. 235 and n.

2. Quoted ibid., p. 234.

3. Johnson to FDR, 13 April 1937 in president's personal file (hereafter PPF), Box 702 in Roosevelt collection, F.D. Roosevelt Library, Hyde Park, New York, quoted in Leuchtenburg, *FDR*, p. 236.

4. Quoted ibid., p. 237.

5. 'Bills in Congress, 1933–37' in president's secretary file (hereafter PSF), Box 28 in Roosevelt collection, F.D. Roosevelt Library, Hyde Park, New York, quoted in Leuchtenburg, *FDR*, p. 155.

6. Quoted ibid., pp. 156–7.

7. Quoted in Richard Hofstadter, *The American Political Tradition and the Men Who Made It* (New York, 1959), p. 341.

8. Marriner Eccles, *Beckoning Frontiers: Public and Private Recollections* (New York, 1951), pp. 231–2.

9. Quoted in Hofstadter, *American Political Tradition*, p. 342.

10. Unedited transcript of presidential press conference 531, 23 March 1939, in PSF, Box 186, Taxes, in Roosevelt collection, F.D. Roosevelt Library, Hyde Park, New York.

11. Currie to FDR, 1 February 1940, in PSF, Box 115, F.D. Roosevelt Library, Hyde Park, New York.

12. J.M. Keynes, 'The United States and the Keynes Plan', *New Republic*, CIII (29 July 1940), p. 158.

13. Quoted in Leuchtenburg, *FDR*, p. 319.

14. Quoted ibid., p. 319.

15. Quoted ibid., pp. 315–16.

16. Thomas Gore to Mary Whyatt, 16 May 1940, quoted in Leuchtenburg, *FDR*, pp. 316–17 n.

17. Quoted ibid., p. 317.

18. Quoted ibid., pp. 320–1.

19. Quoted in Robert Dallek, *Franklin D. Roosevelt and American Foreign Policy, 1932–1945* (Oxford, 1995), p. 224.

20. Quoted ibid.

21. Quoted ibid., p. 335.

22. Quoted ibid.

23. Quoted ibid., p. 336.

24. Quoted ibid.

25. Ibid.

26. Labor Department, PSF, Box 152, Harry Hopkins in Roosevelt collection, F.D. Roosevelt Library, Hyde Park, New York.

27. Quoted in Dallek, *Foreign Policy*, p. 442.

28. *The Times*, 8 November 1944 and PPF, Box 8172 in Roosevelt collection, F.D. Roosevelt Library, Hyde Park, New York.

29. Quoted in Dallek, *Foreign Policy*, pp. 481–2.

30. Quoted ibid., p. 484.

31. Quoted in James MacGregor Burns, *Roosevelt: Soldier of Freedom 1940–1945* (London, 1971), p. 424.

32. PPF, Box 1017, 28 October 1944 (italics in orginal) in Roosevelt collection, F.D. Roosevelt Library, Hyde Park, New York.

33. Quoted in Dallek, *Foreign Policy*, p. 521.

## Chapter 10

1. Quoted in Robert Dallek, *Franklin D. Roosevelt and American Foreign Policy* (Oxford, 1995), p. 76.

2. Quoted ibid., p. 77.

3. W.E. Leuchtenburg, *Franklin D. Roosevelt and the New Deal* (New York, 1963), p. 207.

4. Ibid., p. 203.

5. Ibid.

6. Quoted ibid., pp. 208–9.

7. Quoted in Dallek, *Foreign Policy*, p. 132.

8. Quoted ibid., p. 122.

9. Quoted ibid., p. 137.

10. Quoted ibid., p. 148.

11. Quoted ibid., pp. 148–9.

12. Quoted ibid., p. 149.

13. Alan Bullock, *Hitler: A Study in Tyranny* (London, 1954), pp. 408–9 and Ian Kershaw, *Hitler: 1936–45: Nemesis* (London, 2000), pp. 99–100, 111.

14. Quoted in Dallek, *Foreign Policy*, p. 187.

15. Quoted ibid., pp. 207–8.

16. Quoted ibid., pp. 210–11.

17. FDR to Churchill, 30 January 1942, quoted in Walter Kimball ed., *Churchill and Roosevelt: Their Complete Correspondence*, vol. 1: *Alliance Emerging* (Princeton, 1984), p. 337.

18. Quoted in Dallek, *Foreign Policy*, p. 247.

19. Churchill to FDR, 6 November 1940, quoted in Francis L. Loewenheim, Harold D. Langley and Manfred Jonas, eds, *Roosevelt and Churchill: Their Secret Wartime Correspondence* (London, 1975), p. 119.

20. Quoted ibid., pp. 125–6 and n.

21. Churchill to FDR, 8 December 1940, full text in W.S. Churchill, *The Second World War*, vol. 2: *Their Finest Hour* (London, 1953), pp. 444–50, esp. p. 445.

22. Quoted in Dallek, *Foreign Policy*, p. 255.

23. Churchill to Eden, 2 May 1941, PREM 3/469/350 in Public Record Office, quoted in Kimball, ed., *Correspondence*, p. 8. See also exchange between FDR and Churchill, pp. 178–82.

24. Quoted in James MacGregor Burns, *Roosevelt: Soldier of Freedom 1940–1945* (London, 1971), p. 60.

25. Quoted in Dallek, *Foreign Policy*, p. 334.

26. Eliot Janeway, *The Struggle for Survival: A Chronicle of Economic Mobilization in World War II* (New Haven, 1951), p. 44.

27. Quoted in William Emerson, 'Franklin Roosevelt as Commander-in-Chief in World War II', *Military Affairs*, XXII (Winter 1958–59), p. 190.

28. Quoted ibid., p. 188.

29. Quoted ibid.

30. Eisenhower to Marshall, March 1942 (italics in original), quoted in Emerson, *Military Affairs*, p. 187 n.

31. Quoted ibid., p. 195.

32. For a clear and moderate statement of Stalin's argument, see his message to Churchill, 18 March 1943, transmitted to FDR, full text in Loewenheim, Langley and Jonas, eds, *Wartime Correspondence*, pp. 321–2.

33. Quoted in Dallek, *Foreign Policy*, p. 420.

34. Quoted in Richard Hofstadter, *The American Political Tradition and the Men Who Made It* (New York, 1959), p. 348 and n.

35. Quoted in Loewenheim, Langley and Jonas, eds, *Wartime Correspondence*, p. 403.

36. Barbara Tuchman, *Stillwell and the American Experience in China, 1911–1945* (New York, 1970), pp. 493–4.

37. Quoted in Dallek, *Foreign Policy*, pp. 485, 490–1, 496–7.

38. Quoted ibid., pp. 497–8.

39. Quoted ibid., p. 521.

40. Quoted ibid., p. 528.

# Conclusion

1. Tony Badger, 'The New Deal Without FDR: What Biographies of Roosevelt Cannot Tell Us', in David Cannadine and T.C.W. Blanning, eds, *History and Biography: Essays in Honour of Derek Beales* (Cambridge, 1996), p. 251.

2. Ibid., pp. 251–2 and n.

3. Ibid., p. 249.

4. Ibid., p. 250.

5. Graham White and John Maze, *Harold Ickes of the New Deal* (Cambridge, MA, 1985), pp. 62–3.

6. Quoted ibid., p. 172.

7. Quoted in A.M. Schlesinger, *The Age of Roosevelt*, vol. 2: *The Coming of the New Deal* (Boston, 1958), pp. 583–4.

8. Quoted ibid., p. 557.

9. Quoted ibid.

10. Richard E. Neustadt, *Presidential Power: The Politics of Leadership* (New York, 1968), p. 162.

11. Quoted in Robert Dallek, *Franklin D. Roosevelt and American Foreign Policy, 1932–1945* (Oxford, 1995), pp. 532–3 (italics in original).

12. Quoted in White and Maze, *Ickes*, p. 206.

13. Quoted in A.M. Schlesinger, *The Age of Roosevelt*, vol. 3: *The Politics of Upheaval* (Boston, 1960), p. 656.

14. Text of speech in president's personal file (PPF), 28 October 1944, Box 1017, Roosevelt collection, F.D. Roosevelt Library, Hyde Park, New York.

15. Quoted in Dallek, *Foreign Policy*, p. 552.

# Bibliographical Essay

Though this book is based on secondary reading rather than primary research it could not have been written without spending time at the Franklin D. Roosevelt Library at Hyde Park, New York, the first of the presidential libraries. I made extensive use of it as an American Council of Learned Societies fellow in 1981–82, preparing a book entitled *American Labour and Consensus Capitalism*, and again briefly in 2000, working on this book. Roosevelt is buried in a simple grave next to the library which houses all his private and public papers as well as his personal effects. In addition, the library's location in the beautiful, wooded Roosevelt estate on the banks of the Hudson river and next to the home he shared with his parents, wife and children, helps in understanding the man and his world.

Writing on Roosevelt, though not as vast as on Lincoln, is still very extensive and the following is merely a brief discussion of some of the books I have found most helpful. His personal lawyer Sam Rosenman edited *The Public Papers and Addresses of Franklin D. Roosevelt, 1928–1945* (New York, 1947–50) in 12 volumes. Later volumes in particular have helpful editorial links, written by Rosenman and Roosevelt himself, but the reader must beware that FDR appointed Rosenman to his staff because he was gifted in the arts of political presentation and determined to help fabricate a political myth. The first historian to use the Hyde Park archive was Frank Freidel, *Franklin D. Roosevelt*, 4 vols: *The Apprenticeship, The Ordeal, The Triumph* and *The Launching of the New Deal* (Boston, 1952, 1954, 1956 and 1973). Though it is easy to criticize a biographer who takes four volumes published over 21 years to reach the first Hundred Days, Freidel has put subsequent historians in his debt by his meticulous archive work. The standard account of FDR and the New Deal for many years was Arthur M. Schlesinger Jr, *The Age of Roosevelt*, 3 vols: *The Crisis of the Old Order, The Coming of the New Deal* and *The Politics of Upheaval* (Boston, 1957, 1958, 1960). Schlesinger manages to reach 1936 but says nothing about foreign affairs. Moreover, like Freidel, Schlesinger was inhibited by the fact that Eleanor Roosevelt was still alive when he was working and so says little about FDR's private life. Also, as a leading member of the East Coast intellectual wing of the Democratic party and a founding member of Americans for Democratic Action he never became a completely dispassionate historian. Yet he writes scintillating, powerful prose and gives an incomparable, wide-ranging account of the man and the politics of his time. The most recent multi-volume study, Kenneth S. Davis, *FDR: The Beckoning of Destiny, 1882–1929, The New York Years, 1928–1933, The New Deal Years, 1933–1937, Time of Troubles, 1937–1940* (New York, 1971, 1985, 1986, 1993), is unfinished and was not used in writing this study. Of many other biographies James MacGregor Burns, *Roosevelt: The Lion and the Fox* (New York, 1956) and *Roosevelt: Soldier of Freedom 1940–1945* (London, 1971) is outstanding.

Ted Morgan, *FDR: A Biography* (London, 1986) is a recent complete account by a Frenchman covering domestic and foreign affairs as well as his private life in 830 pages. The best of recent single-volume biographies is probably Patrick Maney, *The Roosevelt Presence: A Biography of Franklin Delano Roosevelt* (New York, 1991). But easily the most useful analysis is William E. Leuchtenburg, *Franklin D. Roosevelt and the New Deal* (New York, 1963). It says nothing about the man's private life or early career, little about foreign affairs and ends before the Second World War, but its clear grasp of the history and politics of the 1930s makes it the best single book on the New Deal. Leuchtenburg, *In the Shadow of FDR: From Harry Truman to Ronald Reagan* (Ithaca, 1983) is a dazzling discussion of how Roosevelt's successors had to deal with the political legacy FDR left them, while the same author's *The FDR Years: On Roosevelt and his Legacy* (New York, 1995) is a perceptive collection of essays essentially on the same subject.

Eleanor Roosevelt, *This I Remember* (New York, 1949) should be read in conjunction with its revision and abridgement in her *Autobiography* (New York, 1961). Both are subjective, as autobiographies often are, and guarded about FDR's personal life. They have been largely replaced by the uncompleted biography (2 vols so far) of Blanche Wiesen Cook, *Eleanor Roosevelt, 1884–1933* and *Eleanor Roosevelt, 1933–1938* (New York, 1997 and 1999). Command of her correspondence and the whole Eleanor archive gives fascinating detail about her private life. However, this biography is less skilled at placing her in the politics of her time. Joseph P. Lash, *Eleanor and Franklin* (New York, 1971) is based on Eleanor's papers and although more revealing than anything written before it now reads like an authorized version. FDR wrote thousands of letters, many of which were collected and deftly edited by his son Elliott Roosevelt, *FDR: His Personal Letters, 1905–1945*, 4 vols (New York, 1970). This lively and readable personal correspondence shows FDR's charming surface. The letters' real significance, however, is that they give nothing away. Max Freedman, ed., *Roosevelt and Frankfurter: Their Correspondence 1928–1945* (London, 1968), despite the toadying tone which often enters into the exchanges, is much more politically revealing and shows how much Roosevelt relied on Frankfurter's fine legal mind and on his extensive contacts both in America and Britain. A bold attempt to get at the 'real Roosevelt' is Geoffrey C. Ward, *Before the Trumpet: Young Franklin Roosevelt, 1882–1905* and *A First-Class Temperament: The Emergence of Franklin Roosevelt* (New York, 1985 and 1989), two massive volumes where much detailed material is in need of a good editor.

Two diaries by important men throw contrasting light on Roosevelt and the New Deal. Harold L. Ickes, *The Secret Diary of Harold Ickes*, 3 vols: *The First Thousand Days, 1933–36, The Inside Story, 1936–39, The Lowering Clouds, 1939–41* (New York, 1952, 1953, 1954) is a detailed, often petty and spiteful daily account by 'the old curmudgeon' as Ickes called himself, while David E. Lilienthal, *The Journals of David E. Lilienthal*, vol. 1: *The TVA Years 1933–1945* (New York, 1964) is episodic, wide-ranging and interpretative as befits one of the architects of TVA. Ickes also wrote an account of PWA, *Back to Work* (New York, 1939), though *Autobiography of a Curmudgeon* (New York, 1948) is largely unrevealing, unlike Graham White and John Maze, *Harold Ickes of the New Deal* (Cambridge, MA, 1985), which uses the unpublished parts of the diary to uncover fascinating links between his private and public life, arguing that there was a homoerotic element in the relationship between some New Dealers like Ickes, Hopkins, Wallace and FDR. David Lilienthal, *TVA: Democracy on the March* (London, 1944) is a spirited defence of his policies which, his colleague Rex Tugwell mordantly said, were more like democracy in retreat. Elliot A. Rosen, *Hoover, Roosevelt and the Brains Trust* (New York, 1977) throws light on these rivalries discussing economic policy during the transition. Rexford G. Tugwell, *The Democratic Roosevelt* (New York, 1957) is a thoughtful reappraisal of the man and his times by one of the sharpest minds in his circle. J.M. Blum, ed., *From the Morgenthau Diaries: Years of Crisis 1928–1938* (Boston, 1959) is a work of exceptional interest about one of FDR's closest friends and cabinet colleagues. Part of the manuscript can be read in Henry Morgenthau, *Presidential Diaries* (Sheffield University microfilm).

An account by the playwright and FDR speechwriter Robert E. Sherwood, *Roosevelt and Hopkins* (New York, rev. edn, 1950) is another insider's book which reveals the role of the man who became the president's closest personal wartime aide with unprecedented influence on making and executing policy. Other accounts by those who worked with

Roosevelt are useful. Louis Howe left no diary or memoir, but his secretary Lela Stiles, *The Man Behind Roosevelt: The Story of Louis McHenry Howe* (New York, 1954) has many tactical details and examples of his personal influence. Raymond Moley, who briefly challenged Howe's position when he chaired the brains trust, wrote a much more critical account, *After Seven Years* (New York, 1972), which every student of FDR and the New Deal has to confront. Frances Perkins, *The Roosevelt I Knew* (New York, 1964), which tries to unravel the most complicated man she had ever known, has become a classic, while Edward J. Flynn, *You're the Boss* (New York, 1947) describes their close working relationship. Samuel I. Rosenman, *Working with Roosevelt* (London, 1952) is a clear but uncritical chronicle by his personal lawyer and speechwriter. Other accounts include those of FDR's long-serving secretary of state Cordell Hull, *The Memoirs of Cordell Hull* (London, 1948) and of the shrewd James F. Byrnes, *Speaking Frankly* (London, 1945). There are two books by FDR's legendary campaign manager James A. Farley, *Behind the Ballots* (New York, 1973) and *Jim Farley's Story* (New York, 1948). Russell D. Buhite and David W. Levy, *FDR's Fireside Chats* (London, 1993), which includes the text of his inspiring broadcasts, is excellent for Roosevelt on radio, as is Betty Houchin Winfield, *FDR and the News Media* (Urbana, 1990) on the wider topic of FDR as a communicator. Franklin D. Roosevelt, *Complete Presidential Press Conferences* (New York, 1972) has the transcripts of all but four of his 1,002 conferences. The crucial political relationship between Alfred E. Smith and FDR is hard to examine from Smith's perspective since he left no papers or diary. The most recent political biography by Matthew and Hannah Josephson, *Al Smith: Hero of the Cities* (London, 1970) is unsatisfactory on the politics of the period but remains the only available account.

Of more general books about the New Deal Mario Einaudi, *The Roosevelt Revolution* (London, 1960) has much interesting analysis, and Anthony Badger, *The New Deal: The Depression Years* (Basingstoke, 1989) is an invaluable survey of the whole subject topic by topic written in the 1980s, while a perceptive essay by Badger, 'The New Deal Without FDR' can be read in David Cannadine and T.C.W. Blanning, eds, *History and Biography: Essays in Honour of Derek Beales* (Cambridge, 1996). David M. Kennedy, *Freedom from Fear: The American People in the Depression Years, 1929–1945* (New York, 1999) is a very useful book which covers the whole period of FDR's years of power from a new and more general perspective. Studs Terkel, *Hard Times* (London, 1970) is a classic of what was then the new approach of oral history, while Don Wharton, ed., *The Roosevelt Omnibus* (New York, 1934) has some first-rate general information hard to find anywhere else, including a detailed article on the Roosevelt family income reprinted from *Fortune* (October 1932).

Roosevelt and the New Deal attracted determined political opposition, so it is surprising that this is not reflected in more of the serious writing on the subject. The nearest approach to considered conservative criticism can be found in two books by John T. Flynn, *The Roosevelt Myth* (New York, 1956) and an earlier working of the subject, *Country Squire in the White House* (New York, 1940). Though they are among the few books (apart from Moley) critical of FDR, their value is vitiated by their bitter and sometimes petty tone. More substantial attacks were mounted by New Left historians published in the 1960s and 1970s. Criticism of Roosevelt for being too kind to corporate interests and of the New Deal for being too conservative can be found in Barton K. Bernstein, *Towards a New Past: Dissenting Essays in American History* (New York, 1968) and in Alonzo Hamby, ed., *The New Deal: Analysis and Interpretation* (New York, 1981), which brings together several perceptive essays by different historians, such as Ronald Radosh, 'The Myth of the New Deal', Richard S. Kirkendall, 'The New Deal and Agriculture' and a radio address delivered in March 1939 by one of FDR's most formidable Republican opponents, Robert A. Taft. A valuable discussion of the New Deal and its legacy to the US political economy can be found in Steven Fraser and Gary Gertsle, *The Rise and Fall of the New Deal Order, 1930–1980* (Princeton, 1989).

The politics of the New Deal are best understood in relation to changes which began during the progressive period. A seminal article by J.J. Huthmacher, 'Urban Liberalism and the Age of Reform', *Mississippi Valley Historical Review/Journal of American History*, 49 (1962–63), which contrasts the middle-class reform agenda with that of organized labour, is expanded in Huthmacher, *Robert F. Wagner and Urban Liberalism* (New York, 1970) to reveal the symbiotic relationship which developed between urban political bosses and liberal reformers. Melvin G. Holli, *Reform in Detroit: Hazen S. Pingree and Urban Politics* (New York, 1969) is an interesting case study of the kind of benign boss who influenced FDR. This symbiosis is examined in three short but useful books by John M. Allswang, *Bosses, Machines and Urban Politics* (Baltimore, 1986), *The Political Behavior of Chicago: Ethnic Groups, 1918–1932* (New York, 1980) and *The New Deal and American Politics* (New York, 1978). Lyle W. Dorsett, *Franklin D. Roosevelt and the City Bosses* (Port Washington, 1977) has a handful of essays on how FDR managed to get along with some of the most corrupt politicians in America. Two excellent books about New York City politics are Arthur Mann, *La Guardia: A Fighter against his*

*Times, 1882–1933* (Chicago, 1959), and *La Guardia Comes to Power* (Chicago, 1965). For the 1920s W.E. Leuchtenburg, *The Perils of Prosperity 1914–1932* (Chicago, 1958) and David Burner, *The Politics of Provincialism: The Democratic Party in Transition* (New York, 1968) are both very stimulating. The most influential single book is Richard Hofstadter, *The Age of Reform: From Bryan to FDR* (New York, 1955), still a convincing argument though now a dated one, while Hoftstadter, *The American Political Tradition and the Men Who Made It* (New York, 1959) has a perceptive essay on FDR and an equally good one on Hoover which have influenced my thinking. Three useful essays on different aspects of the 1920s are: Henry F. May, 'Shifting Perspectives on the 1920s', *Journal of American History*, 43 (1956–57); Burl Noggle, 'The Twenties: A New Historiographical Frontier', *Journal of American History*, 53 (1966–67); and Paul W. Glad, 'Progressives and the Business Culture of the 1920s', *Journal of American History*, 53 (1966–67). However, all these should be read in the light of Samuel Lubell, *The Future of American Politics* (New York, 1952), the first analysis to point out how the election of 1928 indicated the seismic shift which overtook American politics in the 1930s. Richard Neustadt, *Presidential Power: The Politics of Leadership* (New York, 1960) is a landmark study which shows how FDR transformed the presidency. David Bennett, *Demagogues in the Depression: American Radicals and the Union Party 1932–1936* (New Brunswick, 1969) discusses some of FDR's political opponents while T. Harry Williams, *Huey Long* (London, 1970) comprehensively deals with the most dangerous. James T. Patterson, *Congressional Conservatism in the New Deal: The Growth of the Conservative Coalition in Congress 1933–1939* (Lexington, 1967) explains the origins of the Dixiecrat–Republican coalition.

Economics were unusually important during the 1930s. J.K. Galbraith, *The Great Crash, 1929* (Harmondsworth, 1975) is a good place to start and should be combined with Jim Potter, *The American Economy Between the World Wars* (London, 1985). K.D. Roose, *The Economics of Recession and Revival* (New Haven, 1954), Lester V. Chandler, *America's Greatest Depression* (New York, 1970), Mark H. Leff, *The Limits of Symbolic Reform: The New Deal and Taxation 1933–1939* (Cambridge, 1984) and Herbert Stein, *The Fiscal Revolution in America* (Chicago, 1969) are all academic treatments which can be augmented by Marriner Eccles, *Beckoning Frontiers: Public and Private Recollections* (New York, 1951), an account by a key participant in the budgetary revolution of the 1930s. Hearings of the Special Senate Committee on Unemployment and Relief (Sheffield University microfilm) give a taste of the political debate which acompanied this. Robert Lekachman, *The Age of Keynes* (London, 1967) discusses how new ideas transformed economic thinking during the New Deal and after. An article by Patrick Renshaw, 'Was there a Keynesian Economy in the USA 1933–35?', *Journal of Contemporary History*, 34, No. 3 (July 1999) makes extensive use of economic data to argue that there was.

Organized labour also had great significance during the New Deal. Irving Bernstein, *A History of the American Worker*, 2 vols: *The Lean Years, 1919–33* and *Turbulent Years, 1933–41* (Boston, 1960 and 1970) combines vivid drama and detail with careful chronological analysis. Melvyn Dubofsky and Warren Van Tine, *John L. Lewis: A Biography* (Chicago, 1977) is incomparable on the life and times of a key figure in the growth of the CIO. Walter Galenson, *The CIO Challenge to the AFL* (Cambridge, MA, 1960) further orchestrates this theme, while Sidney Fine, *Sit Down: The General Motors Strike of 1936–37* (Ann Arbor, 1969) is the definitive account. For labour after 1940 Nelson Lichtenstein, *Labor's War at Home: The CIO in World War II* (Cambridge, 1982) is the best guide to what was a neglected topic.

The Supreme Court played a decisive role in the New Deal and was at the centre of the greatest political crisis of Roosevelt's presidency. A.M. Schlesinger, *The Politics of Upheaval* has a section entitled 'The Crisis of the Constitution' which serves as a useful introduction, while Samuel Corwin, *The Twilight of the Supreme Court* (New Haven, 1937), Robert Jackson, *The Struggle for Judicial Supremacy* (New York, 1941) and Robert K. Carr, *The Supreme Court and Judicial Review* (New York, 1942) give further detail and argument. A.H. Cope and Fred Krinsky, eds, *Franklin D. Roosevelt and the Supreme Court* (Boston, 1952) offers helpful readings on the subject. But the most useful single book is A.H. Kelly and E. Harbison, *The American Constitution: Its Origin and Development* (New York, 1991), which not only summarizes cases clearly but also places them in political and legal context. Kermit L. Hall, ed., *The Oxford Companion to the Supreme Court* (Oxford, 1992) is the last word in reference books on the Court. John W. Chambers, 'The Big Switch: Justice Roberts and the Minimum Wage Cases', *Labor History*, 10 (1969) examines the critical problem of why one judge changed sides.

The best book on foreign affairs is without question Robert Dallek, *Franklin D. Roosevelt and American Foreign Policy, 1932–1945* (Oxford, 1979, new edn 1995), which is a classic. An older account is Herbert Feis, *The Road to Pearl Harbor* (Princeton, 1952), which should be read in conjunction with W.L. Langer and S.E. Gleason, *The Undeclared War 1940–1941* (New York, 1953), which covers every detail of FDR's diplomacy during the supreme crisis of his presidency. David Reynolds, *From Munich* to *Pearl Harbor* (Chicago, 2001) is an invaluable short and recent account. The best book on the vexed question of why the US Navy was caught by surprise in December 1941 is Roberta Wohlstetter, *Pearl Harbor: Warning and Decision* (Stanford, 1963). A. Iriye, *The Origins of the Second World War in Asia and the Pacific* (London, 1987) is a more recent account, based in part on Japanese sources. F.L. Lowenstein, H.D. Langley and M. Jonas, eds, *Churchill and Roosevelt: Their Secret Wartime Correspondence*, 2 vols (London, 1975) and Walter Kimball, ed., *Churchill and Roosevelt: Their Complete Correspondence*, 3 vols: *Alliance Emerging, Alliance Forged, Alliance Declining* (Princeton, 1984) give the letters of FDR and Churchill, while Herbert Feis, *Churchill, Roosevelt, Stalin: The War they Waged and the Peace they Sought* (Princeton, 1974) is largely based on correspondence. For the military history of the European war, see Stephen Ambrose, *Eisenhower*, vol. 1: *1890–1952* (New York, 1984) and Ronald H. Spector, *Eagle Against the Sun: The American War with Japan* (Harmondsworth, 1987). William Emerson, 'Franklin Roosevelt as Commander-in-Chief in World War II', *Military Affairs*, XXII (Winter 1958–59), is a densely argued but perceptive article on a subject still largely neglected by other historians.

The domestic history of the war had also been comparatively neglected until the 1980s, though it is essential to understanding how the New Deal evolved in the 1940s. It can now be studied in Richard Polenberg, *War and Society: The United States 1941–45* (Westport, 1980), J.M. Blum, *V Was For Victory: Politics and American Culture During World War II* (New York, 1976) and two books by A.M. Winkler, *Home Front USA* (Arlington Heights, 1986) and *The Politics of Propaganda: The Office of War Information, 1942–1945* (New Haven, 1978). Nancy J. Weiss, *Farewell to the Party of Lincoln: Black Politics in the Age of FDR* (Princeton, 1983) explains the decisive shift in black political allegiance. Neil Wynn, *The Afro-American and the Second World War* (London, 1976) examines changes in race relations brought about by the war, while Karen Anderson, *Wartime Women* (Westport, 1986) does the same for women.

US reaction to Jewish persecution in Europe during the war is discussed in David Wyman, *The Abandonment of the Jews: America and the Holocaust, 1941–45* (New York, 1986) while Roger Daniels, *Concentration Camp USA: Japanese-Americans during World War II* (Berkeley, 1962) deals with a shameful example of what war hysteria can do.

Periodical literature in learned journals is vast but the following are examples of useful articles on key areas. Apart from the articles by Huthmacher in the *Mississippi Valley Historical Review/Journal of American History*, 49 (1962–63), by Chambers in *Labor History*, 10 (1969) and by several historians on the 1920s (all noted above), see the following:

W.D. Reeves, 'PWA and Competition Administration in the New Deal', *Journal of American History*, 60 (1973–74), C.G. Wye, 'The New Deal and the Negro Community', *Journal of American History*, 59 (1972–73), J.R. Moore, 'Sources of New Deal Economic Policy', *Journal of American History*, 61 (1974–75), T. Saloutos, 'New Deal Agricultural Policy', *Journal of American History*, 61 (1974–75), W.W. Bremer, 'Along the "American Way": The New Deal's Work Relief Programs for the Unemployed', *Journal of American History* 62 (1975–76), David Brody, 'Labor and the Great Depression: The Interpretative Prospects', *Labor History*, 13 (1972), 'Radical Labor History and Rank-and-File Militancy', *Labor History*, 16 (1975), Daniel Nelson, 'The CIO at Bay: Labor Militancy and Politics in Akron, Ohio, 1936–1938', *Journal of American History*, 71 (1984–85).

# Index